GunDigest
SHOOTER'S GUIDE to
SHOTGUN GAMES

D0940901

NICK SISLEY

Published by

Gun Digest® Books, an imprint of F+W, A Content + eCommerce Company
Krause Publications • 700 East State Street • Iola, WI 54990-0001
715-445-2214 • 888-457-2873
www.krausebooks.com

To order books or other products call toll-free 1-800-258-0929
or visit us online at www.gundigeststore.com

ISBN-13: 978-1-4402-4350-9
ISBN-10: 1-4402-4350-6

Edited by David Draper
Designed by Sharon Bartsch

Printed in USA

RELATED TITLES

Gun Digest Shooter's Guide to Shotguns

Gun Digest Shooter's Guide to Reloading

Gun Digest Book of Shotguns Assembly/Disassembly

Gun Digest Guide to Modern Shotgunning

FOR MORE INFORMATION VISIT
GunDigestStore.com

CONTENTS

FOREWORD

It's been over 40 years since Nick Sisley walked onto the skeet fields at Tarentum Sportsmen's Club and joined us for a round of clay target shooting. I wasn't too impressed. Everyone knows outdoor writers spend all their time indoors on a keyboard and too little time outdoors. After 40 years and an almost uncountable amount of ammo, hundreds of magical grouse hunts, woodcock bottoms and dove fields, and always, an enormous amount of clay targets, I can attest that Nick Sisley is the outdoor writer that is out there shooting, hitting, missing, learning, and teaching more than anyone I ever met. He's hunted one kind of bird or another in just about every state in the U.S. and been to South America more times than even he can count. If anyone is qualified to write this book its Nick.

When we met on that skeet field decades ago it didn't take long to find we had a common enemy, a trouble target. A bird that was hard to hit. Even a mystery. Yet here we are, 40 years later, still friends, still shooting, and still trying to hit that trouble target.

Nor has Nick's enthusiasm waned. He's on the phone a couple days a week. He has got a new gun, a new method, something new he's got to try, so we're out after clay targets again.

Many of my best moments on a skeet field were shooting with Nick. For many years, our team, Tarentum Sportsman, was a tough team to beat. One year we tied for the 12 Gauge State Championship against the famous Holtz squad, the great shooting family from Pennsylvania. Both of our teams had shot sparkling scores, 498x500, and had to shoot off for the 5-Man Team State Championship. Now, we were all friends, good souls all, but make no mistake, everyone was trying to win. Without discussing all the rules of a shoot-off I needed to hit the next bird to win. This was not an easy moment. Big shoot, big pressure. And a tough opponent. I strode up to the station, loaded the gun and readied myself. And then, right before I call for the target, Nick leans over to Ralph Holtz, the patriarch of the Holtz family, and whispers "Pressure shot."

I'm sure Nick didn't mean for me to hear him that day and I doubt if he even remembers. But I hit that bird. We won. And it's one of my best memories in 40 years of competition.

Somewhere in those years Sisley created some memories of his own. Our mutual friend, Donald Lavely and Nick, shot Two-Man Team for many years and at the Mid West skeet shoot at Canton, Ohio. They put together a 200 straight in the 28-gauge event. But to win they had to face a couple of first team All-

Americans that had tied them. Well Nick and Don beat them in the first round and you'd probably have to be a clay target shooter to understand how absolutely galactic that was.

Sometimes, almost comically, Nick's own profession led to problems. One summer he's shows up with a brand new Browning Citori, Briley tubed, high ribbed, all the fixin's. He's hitting everything. Goes to the state shoot, runs 100 straight in the 28 gauge, ends up fifth in the state. Never shoots the gun again. A week later there's something new. And then a week later we ask, "Nick what happened? Why did you change guns?" He simply replies with a grin, "It's my job man."

I will never forget another grin he had during a Pennsylvania grouse hunt. We were hunting in an undisclosed location in the northern part of the state back in the 1980s and the grouse cycle was sky high. It was maybe the best grouse hunt in either of our lives, 27 flushes – but the main memory was 7 double points! Maybe a point and a back are expected on a Carolina quail hunt but in the Northern grouse woods it may not occur even once in a lifetime. These were not points and backs, however, but double points – different grouse pointed by two different dogs at the same time. There was Nick standing in between the two great dogs, on point in different directions, grinning like a possum-eating chicken.

I wanted to laugh out loud when I saw the trio, but didn't want to scare the birds. Finally a flush, a good shot and I never saw a man more at home. When I came through the brush, he's was talking to himself, repeating over and over "What a day. What a year."

Of course one of the central benefits with being friends with a premier gun writer is all the cool guns he shows up with, usually weekly. Shotguns of every price range, weight and use. Shotguns I could never afford or even find for sale are brought to the club in an endless stream of gleaming walnut and blued steel, and these days even shiny plastic. Some we can hit with, some not so well, but every shotgun gets rung out in an honest appraisal. Phrases like "good for this, or good for that", "nice wood," "too light for skeet," great game gun" fly around like clay targets thrown from a wobble trap.

It's a tough job as they say, but we don't take it lightly. Maybe with a smile, but not lightly.

The heady responsibility was illustrated one winter day several years ago where we were trying out some nice shotguns on barnyard pigeons, an activity we share a passion for. The shoot was over for the day and I got the job of carrying some guns back to the car. With a $12,000 Perazzi in one hand and a $5,000 Browning in the other, I slip and go down with a splat on the ice. Holding the guns aloft, wracked in disfiguring pain, I announced, "I saved the guns. I saved the guns."

Nick and I have shared many outdoor pleasures over the years, grouse hunting, bird dogs, of course, shotgunning in all forms, but the one activity we get a big kick out of is pigeon shooting. Not the competitive flyer ring, although we've done that too, but common barnyard pests plaguing the farm. Most farmers welcome responsible shooters in and around the farm and barns to try eradicating the birds.

Testing out guns, glasses and shells, shooting methods and chokes are all part of this pigeon shooting. So along with giving the farmer a hand we'd get to try out all this gear and theory on real birds. They are tough and resilient and hard to bring down. There just can't be a better testing ground for shotguns. But holy mackerel it is fun.

We've shared some of our best times and laughs during these hunts. In the 1970s we found a great shoot near an abandoned U.S. Steel building. Thousands of pigeons lived there and were driving the local farmer crazy. We had to help. We shot hundreds, probably thousands of birds there over the years, but finally, with the demise of steel industry the building was torn down. That meant the pigeons no longer had their roost. If it wasn't for the man-thing, I think we both would have cried.

After a time of deep depression we started, undaunted, looking for other farms plagued by pigeons. Since those years we've found dozens of farms and farmers needing a hand. Sisley, a long-time pilot, has resorted to flying around looking for silos covered with birds. Sometimes we get a few, or more – always trying new guns, equipment, methods. Sometimes sharing spots, sneaking off on our own, but always exchanging advice and wisdom, shot size, choke selection, gun balance, and anything else that can help us hit. After all these years, that common enemy, the tough target in the sky.

Therefore, I can assure anyone wise enough to buy this book and read Nick's advice will never hear guesswork or assumption. Nick is nothing if not humble, questioning and honest. And he will always be trying new things, learning and passing on solid advice, tried and true.

Oh, oh, the phone is ringing. It's Nick and we've got something new to try. Talk to you later. This work is too important to ignore.

Richard Drury

INTRODUCTION

I'm no doubt the luckiest guy who ever lived. I make that claim often to anyone who will listen. Having shot over much of the world (that's real luck), my breadth of shotgunning experience has run the gamut. Serious clay target work began in the late 1970s. For decade, I shot 20,000 rounds at clays every year and still shoot 10,000 per annum, so I guess I'm slowing down. Those numbers don't count the thousands of shotshells I've fired on the real feathered stuff. Imagine hunting ruffed grouse every day of the season – for decades, and making 50 trips to South America to shoot, which I started doing way back in 1972.

Just a guess, but I think I've taken about 50 shotgun shooting lessons. In the first third or more of this book, I've tried to pass on what I've been taught by masters of the shotgunning trade. You can learn plenty about improving your shotgunning skills from this – as I did. Most of the rest of the book deals with shotguns I've tested. Those chapters will have plenty for any reader looking for a first or next shotgun to digest.

Hopefully what follows will be a good read for you and you'll return to these pages regularly to check up on shotgun shooting advice, refresh your memory about a shotgun you might want to buy, and be educated about a subject I love.

Nick Sisley

CHAPTER ONE

THE BIRTH OF WINGSHOOTING

Some claim firearms were used to kill game in the 15th century, but guns that fired multiple projectiles probably hadn't entered any engineer's dreams way back then. We've certainly come a long way since, however, as shotguns have contributed to uncountable amount of game taken for at least the last 150 years, and millions and millions of shotshells are fired at clay targets every year.

Shooting on the wing was originally thought impossible, or, perhaps more to the point, why shoot flying when gunners of yesteryear could shoot stuff on the ground? Further, tremendous bags taken by nobility in the mid 1700s were accomplished not only by shooting, but also by driving game into waiting nets. One of the greatest shotgunners of yesteryear, Lord Walsingham, in his book *Shooting: Field and Covert,* tells of a bag of nearly 50,000 in Bohemia during a big hunt over 20 days in 1753 and the take included few game birds, but also stags, boar, roe deer, rabbits and all manner of non-game birds – including what we call song birds today. Keep in mind such bags were accomplished with muskets, the powder set off via a flintlock. Recently, I shot a replica Colt Walker black-powder revolver with round balls, the powder charge set off by percussion caps. I had forgotten about the "whiz-bang" of such loads – the "whiz" being the sound of the percussion cap igniting and the "bang" related to the charge of powder igniting a fraction of a second later, sending the .44 caliber round ball down the

barrel. With a flintlock there was perhaps even more time involved between the "whiz" and the "bang." So no wonder those old timers didn't think too much about bagging game on the wing.

When percussion caps entered the picture, shotguns followed, or at least more of them showed up in the field. In Cyril Adam's excellent book, *Lock, Stock & Barrel,* Adams shows an interesting chronology of "shooting flying." The flintlock era lasted about 170 years – approximately 1660 to 1820. From 1820 to 1861 was the percussion-cap era, but for 210 years of the earliest wingshooting (much of the game shot on the ground – perhaps sitting) all of the guns used were muzzleloaders. Pour the black powder down the bore, then, in the case of shotguns wadding followed and then the shot and an over-shot wad. It took a while to get all that accomplished.

The so-called "centerfire era" began about 1861 – centerfire meaning a pre-made cartridge could be loaded in the shotgun's chamber. Initially there were a number of different ways the shotgun shell could be ignited. Eventually, a primer in the back center of the shotshell became the most popular and won over the other methods of igniting the powder charge. However, the powder was still black powder – corrosive and accompanied by a big bellow of smoke as the charge was sent on its way. Smokeless powder hit store shelves, and the resultant shotshells loaded with smokeless powder, around 1890. But like many things, newfangled smokeless was not immediately accepted and many top shots stuck with their black powder shotguns for years thereafter. Also, it wasn't a safe practice to shoot smokeless powder cartridges in a smoothbore originally made for black powder – the latter producing considerably less chamber pressure.

I'm getting a bit ahead of myself. Let's return, if only briefly, to talk about "shooting flying." No doubt it was the challenge of bringing down a bird on the wing or a running rabbit that got such shooting started. It was in the late 1700s that Joseph Manton started making beautiful Damascus barrel flintlock shotguns. The barrels were definitely important, but these Mantons were the first shotguns that made up the total package – Cyril Adam's *Lock, Stock and Barrel*. The three were wonderfully wed – to the point that maybe for the first time in history these were shotguns capable of getting this "shooting flying" thing accomplished.

One aspect of these Manton shotguns had to be the lightness of the barrels, as only with reasonably light barrels could the wedding of lock, stock and barrel be such that shooting flying was brought from a possibility to a somewhat probability. There were no metallurgical breakthroughs for better steels then. But gunsmith masters like Manton came up with a method that produced barrels of only .030 in thickness (as Cyril Adams relates, "….about the thickness of today's credit cards.")

How was this done? Manton and similar masters used hard, low-carbon steel in conjunction with soft, low-carbon iron. Thin strips of these materials were wrapped spirally around a mandrill. The smith formed the barrel by rolling, drawing and hammering the metal, along with forge welding of the seams. This technique greatly improved barrel strength and they could be made thinner and lighter. We know such barrels today

as Damascus. Cyril Adams says that about 18 pounds of very high-grade steel and iron were required to produce a 3½-pound set of side-by-side barrels.

Barrels made of steel didn't come on the scene until Joseph Whitworth came up with his fluid-pressed steel. The result was barrels that were harder and stronger than Damascus. The new steel material was better suited to adding choke to the muzzle end – as the two – Whitworth's fluid steel barrels and choke boring – came along at relatively the same time. Smokeless powder – which created higher chamber pressures than black powder – made the new steel's strength a necessary development.

The first wingshooter of note was Sir Peter Hawker. Born in 1786, his introduction to shooting flying was with a Joseph Manton flintlock. He stayed with flintlock shooting well into the percussion-cap era. At some point, he took up shooting a Joseph Manton percussion side-by-side he eventually named "Old Joe." Actually, it was the same flintlock gun converted to percussion by Manton.

The birth and history of shooting flying is detailed in the excellent book Lock, Stock & Barrel *by Cyril Adams and Robert Branden.*

At 28, Hawker wrote his first book *Instructions to Young Sportsmen*. Up until the Hawker-era most all shooting was "for the pot." Peter Hawker introduced "sport" to wing shooting. Reportedly he was an outstanding shot. He began a shooting diary in 1802, which he kept religiously until his death in 1851. George Bird Evans's wonderful book *Men Who Shot* goes into detail about many of the great wing gunners – both of olden days and not-so-olden days. Evans says that Hawker's shooting diary relates that he shot 17,753 heads of game, of which 7,035 were partridges, 575 pheasants and 631 hare. Evans did not go into the critters that made up the rest of the Hawker bag. Keep in mind that this was all "rough" shooting, not the driven shoots for Scottish grouse, pheasants and partridge where such huge kills were made a few decades later by the likes of the Prince of Wales (later King Edward VII), Lord Ripon, Lord Walsingham and others at such game-rich venues as Sardingham, Holkam, Highclere (now of Downton Abbey fame), Merton, Elevden and others.

And so here we are, chronologically, at the beginning of England's magic age of wingshooting where and when the Prince of Wales, Ripon and Walsingham laid the groundwork for decades of aristocratic shooting that has never been matched, and never will be.

SHOOTING FLYING COMES OF AGE: ENGLAND 1880 TO WORLD WAR I

Yes, this is a book about clay target shooting and the vast majority of this book will be devoted to just that. But to get a sense of how shotgunning got started and how it has progressed it pays to look at some history. Clay targets had not even been invented in 1880, nor would they even be seen until decades later.

One way to get a sense of this early England wingshooting would be to read lots about it. There are many books devoted to the subject, but there is one movie that depicts the era well. *The Shooting Party* stars James Mason and takes place just prior to World War I. After the war, shooting by many of the Lords and Princes of that time ended. England was broke. To raise tax money, many of the huge old shooting estates were broken up. Shooting in England has re-surfaced in the last several decades, but today that shooting is done largely by well-heeled businessmen and not by so many Lords, Dukes and Earls as before.

When this period started, Damascus barrels and blackpowder were the "modern" thing. The Lord de Grey (the Marquis of Ripon) was regarded as at least one of the four best shots of that time. Others mentioned in the same figurative breath were Lord Walsingham, Lord Huntingfield and Maharajah Duleep Singh. George Evans divulges that Singh shot 440 Scottish grouse in one day – all over pointing dogs – thus not driven.

Like Peter Hawker, Ripon kept diligent shooting records. Others who may not have kept such records may have eclipsed Rip's totals, but how about his 124,193 partridges and 241,224 well-driven pheasants? Grand total of all game shot was more 550,000! Born in 1852, Lord de Grey died in1923, supposedly just after making a right and a left on grouse he tumbled dead into the heather. What a wonderful way to go.

Ripon was also a writer, and much of what he wrote could be considered "shooting how-to." One of his suggestions was, "don't check," meaning get on the bird and pull the trigger nearly instantly. The more a wing gunner checks, the more he rides the bird and the more likely something not wanted is going to happen.

Another of his gunning suggestions was confidence – a hard trait to incorporate for a beginner shooter. Quickness was also one of Ripon's stated virtues, and these were the days of two side-by-sides and shooting with a loader. Fire two shots, and then pass the gun to the loader while at the same time taking the next loaded gun. No gunner got off all four shots without employing a degree of quickness. While today's clay target shooter doesn't shoot four shots at a time, quickness is still a virtue. Sporting clays, F.I.T.A.S.C., 5-Stand and other clay target games involve mostly two targets. Target setters don't allow a lot of time before the first shot or between

the two, so being ready and taking the shots with some degree of rapidity is just as important in today's clay shooting as it was in Ripon's day.

While huge bags were a part of the Sardingham and other "big shoot" experience, this period was well known and important for another reason –this is when the English side-by-side reached its peak of design. Some say the Purdeys, Hollands, Bosses, Lancasters, and others helped coin the phrase "London Best." These guns were and

We've come a long way since the days of Prince Edward the VII and Lord, but Sisley dons his coat and tie to bring back the days of yesteryear, despite shooting at a modern sporting clays station with a modern Benelli semi-auto sporting gun.

are the epitome of the gun maker's art. Side-by-side shotguns have not been improved upon since before World War I.

What made these doubles so highly thought of? First off, acquiring one wasn't like walking into Hi-Grade Shooters in Youngwood, Pa., to select among a covey of Perazzis or Caesar Guerinis. Buying a London Best was a ceremony of sorts. The knowledgeable person behind the counter probably first made sure you could afford one. From there it was time to the select a receiver type – in most all London Best cases it was a serious sidelock. And how about the walnut? In England and Europe, shotgunners have never been as daffy about a great piece of wood as we are on this side of the Atlantic. Still, a nice piece of wood had to be selected with maybe the most important aspect being high strength at the stock's wrist. And then came comprehensive measurements to ensure the new stock would fit the buyer perfectly. After all you were buying an heirloom, and despite the appreciable cost, your heirloom was not only likely to outlive you, it was bound to increase in value, maybe 10 or more times its purchase price.

But there was more than just the purchase that made a London Best what it is today. You don't have to pick one up. You just have to look at one. You know you're looking at something not only of great value, but, like a Renoir, a piece of art that has totally been hand done. The biggest piece of machinery a London Best had seen was a hand file.

Further yet, the artistry doesn't stop just at appearance. Pick such a shotgun up and you will experience a thrill, a thrill you've never known in picking up any other shotgun. If reasonably fitted to you there will be an awareness of liveliness. You will feel the gun can't wait to get to your shoulder – to get to the bird – especially one of the feathered variety. The balance could take you to new levels of appreciation.

If a London Best doesn't dominate on the clay target fields it is because they are very light. These guns, often in 12 gauge, were built before the days of $1\frac{1}{2}$ ounces of shot in a $2\frac{3}{4}$-inch shell, and before 3-inch magnums. They were built to shoot $\frac{15}{16}$ and 1 ounce loads at probably less than 1,200 feet per second, and many of the 12 gauges only hefted a hair over 6 pounds – maybe between 6 pounds 4 ounces and 6 pounds 8 ounces with 30-inch barrels. Models for waterfowling, as opposed to driven shooting, were a bit heavier and made to fire slightly stouter loads.

Shotguns this light have not worked on clay target venues. Just as we folks do not have the strength, stamina, fortitude and wherewithal of our ancestors from decades past, modern shooters hate recoil. We have become wimps, and I'm one of them. Think of buffalo hunters of the 1870s. They would lay prone and shoot their Sharps and other huge recoiling guns and think nothing of it – hundreds of shots a day on a good buffalo herd.

The over/under first saw the light of day in the early 1900s, when Boss came out with the first one. The shotgunning world has not been the same since. Today the Boss design is largely copied by Perazzi and Zoli, even by the Ruger Red Label. Further, additional over/under designs have also become popular, Browning's Superposed and Remington's Model 32 being only two of many O/U examples. In 1905 Browning came with their Model 5, the first really successful semi-auto. These days we have a myriad of auto-loading designs as well – and many of them are prominent on clay target fields.

We are going to look at many of today's clay target shotguns, but before we do it should help to give some advice on how to "hit" with them.

CHAPTER TWO

THE ART OF SHOOTING FLYING

In many ways shooting flying is a bit of an art form. However, considerable has been learned about the how-to of being successful. The age of the shotgun shooting instructor has been going on for many, many years in England. Why? The most common form of shooting "Over There" is the driven shoot – shooting Scottish grouse, partridge or pheasants with the gunners placed in shooting butts or at specified stands. They shoot flying birds winging overhead, birds driven by beaters who are hired to flush the birds toward the shooters. This type of sport is very expensive. Anyone invited as a gunner is expected to do well. If he or she does not, there is not going to be an ensuing invitation. Since invitees want to shoot the best they can, the British Shooting School was born. There have been many of those dating to way back when and there continue to be lots of such schools in England right through to today.

Until fairly recently, no one considered being a shotgun instructor in the USA, no matter how good and learned the shooter might be. Shotgunners simply were not going to pay money to have someone teach them to shoot. Sporting Clays has changed all that. That shotgun game didn't arrive on our shores until the mid 1980s, but sporting in England had been popular for decades before that. English shotgunners were very willing to part with their dollar (or rather, pound) to learn how to shoot better, and when the top British dudes came here for our sporting tournaments they cleaned American competitors' figurative clocks.

It has taken American shooters several years to catch up, but they have – in most cases anyway. Americans, once beaten soundly on the clay field, were then more than a little anxious to plunk down their dollars for a shooting lesson, and if they really wanted to get better they took shooting lesson after shooting lesson.

I started taking skeet shooting lessons in the early 1980s. Not only had I been interested in improving my own target busting skills, I write about shotguns and shotgunning. Taking lessons was also a subject for me to convey what I learned to my readers. Since those first shooting lessons more than 30 years ago I'm sure I've taken at least 50 different lessons – mostly with a new instructor each time, but not always. Further, I got certified as a National Skeet Shooting Association (NSSA) Level I Instructor, a National Sporting Clays Shooting Association (NSCA) Level I Instructor, plus an NRA Shotgun Instructor.

But I'm not going to teach you much of anything in this section "The Art of Shooting Flying." Instead I'm going to rely on what I've learned over the years from some very great shooters who are equally adept at teaching. So let's get this section started with what I learned from top Instructor/Shooter Will Fennell.

A LESSON WITH WILL FENNELL

Will Fennell shot his first duck when he was only seven, and his first deer when he was only eight. But this many-time member of Team USA (F.I.T.A.S.C.) didn't move directly into shotgun shooting. In high school, he was on the rifle team. After high school he went into pistol competition, including IPSIC, but also competed in the Sportsman Team Challenge shoots.

Then one year in South Carolina he shot sporting clays and became totally hooked. A gifted shotgunner, he moved up to Class AA in sporting clays in only four months. "But I was erratic," Fennel confessed. "One shoot I'd be in the high 80s, even the low 90s, but a shoot or two later I'd crash. Then I got with noted shooting instructor Dan Carlisle, and my shooting world changed forever."

Instead of instructing Fennell, noted shotgunner Dan Carlisle became his coach. Carlisle was an Olympic Gold Medalist, and since becoming a shotgun instructor he has led many a shooter onto the champion's podium. It was Carlisle's coaching that put Fennell on the road to consistency. Carlisle saw that Will also had the many qualities to become an excellent instructor and encouraged him to do just that. Will had a real job, and when he began teaching he didn't think there were enough students for him to switch to full time.

Dan Carlisle had been living in South Carolina (where Fennell lived), but he moved to teach in Texas. He sent his South Carolina students to Will. So Fennell gave up his top-paying job to teach full time in 2004, and he has not looked back. Not only has he enjoyed an excellent and productive teaching career, Will has garnered many, many shooting titles and has been an NSCA All American and Team USA Sporting member often. It's no wonder he's in demand as an instructor.

I met up with the affable guy for a two-day session at his personal South Carolina shooting grounds – where I learned plenty. – much of which will be divulged here. I've

taken many, many shooting lessons, starting in the early 1980s. Naturally, I've been trying to improve my own shotgunning skills, but in those lessons I'm always looking to pass on significant how-to to my readers. When Fennell discovered I was a one-eye shooter, he couldn't believe my previous instructors had not converted me to shooting with both eyes. Because I had shot with one eye for many decades, maybe I had always resisted the change.

"Why don't you use both eyes," Will admonished, probably knowing the answer.

"Because I see two barrels," I said. "I think my left eye takes over, at least on some targets – especially the quartering incomer coming from my right."

"You see two barrels because you're not looking hard enough at the target," said Fennell.

Over the years I've tried shooting with both eyes open (as all beginning shotgunners should) many times, but I'll never forget what Fennell said next. "If I had three eyes I'd use them all!" That's when I decided to just go ahead and do it. I still have trouble with my left eye taking over – called cross firing - on certain targets. Once I started concentrating on hard focus of the target seeing two barrels went away. So if any of you readers are one-eye shooters, you are encouraged to make the switch to both. If you are new to shotgunning, definitely start with both eyes.

As a Dan Carlisle disciple, Will Fennell teaches the same shooting method as his hero. I'll try to condense that method for you here. On crossing targets, mount on the leading edge of the bird, match target speed with gun speed, and then make a very gentle pull-away – with the emphasis on gentle. At first, my pull-away with Fennell was too fast so that I was shooting in front of target after target. My follow through was also too extended as well. Doubles are involved in most clay target games, so if the follow through is too extended the barrels are out of position for most second targets.

A second mantra of this shooting methodology involves quartering away targets. In most instances it's mount on the bird and don't pull-away. Most of these targets require no or minimal lead – as long as your gun is moving. This is especially true if you mount on the escaping bird, briefly match gun speed to target speed and quickly pull the trigger.

For very long crossing shots the Carlisle method dictates mounting slightly in front of the bird, match gun and target speed briefly, and then do the gentle pull-away. Of course this suggestion sounds similar to shorter range crossing targets, but the mount in front maybe differs between say a 40-yard shot and a 55-yard. With the Carlisle method it's critical that the shooter matches target speed with gun speed, if only briefly, before that gentle pull-away. When done successfully there's a smoothness to this swing that is common to all great shotgunners.

Fennell was also adamant about me slowing down my move. My mount wasn't too quick, but my initial muzzle movement was, and that extended follow through further generated too much muzzle movement. "Less is better when it comes to muzzle movement," is the way Fennell put it. That's also my advice to you. In addition to using both eyes (if you don't already), try slowing way down. That 35 mile per hour target can't outrun your 1,200 feet per second shot charge.

If going to both eyes wasn't a major enough change during this two-day lesson, Fennell had another big alteration in my set up. He didn't like *where* I was putting the gun on my shoulder, which was maybe a half-inch inside my round shoulder bone. He thought, especially at my advanced age, that I was going to have rotator cuff or other

shoulder problems, and he wondered if I ever had a sore shoulder from shooting. When he found out I hated recoil he was not surprised.

"Try mounting the gun further inside on your chest," said Fennel. "That way you'll end up with the butt stock farther from your shoulder and rotator cuff and more toward your chest. The gun will be recoiling into a much more stable place on your body. With the stock positioned as I've suggested, the gun and rib will be more *under* your eye, where it should be. You won't have to tilt your head over to be looking right down the rib, like you do now. When you tilt your head you don't see as well. You fatigue faster. If you don't believe me try driving down the highway for about five minutes with your head tilted."

So now I have a much different starting point for my gun mount. When I pull the trigger the butt stock is more toward my chest. Thus I don't suffer from the effects of recoil nearly as much. Previously my neck, wrists, elbows and shoulder would feel the pain after shooting, and the more shooting I did in a day the more the pain level would rise. Now my whole body offers resistance to recoil. My shoulder doesn't get it all, plus the recoil to my wrists and elbows is significantly reduced. Finally, I now shoot with my eyes level, with the rib directly under my right eye – all positives to my shooting.

The Carlisle method references target lead at the muzzle in inches, rather than feet out at the target. Both these instructors believe this type of reference can be less intimidating to a new student. Instead of suggesting a 12-foot lead on a very far target a lead in so many inches is more precise information that is easier for the student to digest, as well as easier for the student to repeat time and time again.

When it comes to lead on a distant target Fennell stressed that there were three things to consider. First is the *angle* of the target, a very important factor. Second is the *speed* of the bird, which is much reduced on a quartering clay. Third in importance, and the least significance is *distance* to the target. I've already covered how a 35 mile per hour clay can't outrun a 1,200 feet per second shot charge.

Let me end your session with a few organized thoughts this champion shooter shared with me. I bet the following seven points will improve your shooting, as they have mine.

On the way to a shoot drink lots of water. Fennell says the eyes are made up largely of water and the first thing to start dehydrating. As the eyes lose water their shape can change, including the distance from your lens to your retina, which cannot benefit your shooting.

How is the target moving? Is it going up, down, perfectly horizontal, or most likely not any one of the above, but some combination. To make certain, use your gun's barrel

as a plumb. Hold the barrel level to the flight of the bird as you observe the target. This information will help you tell where the muzzle should be when you pull the trigger.

If you have selected your breakpoint, hold point and visual pickup point before calling pull – and you break the bird – don't change a thing. You did remember that precise hold point and exactly where you looked for the bird didn't you?

Don't think of *seeing* the target but of *focus*.

Each time you pull the trigger, imagine seeing the shot charge hit the target. Doing this will ensure you have great target focus all the way *through* the shot.

In practice, after you break the bird, next shoot the biggest piece, which, as in the tip above, helps you stay attached to the target with hard focus.

Excess barrel speed and barrel movement makes it easy for the eyes to go to that movement. So slow down. Move the barrel slowly and not excessively.

Will Fennell, a top Instructor/Shooter, shows his gun-ready form - certainly several very nice competition shotguns in the background – all Kriegoffs.

Champion clay shooter and top instructor Will Fennell in teaching mode.

Before this first-timer gets to shoot, she gets detailed instruction on both safety and hitting how-to.

The young instructor in the background has given this new shooter good advice.

Will Fennell looks at how Nick is responding to the instructions.

Fennel, on the left, makes a suggestion to Sisley on how to hit the next target.

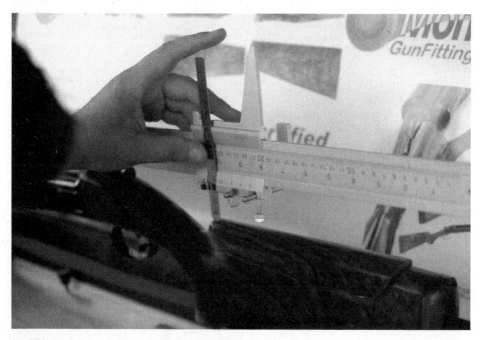

In addition to being a top instructor, Will Fennell is an outstanding gun fitter, and he has the tools to do that job right.

Fennell coaches Nick to mount on the leading edge of the target, briefly match gun speed with target speed, and then pull the trigger.

From tall tower shots to medium and distant crossers, incoming and outgoing quartering shots to springing teal and falling birds – shotgunners can practice them all with a teaching layout like this.

MIKE MOHR HELPS ME HANDLE A FEW TROUBLE TARGETS

Level III National Sporting Clays Association (NSCA) Instructor Mike Mohr teaches at a spectacular sporting clays facility that's imbedded into the Seven Springs Mountain Resort. Seven Springs sprawls over 5,500 acres, and 197 acres are allotted to the shotgun shooting – of which they are so far only using 97 acres. The sporting clays stations are in a wooded setting among slopes galore, thus offering shots at every imaginable angle, including a few I've struggled with.

A slightly curling teal

My natural inclination on this bird started out incorrectly. I had the muzzles meet the rising bird a little more than half way to its peak, and then swung with it as the bird made its curl to the right and started down. Mike watched while I popped two or three and missed two or three.

"Instead of making a 'curling' move with

Fennell has 10 traps set up at his shooting grounds. This allows his students to shoot every imaginable target presentation.

Will Fennell showing off his shotgun instruction wisdom.

the gun let's keep the move simpler, more compact," Mohr suggested. "Try placing the gun initially right above your chosen breakpoint, just after the bird starts down. Don't even worry about tracking this curling target as it is going up."

So this is what I tried, successfully. It was easy to see the rising teal out of my left eye. I waited, and then inserted the muzzles just above my selected breakpoint – and hit the trigger just after the target started downward. It was an easy shot with very little muzzle movement at all, whereas before Mike's tip I was moving the gun significantly.

But sporting clays is always a doubles game, and this station involved a high overhead from behind in combination with that slightly curling teal. Mike's tutoring on this one was, "See the overhead, make your mount and kill it. Then break the gun away from your face without much muzzle movement. You are going to find the gun is already pretty well pointed perfectly for the curling teal, at least as we've just discussed the way to shoot it."

The overhead shot coming from behind is one I've always tried to see as early as possible, often by turning my body part way around. But in most circumstances I think that has been a mistake because I have to get my head and body turned back around, make the gun mount and shoot. As Mike showed me – just look up a bit, find the bird and shoot it. Looking well back on birds like this is only an invitation to ride such a target, instead of just shooting it as Mike told me to do.

Suggesting a negative

One of Mohr's shooting lesson mantras is that he always wants to tell his students something positive, even when they miss or are missing. This is extremely important for Level I NSCA Instructors to realize and adhere to, as well as for anyone introducing a new shooter to the game. Mike is always putting a positive spin on the shot, on the station, on the day. In that vein Mike doesn't tell you what you are doing wrong. Instead he stresses the how-to of doing it right.

Crossers

When experienced shooters come to Mike for a lesson he will typically ask what targets they want to work on. Almost invariably it's crossers. With every individual the long crosser how-to may differ, but one of Mike's constants on this target is to keep the muzzle under the bird. That's so the shooter can see the target. Thus even on a standard-distance crosser the shot pattern will expand to break it. However, just like a bullet the shot pattern is also affected by gravity – and thus the pattern will also drop on those really long shots. On longer crossers how much the shot pattern will drop has to be taken into consideration.

I never realized this one, but Mike says he sees it all the time on crossers – regular distance crossers especially. It all has to do with perception. Some shooters say they require more lead on a right to left crosser – compared to a left to right. Another shooter may comment just the opposite. But Mike sees where the muzzle is when the trigger is pulled – as well as the shot pattern itself in some cases – and the lead is the same right to left or left to right. But some individuals do perceive different leads depending upon crosser direction. I have not noticed this myself. Have you?

Policemen

Mike works with different police departments, plus state and federal agency members, showing these guys and gals the intricacies of shotgunning. Most of these folks are excellent pistol shooters – probably because they have a tremendous amount of handgun training – and they practice with their handguns a lot.

As you might guess these folks typically rely on the front sight of the shotgun barrel all too much. Breaking pistol shooters of this habit is never easy. Usually Mike points out how the muzzle of the shotgun does its start-stop thing during the swing, a sure sign that the shooter's eyes are going from the bird to the gun, bird to the gun. Once Mike has such folks convinced that they are doing this, he switches gears. Now he asks they look at the target – both eyes really working on sharp focus – and just pull the trigger with no concern about lead at all. If these students are listening, the target almost always breaks. Some of you know all this, but remember this suggestion the next time you are giving some instruction to a new student - one you know is looking at the barrel. Don't give advice that the shooter you are working with was behind or in front/above or below. Stress simply looking at the target hard with both eyes.

Long leads

Now we come to long leads. Here's one way Mike puts it. "If I see the back part of a long crosser break, what's that tell me? It means the front of the shot column has broken the bird. To get the bulk of the shot column on the next bird I know even more lead is required to center the bird."

Mike's point here is to watch our breaks carefully. If we know what to look for, that broken target can give us good and useful information. We'll have a better idea of how to perform even more effectively on the ensuing shot.

In that same vein, how we position our hands on the forend can help or hinder us with the target. Mike suggests experimenting with slight changes in your placement of the hand on the forend. See if this might make sense during your next practice session. Put your hand more under the forend. Doesn't

this tend to help you move the gun up? If so, could that help you on a rising target? If you put more of your hand on the left side of the forend, does that help you move the gun easer to the right – especially on long cross-ers? Most of us are self-programmed to put our forend hands in the same place for every shot, which sounds like the correct idea. But is it for all targets?

Setting up the pool shot

"Setting up the pool shot," is a comment Mike Mohr makes with many of his students. Obviously, this has to do with where you break the first target to make the second shot easier.

Despite the advantages of setting up the pool shot, it's my bet that too few of us do it religiously. As we know, a good pool shooter not only puts one of the balls in the pocket, he also hits the cue ball so it stops right where he wants it to stop to make an easier shot on the next ball to be taken.

So before you step into the station why not let this thought roll through your mind: "I'm going to set up the pool shot."

Seven Springs sporting clays stations are in a wooded setting among slopes galore, thus offering shots at every imaginable angle. Further, with 101 Lincoln traps at 30 stations this layout is a target setter's dream. Cart paths run to every station, and for inclement weather shooting there's a covered, heated 5-Stand. Take your wife, kids, and/or significant other along. Even if they don't shoot there are activities galore for them to enjoy at this mountain resort. Contact NSCA Level III Instructor Mike Mohr via email at mmohr@7springs.com. Seven Springs Mountain Resort: www.7springs.com.

Mike Mohr, a Level III NSCA Shooting instructor who teaches out of Seven Springs Resort in the mountains of Pennsylvania, really knows his stuff.

Mike Mohr watches from behind as Sisley tries to break a high incoming target.

Mike Mohr pontificates about shooting to students working toward for their Level I NSCA Shooting Instructor Certificate.

The shooting lodge at Seven Springs resort and shooting complex.

Part of earning a student's Level I NSCA Shooting Instructor accreditation requires the students to instruct one another. Here Sisley suggests to one of his fellow students the how-to of breaking a quartering shot.

This top student is about to shoot his Perazzi Sporter as the Level III NSCA Instructor looks on.

GOLD MEDAL SHOOTING ACADEMY

The four principals of the Gold Medal Shooting Academy at Dover Furnace, N.Y., are Dan Carlisle, Haley Dunn, Scott Shinneman and Mark Weeks, all of whom are champion shotgunners as well as very experienced instructors. The Dover Furnace Gold Medal Shooting Academy is graded pass/fail. No attendee is rubber stamped as passing. A written test with questions is given on the final afternoon, plus the students have to pass an interview test with Carlisle to receive their accreditation. The course is for Level I and higher NSCA Instructors to bring their teaching skills to even higher levels, and relatively experienced shooters to bring their shotgunning game to championship or near championship status.

How does Gold Medal accomplish this? The book that comes with the course is one key. How the book is so intensely covered in the twice-daily skull sessions is another. Obviously, the shooting under the watchful eye of the Gold Medal Academy principals is extremely important as well. Each of the shooting days students are paired off with three instructors – so pupils are viewed and helped by all three – every day. But my take after only one day of the academy was the extreme importance of the skill sessions.

After Lesson I (Safety) comes Lesson II – Basic Fundamentals. While most Level I and Level II Instructors are very familiar with basic shotgunning fundamentals all those taking the course learn a lot more here. The Basic Fundamentals chapter wasn't an "I already know it all" thing. We were shown how stance is a lot more complicated than simply how you position your feet. Knee position, waist position and head position were all stressed here, along with various gun mounts and positioning of the elbows.

While bending forward is encouraged, this movement was to be from the hips only – not leaning forward from your knees. Dan talked about how many new shooters do the reverse, bend back from the hips and/or knees. Maybe some are doing this fearing recoil, but Dan thinks most of this is done by young and smaller shooters who do not possess the strength to hold the shotgun up properly so they lean backwards. When you find this with someone you are teaching why not suggest some exercises to improve arm strength, which might be only practicing their gun mount over and over to strengthen the arms and get accustomed to the weight of the gun.

Also in the gun mount, Dan wants our head to come forward and down slightly. He says, "When done properly the head will be as far forward as possible." I've always been accustomed to raising the gun to my face, but moving the head down and forward allows a better (maybe more athletic) position in the gun. Further, Dan wants the fat or skin of the cheek over the comb to create a bit of a cushion. So look for part of the cheek hanging slightly over the comb of the gun on someone you are introducing to shotgunning, as well as thinking about such a face position for yourself. Done properly this means such a shooter is really hard into the gun. This type of mount probably also puts your nose closer to your thumb than you have done in the past.

More on fundamentals covers where your finger should contact the trigger and the proper way to hold the gun with the forend hand. Even further, precise placement of the stock on the shoulder is stressed – e.g., if the stock is slightly high on the shoulder the gun will lose its uphill pitch (more on that shortly). If the gun is placed too low on the shoulder, it's just about impossible to achieve a correct head position. Also stressed is that it doesn't take much of a low or high position of the butt stock on the shoulder to negatively impact the shot. Elbow position is also given its due.

The Fundamentals part of the Academy isn't over yet. There's still gun fit, natural point of aim and dominant eye. You can bet the instructors at the Academy had plenty to say on all three, as well as on shooting vests, pouches, headgear, footgear and chokes.

Lesson IV gets into the "meat" of what's taught at Gold Medal. Fifteen years ago Carlisle developed his "Secrets of the Triangle," and this is what Lesson IV is all about. Let's break this "triangle" down to its individual parts – and what the shooter should do first, second, third and so on.

Break zone

First locate your break zone. Do this by finding the area where the target(s) looks clearest with your hard focus. That hard focus area will vary with target speed and other factors. Where the target is most clearly defined is a very short zone. So when the bird goes into sharp focus, that's the start of the break zone. As the target moves from clear to just a bit fuzzy, that's your end of the break zone.

Hold point

Obviously, this is where you place the muzzle before calling for the bird, maybe $\frac{1}{3}$ to $\frac{1}{2}$ of the way back to the trap from the break zone. Farther back for slow birds. Farther out for fast birds. A key here is to never allow the target to get in front of the gun.

Speed

This is the start of the "triangle." The gun moves to converge with the target. Next target speed and gun speed must match.

Placement

Where you mount on the target controls the lead. In all cases the mount will be on the leading edge or somewhere in front of the target dependent upon target speed, angle and distance.

Feel

While watching Carlisle coach the father and son team preparing for the US Open I kept hearing the words "connected" and "connection." In my notebook I wrote those words over and over. Such a "connection" (between the gun and the target) seems a very basic ingredient to the Carlisle method. The idea is to "connect" with the target – keep the gun and bird moving at the same speed and then simply wait for the target to enter the break zone.

Focus

Hard focus, as already covered, starts when the target enters your break zone. The Gold Medal course suggests putting a colored dot on a ceiling fan. Turn the fan to medium speed. First you will see the entire fan as fuzzy. Keep looking and next you will see the whole blade with the dot. Finally you will see the dot itself – and the fan will slow down in your mind's eye. This is the way Dan expects to see a target; first fuzzy, next the whole clay, finally sharp detail. Sharp focus like this doesn't come easy. We have to work at it.

Executing the shot

Gold Medal says don't think about shot mechanics before calling for the target. Think only about achieving hard focus as the clay enters your break zone. The harder you can focus the more your hands will listen to what the brain is telling them to do. Carlisle and his team are first to admit that telling yourself to focus hard on every target is extremely difficult to do

But after the shot there's more work, and Dan and Haley were quick to confirm this. Ask yourself some serious post-shot questions. First off might be, "How did I really see the target?" Be honest. Did you see the front curve of the bird? Or the dome? Or the center circle? Or what? If you hit the back half that probably means you could take even more lead to center the bird – and vice versa. Post-Shot Analysis is on the last page in the Gold Medal book. This is where you are reminded that a "routine" has a beginning, middle and an end. Post-Shot Analysis is the end or final part. According to the Gold Medal folks, there's not a single professional shooter who does not run a post-shot routine.

Mental routines

Some of you already know a bit about your conscious and sub-conscious mind,

and how they work, but more is explained in the Academy's final chapter. Here you learn there are four "routines" – not just one. First there's your mechanical routine – where you locate the break zone, realize the bird's angle, distance and speed – and determine your placements.

Second comes your pre-shot routine – where you go over what you can control. Make this one short, as Dan says, "Something that you can remember under pressure." Try a word that triggers a feeling or a focus. Visualize the target moving and breaking. Demand of yourself that you look for (hard focus) a specific part of the target.

The shot routine is maybe even shorter. Have no mechanical thoughts – maybe only

Sisley steps into the shooting box after receiving some of the Gold Medal Shooting Academy advice.

something like "front edge." Thus allow your sub-conscious mind to make the shot. Finally, there's your post-shot routine – which has already been discussed. Don't allow yourself to get away without going through your post-shot routine.

Reading about some of what happens at the Gold Medal Shooting Academy is only an infinitesimal part of actually attending that school. I promise, you will learn much more than you ever thought possible. The contact is carlisleshooting@aol.com; Website: www.shooting4gold.com.

Instructor and Gold Medal Shooting Academy principal Haley Dunn watches closely as one of the academy's students goes to work on a target.

Dan Carlisle inspects Sisley's trap shooting prowess as Nick shoots the then-new Beretta DT11 trap gun.

Before every shot, Carlisle typically suggests good shooting wisdom to his student.

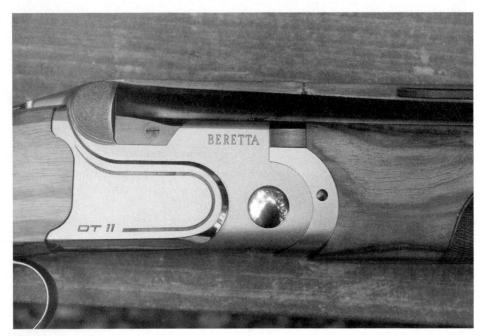

Close up of the DT11 receiver some of us shot during our learning session at the Gold Medal Shooting Academy.

Dan Carlisle showing us how it's done.

Shotgunners can keep learning about the how-to all their life. Carlisle Teaching. This is the cover of Carlisle's famous shooting instructional DVD – "Secrets of the Triangle."

CHAPTER THREE

CLAY SHOOTING HOW-TO

THE QUARTERING SHOT

At our first shot the pintails wheeled in reverse. Both Neil and I had knocked down easy birds that had been extending their feet for landing in our spread. But there was a significant wind blowing that day, so a quick second shot, if successful, was going to be difficult. I got lucky and bagged my second bird, and my two shots had rung out very close together. For some reason Neil didn't get to his second shot as quickly. I can't remember the reason for that, but I do recall looking over to my right – to watch his barrel swing too far ahead of one escaping drake in beautiful, full plumage. Next Neil shot even farther ahead with his third shot.

As his chocolate Lab, Hershey, set about the fetching chore, Neil started whining about not killing that magnificent drake sprig, "Gad what a beautiful bird," he lamented. "And an easy one, too," he scolded himself further. "Even after I missed him the first time, I was telling myself what a great bird this will be to mount. I just knew I was going to kill him with my third shot"

Within minutes we had changed the subject, and after Hershey had brought us three spectacular pintails the subject changed to something else. Those few seconds happened several years ago. I didn't think too much about Neil's miss until long after that day.

One of waterfowling's or clay shooting's toughest shots is the left to right crosser – for a right-handed shooter, of course. I think the quartering away shot can also be a tough

one, particularly for those whose natural tendency is to be a sustained lead type of shooter, i.e. get the muzzle ahead of the target, track only briefly until one is certain of the correct sight picture (lead) and then hit the trigger.

This philosophy of shooting, known as sustained lead, works very well on any number of clay targets – as well ducks, geese, doves and other birds – most crossing shots anyway. But I think another ideal way to shoot the quartering away clay bird is to use the swing-through method. Why? I think it's too easy to dial in too much lead on this shot via the sustained lead. A quartering away bird does not require much lead at all. Naturally, target speed and distance to the bird are factors in the required lead, but I still think, generally, a quartering away clay does not require much lead. Consequently, if the shooter simply swings the muzzle through this target and hits the trigger when he or she first sees a bit of minimal daylight between the target and the muzzle, the bird will fall. If the bird isn't very far or if the bird is fighting some wind you probably don't even need to see daylight.

The idea with using the swing-through shooting method is that you use muzzle speed to counteract the need for lead. Because you start from behind the target the muzzle has to play catch-up with the bird. So the muzzle has to move faster than the target. Two of the tougher targets in skeet would be Low 5 and 6 – and High 2 and 3. These are the quartering away birds on the skeet field and are four good targets to practice the swing-through technique on. At 20 yards or so you might not think any of these four birds would be that difficult, and I would agree with you.

But, assuming it's safe to do so, start stepping back from these four stations. Add five yards to the distance and the shot becomes slightly more difficult. But as you add 10, 15, 20 and more yards to say a Low 6, I think you're going to find two things. First, the quartering away shot becomes one heck of a lot more difficult, and, secondly, it's just easier to hit this bird with a degree of consistency using the swing-through method compared to the sustained lead. Staying on the front edge of the bird can also be effective, but that's in another chapter.

Your first shot at an incoming 20-yard clay is relatively easy. But if the next shot, especially if there's some wind, is a quartering shot your muzzle may not be in an ideal position to set up for the second bird, especially using the sustained-lead method. If the clay you have to shoot next is already significantly ahead of your gun's muzzle you'll get to that bird a lot quicker (before it gains additional distance from you) if you now incorporate the swing-through method. If you have to take the time to get the muzzle ahead of the bird, sustain what you think is the ideal lead that takes a few extra milliseconds, milliseconds in which the bird is getting farther away from you. And don't forget what Neil did at the start of all this – shot too far ahead with his sustained lead.

I think the toughest bird to kill (though not the toughest to shoot) is the duck (or any other real bird) that's flying directly away from you with some distance between that bird and the gun. You can break a wing, yes. That's not likely, however. But it's tough to drive shot up into the vitals far enough for a sure kill on this bird that's flying directly away from you. Similarly, a straight away

clay target offers its thinnest profile – making it easier for the clay to escape through a hole in the shot pattern. It's not as tough to kill (penetrate) the quartering away bird as one flying directly away, but the quartering clay is a close second if there's any distance involved. So the quicker you can get a telling shot off, before too much distance becomes involved, the better the chances of shattering the clay into tiny pieces. Among skeet champions the sustained lead is used by most on every target. But a few of these super shooters rely on the swing through. I swear the best of the best swing-through skeeters break the bird coming out of the Low House at Station 6 faster than the best sustained-lead shooters. World Skeet Champ Charlie Parks comes first to mind in this regard. My point is that using the swing through for your second clay on a quartering away bird should be slightly quicker, plus there will be less chance to over lead.

Conversely, the incoming quartering target – say a Low 1 or Low 2 bird on a skeet field or, on the other side of the field, a High 7 or a High 6, these are easy targets for most shooters, whether we're talking a skeet, sporting clays or 5-Stand clay or in duck or goose shooting. Further, I firmly believe most will naturally shoot these quartering incomers easier with a sustained-lead type of swing. Get the muzzle in front to start with, keep the muzzle ahead, track the bird briefly until the ideal lead is seen, and then immediately hit the trigger.

If you dally on the trigger a bit with the quartering incomer, there's usually no problem as the bird is flying closer to you. Hopefully, you won't be choked up with a tight full choke for this one, especially if you're prone to maintain your lead as the clay gets closer and closer.

Hard focus on the bird's head is critical on any shot, but you have more time to do that hard focus with the incoming quartering bird, compared to the departing quartering duck that's getting farther and farther from you every millisecond. Still, those who can train themselves to hard focus on the quartering away bird's head will certainly make their shot easier.

Staying in the gun is always important, but I think this is particularly true on any quartering bird – incoming or outgoing. It's easy to peek a bit on any bird, but I think this is easier for anyone to do on a bird that's getting farther away.

Follow through is equally important. This might be obvious on the going away quartering bird, but a good follow through on the incoming quartering clay is also very important. You don't have to follow through much, but you should follow through at least

a bit after the trigger is pulled. Those who get lazy with following through tend to do one of two things: stop the gun, or slow the gun. Both are likely to result in a miss.

The incoming or outgoing quartering shot is easy to practice on any skeet field. Many sporting clays and 5-Stand layouts also offer ample opportunity for practicing these shots. I suggest, where safe and possible, to practice both shots at distances farther than the typical skeet station. Work on these quartering birds when they are 30 and 40 yards away. You'll certainly find them challenging, especially the going away quartering bird. Shoot it both swing through and sustained lead. See if you don't agree with me that the swing through works better on this going away quartering bird.

Instructor Gil Ash explains some how-to of breaking an escaping quartering target to Sisley.

Sisley works on his swing-through technique on a quartering away clay.

Vicki Ash, Gil's wife and a top instructor, explains what she wants this student to do on a quartering away clay.

Before starting a shooting lesson in the field, Gil Ash typically conducts an indoor skull session on the how-to he will be working on with his students.

Vickie Ash uses her hands, imagining she's holding a gun, to explain what she wants her student to do.

Getting ready for the gun mount. Start the muzzle moving first on the clay's flight path, then blend in the gun mount.

Champion sporting clays shooter Brad Kidd shows his smooth and steady form.

Staying smooth and making the turn and gun mount appear as one unit – that's what you should be striving for.

Wendell Cherry, top clay performer and instructor, loves his long 34-inch barrels on his Perazzi 2000. He thinks the long barrels can smooth out his swing.

Wendell Cherry instructs Sisley on making sure both hands are working together to better see, and hit, the target.

THE "SWING" IS A MISNOMER

"Swinging" a shotgun. It's an easily recognized term. Everyone "swings" a shotgun as they are tracking a target, right? Well, yes, but a qualified yes. That's because a proper shotgun move should be more of a "turn" than a "swing."

Here's my point. If we swing a shotgun with only our arms, and never turn our bodies (which is what a great many shotgunners do - swing without turning), the end result can be a lot less than perfect. Whether in the confines of a waterfowl blind, at a sporting station, on a skeet pad, or a F.I.T.A.S.C. hula hoop, it's important to incorporate this body turn into your so-called swing.

Why? Number one, a proper body turn is simply a good fundamental of shotgun shooting. It adds a lot of positives to the endeavor. Anyone who shoots mainly via swinging of the arms is bound to experience a number of problems. Try this experiment. Let's assume you're right-handed. If you're left-handed, the reverse of what I'm going to say will apply. Practice swinging a shotgun with only your arms and no body movement on an imaginary clay target that's flying from left to right.

One negative that's going to be obvious is that you won't be able to swing as far to the right as might be necessary. A body turn, at least the waist up, but preferably even from the ankles up, will allow you to turn farther to the right.

Not so obvious to most shooters will be the right shoulder is dipping lower than the left shoulder as you're beginning to complete the arm-only swing. This shoulder dipping is a very strong negative. It won't allow consistent results. What shoulder dipping does is bring your gun's muzzle away from the target's flight path – actually below the target's flight path. When we miss a bird our shooting partners most often say, "You were behind."

Well, maybe you were and maybe you weren't. Many shooters tend to think of missing the target only by being in front or being behind, mostly the latter. But I assure you one of the most critical factors in successful shotgun shooting is staying on line with the bird. Yes, in addition to missing in front or behind, misses can also occur because the shot cloud passes above or below the bird. When the sight picture looks just perfect as you hit the trigger and you still miss – guess where you probably missed. Above or below. In the shoulder-dipping scenario I discussed above it's almost impossible to hit the target in question – because the shot cloud is going to end up going below the target. So you won't make a telling shot, even if your lead on the bird looks perfect.

If you tend to swing a shotgun, with minimal, if any, body turn, it's easy to practice the proper maneuver. Do it at home, practicing with an unloaded gun. In addition to learning to turn your entire body as you swing the shotgun, you'll also be practicing a proper gun mount. Without a proper (and thus consistent) gun mount, it's very difficult to be a consistent shooter.

The tendency for so many is another dip maneuver. As the gun is mounted, the right hand gets too active in bringing the butt stock to the shoulder. When that happens the muzzle dips down away from the target's flight path, whether the bird in question is flying straightaway, offers a quartering or a crossing shot. What you want is a smooth move to the bird, not just with your hands, but also with the ever-so-important muzzle.

How do you do that? The mistake so many make is that they start the butt stock to the shoulder first. This move almost guarantees that the muzzle will come down, probably away from the bird's flight path. The additional negative here is this. As this shooter is getting the butt to the shoulder the muzzle isn't moving yet. Thus the bird is getting further ahead of that muzzle.

What makes a lot more sense is to start the muzzle moving with the bird so that the pitch or feathered target doesn't get that jump on you. Then bring the stock to the shoulder as you keep swinging and turning. You may still see some muzzle dip as the butt stock nears your shoulder. If this happens, try less gripping pressure with the right/pistol grip hand. Also, work on smoothness as you practice at home. If the muzzle dips down, slow down until you become more accustomed to this move and comfortable with it.

It's a good idea to initially practice this move on an imaginary straightaway clay. Get the feel of having the muzzle move smoothly and unwaveringly to the top corner of your office or den wall. One company sells a special flashlight that you can insert in your practice gun's muzzle. It has a tiny red beam. The slightest incorrect move to the imaginary bird can thus be seen easily via the light on the wall corner.

Once you're comfortable with this smooth move to the straightaway target, it's time to work on a crossing shot. Here you can use the seam where the wall meets the ceiling. Start the muzzle at the room's corner, gun down. Start swinging along that wall/ceiling seam, blending in the gun mount while turning, hopefully from the ankles up. As the stock hits your shoulder and cheek, this is when you should be hitting the trigger in a real clay-shooting situation.

How often should you practice this gun mounting and body turning scenario? I don't think any of us should ever stop. This practice should be done every day, at least several times a week, - and not only in the days or weeks leading up to an upcoming tournament.

Why? Because the proper gun mount and the proper turn in your swing hits at the very fundamentals of shotgun shooting. Watch any how-to video on shooting, golf or the stock market. What do the extremely successful pros go back to day in and day out? It's the fundamentals. I recall watching a golf video years ago - done by Gary Player. He kept going back to his grip. To his caddy and other close golfing friends he would say something like, "Keep an eye on my grip. It has to be perfect. If you ever notice the slightest change in my grip, tell me right away."

It's the same with practice sessions using a shotgun on imaginary targets. Your move need only be off minutely to affect your success. Because it's a shotgun you might still get the bird with a slightly poor move, but you won't center that clay. So in your gun mount and turn/swing practice sessions don't be satisfied with anything but perfection.

Professional golfer Vijay Singh is considered one of the hardest working pros when it comes to his practice ethic. He hits balls for hours on end, knocking them out of sand traps hundreds of balls at a session He putts hours after others have gone home. Why does he do this? There's no secret here. He's practicing the basics, the pure fundamentals of his game. He's working on his grip, perfecting his swing so it's nearly the same every time, giving his follow through thorough attention, and he knows his putting stroke has to be consistent – day after day, week after week, month after month.

So many shotgunners pick up their gun and go to shoot with no thought to proper shooting fundamentals. Some of them do fine. They can thank their lucky stars for God-given talent if they do. Guys like Vijay Singh, Tiger Woods, Michael Jordan and other sports stars have a great deal of God-given talent, too. But they augment that talent by practicing the fundamentals over and over and over. Make no mistake about it these guys are not working on something the rest of us don't know about, something we aren't aware of. They are working on basics, fundamentals. It's that simple.

It's easy for a shotgunner to work on fundamentals as often as he wants. You do it in the comfort of your own home over and over and over. Tiger Woods doesn't make a perfect golf swing every time, but because he spends so much time on the simple fundamentals he makes of a lot of great swings. If you practice your gun mount and turn/swing 100 times a day, 365 days a year, do you think you'll increase your shotgunning skills? You better believe you will.

A "DIFFERENT" GUN MOUNT

I have a good friend who mounts the butt stock of his shotgun way out past his shoulder, actually on his upper arm. I've never seen anyone mount that far out. Despite this out-of-the-ordinary gun mount I have to admit that Leonard is a pretty good shooter. I always thought my gun mount position was correct, which has always been just inside the ball and socket of my shoulder, but I had my comeuppance with regard to this position - via a two-day shotgun instruction session I had with Will Fennell in South Carolina.

Will had me change a number of major things with regard to my shooting, and he tweaked quite a few others. But the main thing I want to talk about here is how he changed the position of my gun mount, why he did this, and explain the benefits.

After watching me shoot maybe 10 or 15 shells at mostly crossing targets, which I was hitting by the way, Will posed, "How about recoil? Do you suffer from a sore shoulder or neck at all?"

Like a good lawyer, I think Will Fennell knew the answer to his question before he posed it. I told him that I had a lot of recoil problems, like not only shoulder pain, but right wrist and right elbow pain. I also told him that in my writing I had always ac-

knowledged to my readers that I was a recoil pussycat. Maybe once or twice per hundred clay target shots, I'd also flinch.

"You know Nick your rotator cuff is a very thin muscle. It's very easily injured. And the older we get, the more prone we become to a shoulder injury, especially to that thin rotator cuff," he explained. "Would you like me to cure your pain caused by felt recoil?"

Boy, did I. Just in the months before this lesson I had been putting shotguns I had previously loved in the gun safe specifically to try others that would not hurt me so much. I know I'm coming off sounding like a wimp with this recoil thing, but I'm no spring chicken. I was having serious concerns that I was going to have to cut my shotgun shooting way back, switch to shooting only 2½-inch .410s for a while, or, horror of horrors, have to quit shooting altogether. I didn't like any of these three alternatives, so I couldn't wait until I heard what Will Fennel had to suggest to me. I also remember thinking, "If this works my readers are going to love me for it."

For the lesson with Fennell I was starting from a low-gun position. I think I can see the targets quicker and better with the gun un-mounted, and Will agrees with that premise, as do most all of those with whom I've taken shotgun shooting lessons. I take a lot of instruction – all in the hope of securing good information for my readers – and, of course, it's always great to learn more from an expert.

"Place the stock in closer on your chest," he instructed.

I moved the stock well in, but Fennell chided, "No, that's not far enough. This is going to be a totally new and different feel for you. You aren't going to get accustomed to it today or even tomorrow. But we're going to work on this new pre-mount stock position for the hundreds of targets we are going to shoot this afternoon and tomorrow morning."

So I moved the stock even further in toward my chest. "Now start making some practice mounts for me," Will suggested.

When I did this the motion felt very different. Further, it wasn't as easy to get the stock all the way up into my face. Often the butt stock would snag a bit on my clothing. Will saw what was happening with this, so he suggested, "Look, you don't have to have the stock touching your shirt or sweater as you mount. Move the gun out just slightly away from your clothing so the recoil pad isn't touching anything. Don't move the stock away an inch or two, just a little. This will eliminate the stock hanging up on clothing. Further, you will be more inclined to mount the comb to your face. Your tendency has been to mount the gun to your shoulder. Depending upon where the stock stops on your shoulder you may or may not be getting the comb all the way to its proper sweet spot, which is right under your cheekbone.

It has been some time since I had this instruction. I'm still working on my gun mount – starting from the new position and ending up in a new position, and I'm going to have to work more at it. The key is that the butt stock ends up being even further in toward my chest compared to what I previously thought was the proper spot, say just inside the ball and socket area of the shoulder. Feel up there on your shoulder right now to see what I'm talking about.

From that spot my new Will Fennell gun mount is approximated $1\frac{1}{2}$ inches closer to the center of my chest. Now how could this new position have anything to do with reduction in felt recoil? Maybe you are already surmising the answer.

First off, my sore (and old) shoulder is no longer involved in recoil. Now my whole body is absorbing the recoil (more or less). This is because the whole mass of my body,

or at least a heck of a lot more of it than my shoulder, takes the brunt of the shove. I no longer feel any shoulder pain at all, even if I shoot say 100 12-gauge rounds in an hour or less, if I concentrate on this different gun mount.

Further, my wrist and elbow are no longer sore at all. Fennell says the reason why is when the gun recoiled against my shoulder there was more gun movement rearward, movement that was in part absorbed by my right wrist and right elbow. Now with my whole body absorbing so much recoil, my wrist and elbow are treated more tenderly. Thus the reason there's no pain in the wrist and elbow joints now. I probably have at least some minor arthritis in both joints, considering my age. Arthritis in the shoulder has to be a problem for many other old timers as well. Couple all three joint problems with the thin, vulnerable rotator cuff muscle and it's no wonder so many of us become so recoil intolerant. Of course, you don't have to be approaching old age to experience recoil pain.

When most of us mount the recoil pad to our shoulder the pad does not contact with 100 percent of that part of our anatomy. Some place the butt too high and get the top of the pad somewhat above the shoulder area. Others finish the mount with the stock too low, so the bottom of the recoil pad essentially touches nothing but air. But when you mount to your chest the recoil pad touches everything. You get 100 percent of the recoil pad touching something, and that means the recoil is spread out over a wider area, which is a very good thing.

Another benefit of this "different" gun mount position is that those who use it or will try it discover something else very positive. With the stock just inside the shoulder ball and socket area it's almost impossible to shoot with your head level. The tendency is thus to tilt the head. Depending upon how long your neck is (mine is long) and how high your cheekbone is the more head tilting tends to take place. Otherwise you can't be looking down the rib unless considerable cast off is built into the stock. And let's face it, not many factory stocks have enough cast built in for long neck/high cheekbone shooters.

But with the butt stock much further in toward your chest you can shoot without the head tilt. Everybody is built differently, but with this new gun mount final position I found I was looking right down the rib of both the guns I took along to shoot for this instruction in South Carolina – while keeping my head perfectly level. Few of us have perfect vision, but there's no one who has better vision with a head tilted right or left. This is especially true over time. Try driving a car with your head tilted to the side. It takes a very short time for fatigue to set in.

If you have had your shotgun fitted professionally – and mounted to what I once called the normal shoulder spot – just inside the ball and socket area – your gun may not fit perfectly when you starting mounting well inside the area to where I have suggested. Then again it isn't written in stone that you will have to be refit from a cast standpoint. What may change is the amount of pitch you now require. This is because the toe of the butt stock is not in your shoulder – but on your chest. Frankly, I experienced no "digging in" of the toe of the stock with any of the guns I have shot so far. The two I used in South Carolina were carefully measured by Will Fennell (he's also a gun fitter), and there was minimal pitch in those two over/unders. If you ever shoot with him he has numerous ways he can change the pitch on the gun you're shooting with him, and he thinks pitch is a very important measurement.

Back to my friend who shoots with the stock way out on his arm – well out from the shoulder ball and socket. One year he took

a 12-gauge over/under to Colombia, South America. It was a light one, from a famous maker, and well in demand on the used market these days. That friend shot for less than an hour the first morning of our hunt – and had to quit – virtually quit for the rest of the day, the next two full days and the final morning of our trip.

Lots of folks go on these high-volume dove shoots and experience plenty of pain, resulting in some unbelievable black-and-blue bruising. Competitive and casual clay target shooters also suffer a great deal from what the effects of recoil dish out. A new, different gun mount can cure these problems. No one is going to make this change and be comfortable with it immediately, but for any of you who try it and stick with it – I bet your fear of recoil becomes history.

Will Fennell can be reached at willfennell@willfennell.com.

This is author's old pre-mount gun position – with the butt stock between arm and chest.

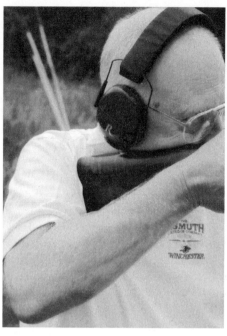

This is author's new pre-mount gun position – with the butt stock much closer in to chest.

The final position of the new gun mount is much closer in on the author's chest, well inside the ball and socket area of the shoulder.

Here the butt stock is just inside the ball and socket area of the author's chest, which was his previous final gun-mount position.

The head tilt is exaggerated a bit here, but it is typical, yet poor form, to allow you to see straight down the shotgun's rib when the butt stock is too far out on your shoulder.

By moving the stock well in from the ball and socket area of the shoulder it's much easier to end up with your eye looking right down the shotgun's rib, exactly where it should be.

HOW TO BE A BETTER SHOTGUN SHOT: PRE-SEASON PREP

Practice your gun mount. Often. Make certain your gun-mounting basics are correct. Get professional help to make sure. Until you're making the same, consistent gun mount don't go overboard thinking about gun fit. Gun fit is extremely important, but as long as your gun mount is inconsistent it will be very difficult for anyone to fit you perfectly.

Practice gun mounting tips. Imagine straightaway targets first. Work on smoothness. No bobbing around of the muzzle. Especially avoid muzzle dipping, usually caused by getting the pistol gripping hand too involved. Start your gun mount move from the same low-gun position every time. Get the butt stock to the same place on your shoulder and cheek every time. Practice your gun mount every day.

Next, work on imaginary crossing shots. Start the muzzle moving along the bird's imaginary flight path first, and then blend in bringing the stock to your shoulder. This move is the centerpiece of top instructor John Bidwell's well-known book *"Move, Mount, Shoot."* So many mistakenly do the opposite – mount, move, and then shoot – which is fundamentally in error. Think smooth. If you're not smooth, slow down in your practice gun-mounting sessions. Smoothness will come if you work on it.

Here, the shooter's face is a little too far back on the stock.

Anywhere you can shoot clay targets will be helpful, but fine tune your gun mount. When you shoot clay targets start from the same gun-down position you found worked during your practice gun-mounting sessions.

Try this for a crossing clay target shot. If you're right-handed place a little more weight on your left foot – say 60 percent. Bend at the knees slightly. Point your left toe at the spot you want to break the target. You know where the target is going to emerge. Place the muzzle half way between where you want to break the target and where the clay emerges. Place your eyes half way between where your muzzle now is and where the target is going to emerge. These suggestions simply put you in a perfect or near perfect position, making it easier to break the target.

Pat Lieske and all other shotgun instructors will stress practicing your gun mount.

Think smoothness in the gun mount. Slow down. Don't rush.

SHOOTING TIPS FOR THE FIELD

Let's say there's a dove winging toward you, or the mallards are making their final swing for the decoys, or you're walking in on a staunch point. In each of these scenarios, and others, you can be physically ready by getting your shotgun in the perfect position, the same start position you have practiced hundreds of times during your gun-mounting sessions at home. That's an edge, a genuine shooting edge.

Think about your feet and how you want them positioned. Think about the muzzle. If possible move it into the most advantageous position before it's time to shoot. Recall how you moved the muzzle half way back from where you expected to break the clay bird – toward the target's emergence point. Do this just before you're ready to shoot a real bird. It just makes the shot easier. Do it often enough and you won't have to think about it. Practice this philosophy and you'll discover that you can use it more frequently than you might now suspect.

Of course, we can't be so thoroughly prepared for all the shots we encounter in the field. Birds burst forth or appear with no warning, so there's no time to incorporate what I have suggested. For these types of shooting situations the best advice is to think

about your feet. Right-handed shooters want that left foot leading at trigger-pulling time. So they need to be stepping over logs and other items in their path with their left foot first. When you hear the roar of a grouse flush or the twitter of woodcock wings you often have to turn your body somewhat. As you turn, perform the proper footwork, getting that left foot in the lead.

THE TOUGHEST SHOT

I don't think there's any question here – it's the very, very long shot. Most folks don't even try them. The game of sporting clays has shown that expert shotgunners can break these super-long shots – and do it consistently. I'm talking 60 yards and more. In South America some experienced dove shooters don't even bother with the 15 to 40 yard shots. They think they're too easy. Making a 55-yard shot on a wind-driven dove requires an unbelievably long lead, but a few experts have learned how to do this.

However, if you're having trouble with doves or clay targets at 25 yards there's little sense in attempting to master a 55-yard try. Consistently making the shorter-range shots is what you need to learn first. If you can't break 9 out of 10 from Station Four on a skeet field, shooting from the gun-down position, you need to work on your basics, most of which have been discussed already. Shotgunning is no different than any other sport. They all get down to basic fundamentals. The person or team that performs the fundamentals best will always be a force to be reckoned with. There's no more important basic fundamental in shotgunning than the gun mount. You have to use proper gun mounting techniques, and you have to make the same gun mount every time. Combine a perfect gun mount with proper body, foot and muzzle position, and look at the ideal spot – the birds you're after will certainly be in trouble.

PRACTICE SESSIONS TO IMPROVE YOUR WINGSHOOTING

It was amazing to watch Bill shoot. We were in Colombia, South America's Cauca Valley. Though what I saw took place over 30 years ago, I can still picture this shooter's movements in my mind today. He was so smooth. He seemed to be hardly trying. He moved his barrels and his body minimally. And doves kept falling from the sky – dove after dove after dove, many at significant distances. Plenty of birds were passing over my head, but I was so intrigued with this guy's shooting that I kept passing shot after shot after shot.

At the time I thought I was a pretty good shotgunner. Watching Bill was my comeuppance. Ever since then I've tried to become a student of the game, a pupil of consistent smoothbore shooting. If I have learned anything during this time it's that being suc-cessful with a pump, semi-auto, over/under or a side-by-side boils down to the basics. If we don't know the basics, if we don't utilize these fundamentals every time we pull the trigger, we're going to have a very tough time with consistency.

SEEK OUT A SKEET FIELD

There are literally thousands of gun clubs across the country with one or more skeet fields. If you're not already a member of one, find such a club and join. But don't do what everyone else does – shoot a regimented round from all eight stations. Instead, try this regimen. Maybe you can do it with a friend or relative, then both of you will be learning and practicing these fundamentals. Go to Station 7. Note skeet field sketch if you're unfamiliar with this clay target game. I suggest skeet because it requires the least expense, so you can practice the fundamen-

Work on straightaway or nearly straightaway targets first. Next try quartering shots, and finally crossers.

tals over and over.

Although the formal game of skeet permits a mounted shotgun, I'm going to always have you starting from the low-gun position of your choice. More about that gun position shortly. You can throw a high target from above Station 1 or a low target from just to the right of Station 7. We're going to work on that low target first while standing at Station 7. This is a going-away bird, typical of many shots you will get in the uplands – pheasants, quail, grouse, woodcock, chukars and so forth. Naturally, you get other angles on these birds, but let's walk before we run, practice the easier straightaway shots.

Start by placing your gun's muzzle where you think the bird is going to be when you pull the trigger. Of course, you can simply ask for a low target to be thrown (they all have essentially the same path) to help you determine where you should place the muzzle. Also, place the butt stock in the appropriate low-gun position. Assuming you're a right-handed shooter, point your left toe in the vicinity of where you expect to break the bird. Place about 60 percent of your weight on that left foot. Bend both knees slightly. Call for the bird.

When the bird appears you need to be staring at it so hard that you can easily see the rings on the target's dome. This hard focus is one of the fundamentals we all must always try to improve upon.

As smoothly and effortlessly as possible start the gun to your shoulder as you see the target. One key to hitting a straightaway bird consistently is to make sure the gun's muzzle does not dip down away from the bird's flight path as you mount. Doing so takes away from the smoothness you're striving for, as well as taking the muzzle away from where it's supposed to be in the first place and when the trigger is pulled. If the muzzle dips down, you have to make another move to get the muzzle back where it's supposed to be.

Right here is a good time to stop our shooting for a bit and talk about the gun mount. Most formal clay target games allow a fully mounted gun. Why? It's simply easier to hit targets if you mount the gun first. But you can't mount the gun first in the hunting field. So how do you cover this base? No wingshooter will ever be very successful without a proper and consistent gun mount, another of these fundamentals we're trying to stress here. Of all the fundamentals involved in field shooting, a proper and consistent gun mount heads the list. I know, I'm being redundant, not only in this chapter but others as well, but a great gun mount is that important. So I'm hoping I have your attention on this.

You develop a proper and consistent gun mount at home. You practice mounting your shotgun every day, and as often as possible every day. Start by practicing on an imaginary Low 7 target – using the top corner of a room where two walls and the ceiling come together. Place the muzzle at the corner. Place the butt stock where it's most comfortable for you. I like my butt stock tucked in about ½-inch under my armpit. If you're more comfortable with some other butt-stock position, no problem, go ahead and use it. Just make certain you get that butt stock to the exact same starting place every time.

Now simply raise the stock to your shoulder, without allowing the muzzle to deviate from that wall corner where you started. Work on being smooth. If the muzzle does dip, even the slightest, slow down your next mount. I'll come back to more gun-mounting basics shortly, but let's get back to shooting that easy Low 7 straightaway.

Incorporate everything you learned mounting on your wall corner into the Low 7 shot. Shoot it over and over. Remember this. There's no sense practicing a more difficult shot until you master the easy shot. That's what we're doing at Low 7 – shooting an easy target over and over and over. Get to the point where you can consistently break nine out of 10, even 10 out of 10.

Only then are you ready to switch to a slightly more difficult shot. Stand half way between Station 7 and Station 6. Continue shooting only the low target. From where you're now standing a very slight quartering shot is offered. Again, this is the type of shot you will get many times when shooting the various upland game birds. Place the gun's muzzle where you expect to break the bird, then move the muzzle back toward the Low House slightly. Move your eyes back a bit more. As the bird emerges make your hard focus on the leading edge. Start the gun's muzzle moving along the flight path first. Only then blend bringing the butt stock to your shoulder and face.

Let's stop again and go back to some more gun-mounting practice at home. This time we're again going to start the gun's muzzle at the wall's corner. Instead of point-ing our lead foot at the wall corner, however, we're going to point that foot midway across the room. Now our in-house practice is go-ing to be for a crossing shot. Muzzle in the wall's corner, start that muzzle moving along the wall/ceiling seam. Only after the muzzle is moving, start bringing the butt stock to your face and shoulder. Don't lower your head to the stock. Bring the stock to your face and shoulder. The idea is to swing the muzzle exactly along the wall/ceiling seam, no bobbing up or down at all. If you can't keep the muzzle moving smoothly along that wall seam try slowing down. This is your basic, fundamental gun move on any target that's not a straightaway. You can't practice this move enough. It's similar to a profes-sional golfer grooving his swing by going to the practice range and doing it over and over. The one thing virtually anyone can do to best improve his wingshooting is to practice the gun mount over and over. Of course, it must be a proper gun mount first. Then it has to be consistent time after time.

Gun fit becomes extremely important now that you have a proper and consistent gun mount. Some new shotgunners rush right into a so-called custom gun fit. This is not a good idea – until you have a proper and consistent gun mount. Only then can a professional fit you perfectly. If your mount is inconsistent there's no way anyone can fit you well, unless you get fitted while the gun is already mounted. But an already mounted gun position may not be the same as the one you have as you develop a proper and consistent gun mount.

Now let's go back to that shooting position halfway between Stations 6 and 7. Fundamentals – toe aimed toward the break point, 60 percent of your weight on that lead foot. Knees slightly flexed. Muzzle to the break point. Bring the muzzle slightly toward the house. Bring your vision a bit closer to the Low House than where you have the muzzle. When the target appears, start the muzzle moving first. Blend in the gun mount to your face and shoulder. Get to the point where you can smash nine or 10 in a row from this position. Remember, you're practicing the easy shots, incorporating proper fundamentals into shot after shot.

Now move to Station 6. This increases the angle of the shot more. But the basics remain the same. Remember your foot and body position. Muzzle $\frac{1}{3}$ back. Vision – hard focus $\frac{1}{3}$ back from the muzzle. Start the muzzle moving first, but only after the clay appears. Blend in getting the butt stock to your shoulder and face. Again, work on breaking nine and 10 in a row. Make the shot using the same fundamentals every time. Get to this point and you're going to discover the clay targets you're after are going to be in a lot more trouble.

But how do you hit the various incoming clay targets consistently? Go back to Station 7. Now you're ready to shoot the High House target. This is an easy, lazy incomer, but the basics, the fundamentals are the same. Butt stock in exactly the same pre-mount position, every time. Muzzle in the same pre-shot position every time – $\frac{1}{3}$ of the way back from your break point, vision $\frac{1}{3}$ of the way back toward the High House from the muzzle. Left foot pointing at the break point. A bit more weight on that foot. Knees slightly flexed. Call for the bird.

Hard focus on the clay's leading edge. Start the muzzle moving along the flight path first. Next, blend in bringing the butt stock to your shoulder and face. Maintain that hard focus throughout. This is a short-range, easy shot but just keep shooting it over and over. Break it 10 straight times, and then increase the angle of the shot, making it slightly more difficult, by moving to a position half way between Stations 6 and 7. You'll discover this bird now requires just a little more lead. Learn how to break ten straight, but incorporate the same fundamentals every time. Don't forget that the fundamentals are more important than actually breaking the bird. You begin to realize when you have not performed all the fundamentals perfectly – whether you break the bird or not. Make the same move on every bird.

Next simply move to Station 6 and shoot that High House target. You've increased the angle more, so a tad more lead will be required. Same deal. Consistency. Make the same move every time. Get to the point where you can break 10 in a row.

A one-time trip to a skeet field for these practice sessions might help a little, but in reality, it pays to do it as often as possible, for months, even years. If you're interested in becoming a better shot, don't ever stop these simple practice sessions that I've suggested. They are all easy shots, and I think you'll quickly develop the skill to be very consistent, breaking quite a few of all these

targets in a row. Because you are hitting so many of them, your confidence level is bound to soar. Unless you have a skeet field in your backyard, you're probably going to travel some distance to reach such a shooting facility. If that's the case take at least four boxes of shells. Shoot those 100 targets in the manner I've suggested as often as possible, not just a day or so before an upcoming competition. If you tire before shoot 100 targets, rest for a while.

Occasionally you won't always be able to get the muzzle perfectly established, the butt stock in the perfect pre-shot position, your vision exactly where you want it, but you're going to find you can break targets on a surprising number of these occasions. But if you had not been aware of all these fundamentals, or practiced them over and over, you wouldn't have a clue where to start, even if the opportunity for incorporating those fundamentals existed as you walked in on a dog's point, watched the ducks swinging for your spread, or zeroed in on a dove winging your way.

Further, even if you are not able to get everything set up perfectly before the shot in the field you're going to find that your fundamentals will take over. All the gun mounting practice you've done, all the easy targets you've broken using great fundamentals, will take over.

Fundamentals, fundamentals, fundamentals. These were what made Vince Lombardi a legend in his own time and ours. Ditto for sports champions worldwide. Obviously, talent is very important, no matter the endeavor. But it's by practicing fundamentals over and over that we all achieve a skill level that we could never attain otherwise. Talent and proper fundamentals made Bill a fantastic wing shot in Colombia. After watching him I started concentrating on fundamentals. While I may never have the talent to match Bill's skills, I became one heck of a lot better than I ever thought I could be. You can do the same.

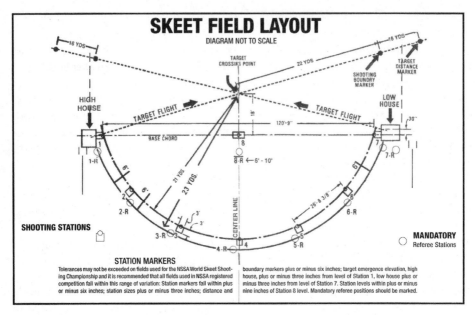

SKEET FIELD LAYOUT
DIAGRAM NOT TO SCALE

For any readers not familiar with the layout of a skeet field, here's a schematic. Note Station Seven – where Sisley suggests starting your practice.

ONE EYE OR TWO?

Do you shoot with one eye or two? I don't think there's any question that the majority of shotgunners, especially the good ones, shoot with both eyes open. But it's also a fact that some very good shotgunners bang away with one eye shut. A Hall of Famer that comes to mind is Nora Martin, one of the great one-eye trap shooters of all time. There are, of course, other excellent shooters who shoot with one eye.

Maybe the tendency to shoot with one eye or both eyes centers around how a person began with a smoothbore in his or her hands. Maybe it was natural to go one way or the other. If any early instruction was involved with an experienced shotgun shooter, the neophyte was probably strongly urged to shoot with both eyes open.

Obviously, I did not have that early-on instruction from a good shotgunner or shotgun instructor telling me to shoot with both eyes open. Unfortunately, I shot with one eye closed for decades. It only makes good common sense to shoot with both eyes open. We wouldn't consider driving down the road in a vehicle with only one eye open. We don't look at the computer screen with one eye. We don't eat our food with one eye, assuming we have two good eyes to perform our daily tasks with. So why would anyone shoot a shotgun with one eye closed?

Again, I think the only reason those of us who have shot with one eye is that we started incorrectly. And it can be very difficult to change from one eye shooting to using both eyes. I can guarantee you I've tried to make the switch many times. A past President of the National Skeet Shooting Association, Louise Terry, made the change successfully, but it took her at least a year, and it was a frustrating at times. But Louise was already a world-class shotgunner shooting with one eye before she made the difficult switch.

Years ago I took a trap shooting lesson with the previously mentioned Nora Martin. When she discovered I was a one-eye shooter it was no problem with her. She simply had me adjust my hold points before calling for the target. I assume Nora still shoots with one eye because, as I said, I took that lesson with her many years ago – probably in the early 1980s.

Since the early 1980s I've taken many, many shotgun lessons. I always thought the information I received taking lessons would transfer over well to my readers. Some instructors, but not all, have suggested I make the switch to two eyes, that is until I took a lesson with Will Fennell. He was very diplomatic about me switching initially, but after an hour or so it became apparent that he would not take no for an answer.

So I committed to making the switch. We shot for two days at his sporting clays layout between Charlotte, North Carolina, and Greenville, South Carolina, and I could not believe how well I was doing. I was breaking hard crossers, incoming and outgoing quartering targets, very long shots – all by looking hard with two eyes open.

I had told Fennell that my nemesis with two eyes was the incoming Low One target in skeet. I could shoot 50 of them and miss them all. Shooting with one eye, I almost never miss this easy incomer. I always figured my left eye was taking over on that bird, even though I am right eye dominant. (I'm a right-handed shooter.)

But Will Fennell convinced me that the reason for the Low One missing was that I was not looking at the target hard enough. "You see two barrels out there shooting with two eyes, right?" he posed.

I sure did, as do many of the one-eyed shooters trying to make the switch that I've questioned on this. They, too, see two barrels when they try to shoot with both eyes open. But Fennell instructed, "Trust me. Just look

at the target harder and harder. It won't be long before that two-muzzle thing disappears. The target will be brighter and slower, and you'll be smoking bird after bird."

Near the end of our second day of instructional shooting Fennell presented me with a long incomer – coming from in front and quartering very slightly to my left – a lot like a Low One Skeet Target. I started missing bird after bird shooting with two eyes. Will really worked with me, but he became frustrated, too. Like me, he couldn't figure out why I was missing this target, according to him way in front – often four to six feet in front, and this clay was less than 20 yards away!

We never did figure that one out. We simply ran out of time. The next day I took a lesson with another top pro – Chris Batha. We shot at the Deep River Sporting Clays layout at the start of the Southern Side-by-side Championships. We shot all crossing and going-away quartering shots, as well as plenty of rabbits. I learned a number of things from Batha during that lesson, but I continued to shoot – fairly successfully – with two eyes open.

Back home in Pennsylvania I don't have a sporting clays course close by where I can practice, so I use a skeet field. The first practice session or two, aside from the nemesis Low One, I was doing as well with two eyes as I had been with one, breaking most all the targets.

But then my two-eye shooting went sour. I don't know why. I started missing crossing shots when everything looked good. Inexplicable. Frustrating. But not long after that two-eye shooting downfall I made a trip to Argentina to shoot doves, ducks and pigeons. I vowed to shoot with both eyes open down there.

And I did. At least at the start. But then I'd try a bird or two with one eye. With one eye it just seemed easier. On those South

American birds I could *measure* the lead so much more precisely shooting with one eye. I guess measure is the definitive word here, maybe precisely as well. There are so many birds in Argentina, Uruguay and Bolivia that a shooter can pick his or her shots. In most instances you can pick a bird in the distance. Stare at a single bird, usually among many, as it wings toward you, make a slow, precise gun mount and hit the trigger, all the while continuing to try and stare a hole through the bird. Actually, I try to zero in on the bird's eye. If the bird is too far away for that I concentrate on the bird's head.

But my point here is, for a one-eye shooter, it's easy to see a very precise lead on the type of shot I've just described. But on a sporting clays course, as well as in many types of bird shooting, including a lot of the duck stuff, you don't have this luxury of time. The deal with what I'm talking about is that you see the bird, mount the gun and pull the trigger, all in one motion. This is the type of shotgunning scenario where I'm convinced two eyes are better than one, and why I'm committed to continue to make the change over from one eye to two. It took Louise Terry a year, so there's no reason for me to give up.

Instructors have stressed time and time again about how well a shooter sees a target is so important. I think everybody sees a little better with two eyes. Two-eye relationship with the barrel (muzzle) is not as good as with one eye, but the increased clarity of the bird when using two eyes supersedes that.

On another shooting lesson, this one with Wendell Cherry, arguably the best American shotgunner at that time, he pointed out how your hands work can help you see the target better – or how your hands work can negatively affect how you see the target. I think Wendell makes a good point here, and it's something that I never realized before, so I'm guessing most of you haven't realized this either.

One of Cherry's mantras is *for the eyes to perform at their best, the hands must be working together*. When the hands are not working together, that's when you see how the target deteriorates. Assuming a right-handed shooter, most of us get too much right hand involved early in the swing/mount scenario. So, when the right hand moves quicker than the left jerky things happen out at the muzzle. This muzzle movement is a visual attractant that takes your eyes, if only slightly, away from the target you are trying so hard to stare a hole through. But if the right hand works at the same speed as the left hand there are no distracting jerky movements with the muzzle, and your eyes are not drawn away from the target, so you are able to see it better throughout the shot stroke. In many chapters I've talked about developing a great gun mount. What Cherry instructs is just one more aspect to gun mounting practice. Get the hands working together at the same speed.

There are so many doves in Argentina, it's a good place to practice with both eyes.

Will Fennell gives Sisley some instructions about using both eyes.

For the eyes to perform at their best they need to be working in conjunction with the hands.

HOW IS YOUR GRIP?

After shooting 50 to 100 targets, I find that my right hand and wrist get really sore. This has been happening for a long time. I previously attributed the problem to gripping the pistol grip too tightly and/or just getting old with arthritis being a significant factor. Both these could be causes. I can do something about the former, but the latter I have to live with. Recently I've come up with a third possibility for hand/wrist soreness, and I'm convinced it is the most important factor of all. Finally, I'm relatively hand/wrist pain free during and after shooting, and I'm also breaking more targets.

I learned about this possibility from a monthly Internet newsletter put out by Dennis DeVault. Dennis is a great trap shooter and a trap shooting instructor. He's also an accomplished stock fitter, plus this guy was probably one of the pioneers that first installed very high ribs, not only on trap guns but on sporting clays shotguns as well. Sporting clays star Jon Kruger began using a high DeVault rib in the mid-1990s. You are probably already aware of the new high-rib sporting guns like the Krieghoff Pro Sporter, the Caesar Guerini Impact, the Kolar MAX/ SC, the Rizzini BR 320. Others appear to be at least on the drawing board.

But this isn't about those high rib shotguns. It's about your hand position on the grip, usually referred to as the pistol grip. The way you grip your shotgun has many ramifications, like alleviating hand/ wrist pain. Again, I learned all this from the DeVault newsletters. Put these ideas into practice, and you are going to be very pleasantly surprised with the results.

Typically, many shotgunners have the thumb well up over the top of the stock. The result is that the palm of the hand rests too high on the grip and the trigger finger pulls up on the trigger, rather than straight back.

Depending upon how long a shooter has been shooting with one eye, the transition to two-eye shooting can be difficult and frustrating.

Work on getting both hands working in unison. The tendency is "too much right hand" – with right-handed shooters, of course.

Shooting instructor contacts

Will Fennell – willfennel@willfennel.com,
803-328-9321 – cell 803-517-4216
Chris Batha – chrisbatha@aol.com
Wendell Cherry – wcherry@twlakes.net –
931-258-3707 – cell 931-529-1802

Louise Terry's comments on the switch

"It took me a full year to make the switch. I ended up changing most all my skeet hold points, my foot positions, as well as where I look all because I was seeing the targets so much sooner. Shots actually looked different – better, easier. The time-table for making the change also probably has to do with how often you practice the new two-eye way.

"I was convinced that as I grew older two eyes had to be a benefit to my shooting since vision typically suffers with age. You really have to stick with the change. You're going to have inexplicable misses for a time. This change does not provide instant gratification – call it character building instead. My skeet averages went down for the one season, but then they came back better than ever."

Such a hand position also makes it tough to get the stock high enough and into the shoulder properly. "The wrist is made to bend from side to side, not up and down," said DeVault. With this hand position the wrist is already cocked about as low as it can go. This is what makes it difficult or at least uncomfortable to get the stock into the correct position in the shoulder.

Perhaps most importantly, with this hand/wrist position that body part is absorbing a significant percentage of the recoil. So no wonder I experience hand/wrist pain. How about you? So what is the proper hand/wrist position on the grip?

The answer is extremely easy, so easy I now say, "Why didn't I think of that. This is obvious."

Simply slide the palm of your hand down and to the side of the grip. Your thumb might still be over the top of the grip, but just let it settle where it may – perhaps even on the side of the grip. The key is to have the hand (palm) on the side of the stock. Now when the gun recoils the grip does not come back into your hand/wrist. Instead the pistol grip slides more through your hand and into the shoulder where your recoil reducer, recoil pad and broad butt of the stock is in a much better position to take that recoil. You will find your hand/wrist pain will be essentially gone or at least vastly reduced. A very recent instructional DVD by Instructor and Champion John Wooley also advises this grip palm on the side of the stock.

Further, you will be pulling the trigger straight back instead of up. Further yet, you will find your middle finger is now well back from the rear of the trigger guard. With the hand position high on the pistol grip your middle finger rides right against the back of the trigger guard, which, too, can be painful when the gun recoils. With the new suggested hand position on the grip you will also discover that your eyes are in a more horizontal position and head less tilted. Also, your thumb on the grip does not restrict your vision of the target nearly as much as with a typical high hand on the grip. You can readily see this in accompanying photos.

Another positive of a proper grip position is that the right hand on the side of the stock is in a much better location to help move the gun to the right or left. With the high-hand position many of us use the wrist cannot move as far to the right or left, plus it is uncomfortable and unnatural for the wrist to move right or left when the wrist is cocked downward, as with the hand high on the grip.

Just pick up your shotgun to prove this to yourself.

With the hand on the side of the stock it's easy to raise the butt stock to the proper position in the shoulder, plus it's natural to pull the stock straight back into the shoulder. Yet another benefit is that you will not have to turn your face as much into the stock if you have an adjustable stock and can adjust the comb properly. It will be more natural for you to simply mount the gun. It will feel right. It will feel more natural. Anyone who turns their head significantly into the stock is going to feel more facial recoil. As with any new habit, it will take some time to develop this new correct grip position. But if you give this new grip position a try, I believe you will be both happy and surprised with the results.

You can go to the Dennis DeVault Website at www.devaultind.com. If you will email him at dennisdevault@scglobal.net, you can ask him to put you on his list to receive his free monthly newsletter, which I have always found to be thought provoking and filled with plenty of how-to information.

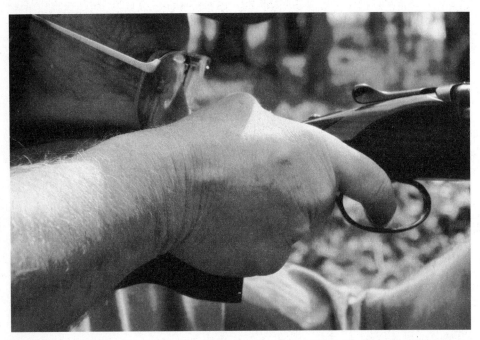

If your grip is similar to this maybe you, too, are experiencing some hand/wrist pain. Note also how the thumb definitely gets in the way of your vision, as well as how the trigger finger pulls up rather than back. In this position your hand/wrist is going to take a lot of the recoil.

Here the palm of the hand slides down on the grip. Now the palm is more on the side of the pistol grip. This allows the recoil to slide more past the hand rather than up into it. Note also the straighter pull on the trigger, plus the thumb is not in the eye's way as much.

You can slide your thumb all the way to the side of the stock, which takes the thumb even further away from your forward vision.

SWING THROUGH, SUSTAINED LEAD, PULL AWAY

Most every shooter tends to shoot a single way, at least most of the time. Looking at clay target shooting, trap shooters tend to swing through their targets. Most skeet shooters, by far, utilize the sustained-lead method. In sporting clays, some folks rely on the sustained lead, while others opt for the pull-away style. Is it 50 / 50 in sporting clays? Nobody knows. But this much most experts will agree on, whether you are shooting a shotgun at any manner of clay target, or caught up in the real thing, like ducks, grouse, geese, quail, pigeons, whatever – it pays to be able to comfortably shoot all three of these methods.

I spent a number of years teaching shotgun-shooting skills, mainly to hunters. We'd spend two days shooting 500 targets a day, but I always started my students with a High Seven on a skeet field. Skeet fields were always used because of the convenience of shooting all the angles, although I did not always have my pupils shooting from one of the skeet stations. What I learned by taking these folks to Station Seven and shooting the High Bird was that most everyone is a sustained-lead shooter, at least on this particular target.

What does sustained lead mean? Just what it says. You place the muzzle in front of the target initially. You track that target with a specified lead, which depends on the angle and the distance, and when the sight picture looks right you hit the trigger.

This shooting method works well any time you have advance notice, like when you see ducks, geese or doves coming, and thus have time to make your gun mount with the barrel out in front of the bird. Tracking the bird, at least briefly with the sustained lead, allows you to match gun speed to target speed, and, secondly, to decide the distance

In the field or on a clay target station – think about foot placement.

and angle – and thus put the properly lead on the target. Sometimes it's very little lead, as with a slightly quartering away shot, but even a harsher quartering target requires little lead compared to a crossing shot.

But in most all upland shooting, especially in thick cover, it can be impossible to initially get the gun in front of the feathered escapee. The birds are quick. There's intervening vegetation. You probably are not expecting the flush, unless you are working with a pointing dog. Even with a dog flushes can surprise any of us. Further, many of these shots are going away or quartering away, the antithesis of the High Seven incomer where it's so natural to use the sustained lead style. In close-cover upland situations, it certainly pays to be able to swing through the target. If you have never done that before, performing well may be pretty tough.

But you can practice swing through on practically any skeet field target. One of the best to practice on is the Low Six clay. Like a lot of upland birds, this one starts low, rises, travels fast, and it's quartering away a bit. The key to practicing the swing through on this bird is to place the muzzle somewhere closer in toward the Low House window. When you call "pull," the clay will certainly jump in front of the barrels when you place them in this position initially.

So now you're behind. What do you do? Force the barrels ahead, sustain the lead a bit, and then pull the trigger? No. For this, practice swing-through shooting. You want to simply put a very hard focus on the bird. Keep the muzzle swinging right along the target's flight path, and when your barrels hit the back end of the clay, pull the trigger. Because the gun is moving faster than the bird, the lead is built in. Don't ever look at the barrel. Look at the bird only. You'll see the barrel in your peripheral vision plenty, enabling you to hit the trigger as you get to the bird.

But if you shoot this low bird swing

through from Station 5 you have increased the angle. Now you'll have to hold off pulling the trigger until you see some distance in front of the target. Station 4 is a full crosser. Shooting swing through you will need even more daylight in front of the target. If you move back 10 yards from either of these stations you have increased the distance and even more daylight will be required. Of course, if you are shooting sustained lead on Stations 6, 5 and then 4 you are again going to require more lead as the angle increases and as the distance increases.

The bottom line with swing through is that grouse, woodcock and quail hunters will have to use this method quite often, despite perhaps their preference for shooting sustained lead. One problem with swing through is that the target may dip down and under the barrel just at the moment the trigger is pulled. Such a problem can be more common and pronounced on a clay target field (especially on a windy day) than it is with a real grouse, woodcock or quail.

Dan Carlisle and Will Fennell are two of the most in-demand shotgun instructors that often teach the pull-away technique. These instructors feel the pull-away method best allows the shooter to most easily match target speed with gun speed. When this can be done for a short period of time – a very gentle pull away from the target with the muzzle provides the necessary lead.

Not only does this method work very well with many clay target presentations (almost all of them really), the pull away is tough to beat on ducks, doves, geese, most of the time anyway. As long as you can plan the shot, either the sustained lead and the pull away are the way to go.

Let's say it's opening day of dove season. You are using your normal sustained lead, but things aren't going your way very often. There are a lot of empty hulls on the ground and too few doves beside them. Why not try

For excellent pull away practice shoot the High Target from Station Seven on a skeet field. Start from the low gun position. As the target comes out, start the muzzle to the clay's leading edge as you blend in your gun mount. Match gun speed to target speed. After you have done that make a very gentle pull away from the target and pull the trigger. You can also use this High Seven target for sustained-lead practice.

Shooting the Low Bird from skeet Station Six can be excellent practice for the swing-through method. Starting with a low gun, swing the muzzle far enough toward the Low House window that you are sure the target will get the jump on. Don't panic when the target gets in front of you. Swing faster than the clay, and as you catch up to it, pull the trigger.

You can do further swing-through practice by moving to Station Five on the skeet field. Again, start with a low gun and place the muzzle in close enough to the window that the clay will jump in front of the barrels initially. Because you have increased the angle on this station, you will have to actually see daylight in front before pulling the trigger.

Here the shooter has moved about 10 yards behind the skeet station. Thus the distance to the target has increased. With swing through you will have to see a bit of daylight in front of the target before pulling the trigger. With sustained lead you will have to see more lead compared to shooting from a closer position. With the pull away you will have to pull slightly more in front before triggering off the shot. Bottom line: as distance and/or angle increases, more lead is required.

This shooter might be thinking, "Should I maintain lead this dove or use the pull-away method? Then again, might a swing through be the ticket?"

Looks like a sustained lead is going to work on this dove. But it pays to learn and practice all three methods – sustained lead, pull away and swing through.

one of the other shooting techniques? Doing so may not only break your bad luck spell, it will be fun to try.

If you have not tried the pull away before, I think the High Seven target is the one to try initially. As with all this practice, start from a low gun position. Call for the bird. As the target comes out start the swing about the time you start your gun mount. Visually focus on the target's leading edge. That's where to place the muzzle, without, of course, looking at the muzzle. Focus only on the target. Track that bird, matching gun speed with target speed, until it passes the center stake. As soon as you are comfortable with matching gun speed to target speed, make a very gentle move ahead and pull the trigger.

You will have to see minimal daylight on this pull away because the target is close and it's not quartering in much at all. Further, any time you pull away from a target, feathered or pitch, that move should be a gentle one. Why? It comes down to the eye wanting to go where the most movement is. If your pull away is too pronounced, the eye will go to that quick movement – i.e. the barrel. But you must maintain full visual focus on the target. The same goes for your initial move to this High Seven skeet target. Slow down. You have plenty of time. Focus on the target. Don't allow the muzzle to move anything but slowly. Otherwise your eye is going to naturally go to that fast muzzle movement.

This is one of the downfalls of the swing-through method. The muzzle is moving faster than the bird, so it will be natural for our eyes to go to that faster movement. But sometimes you can't get ahead of the target initially, for reasons already stated. This is when to use the swing through. If you practiced the swing through on clay targets, you're going to have more experience at staying with a hard focus on the bird despite the muzzle moving faster than the bird.

This is another reason why I think the sustained lead and the pull away are better for most shooter, or with birds that you see in time and can make a very brief plan – especially a plan allowing you to start the muzzle ahead of the bird (sustained lead) or on the bird's head or front edge (pull away).

If you haven't practiced the pull away it's not all that easy to place the muzzle properly. You may start too far in front or too far behind. Both practice and hard focus on the bird's head or target's leading edge will be a big help in starting the muzzle in the perfect place.

Depending upon what game species you hunt most, you may only be familiar with one of these three shooting methods. But if you practice all three you will find you can soon use any of the three as a specific hunting or clay target shot presents itself – and you'll do this naturally.

CHAPTER FOUR

SHOTGUNS AND SHOTGUNNING – THE DIFFERENCE

"**S**upposedly, the Han'werker blind was right over there," Will Owen explained with a wave of his free hand. His other hand was controlling the outboard motor as we putted away from the northern end of storied Old Beaver Dam. This body of water is storied because Nash Buckingham had made the lake and the blind forever famous in perhaps the most enduring hunting story ever written, "De Shootinest Gent'man." That story captures a morning with outstanding wingshot Harold Money and Beaver Dam guide Old Horace – and the bottle of Brooklyn Handicap that sat between them in the Han'werker blind.

Will Owen had his boat motoring toward his own Beaver Dam blind, which he calls The House of Death. I could have taken a modern, high tech auto-loader for this duck hunt. But doing so would have bordered on sacrilege. It seemed more fitting to bring along a very old shotgun for a duck hunt that was so steeped in the tradition of so many years. So when we reached Will's blind, I uncased my prize. It wasn't the first time this side-by-side had seen the pale light of early morning. The gun had perhaps seen hundreds of such daybreaks, maybe thousands. But here I was at Old Beaver Dam giving the old trooper of a gun another look back into waterfowling history. I sensed this old Lefever was thankful to be in such a place. I know I was.

But let's get back to the title of this piece. A typical shotgun brought along for a hunt on Old Beaver Dam would have been just that – just a shotgun. But this was to be a day filled with memories of past days at Beaver Dam, of old traditions. No game warden would have to check my Lefever to see if the magazine was properly plugged. This was a simple two-holer. This day's shooting would not be about a shotgun and how it faired. No, this day would be much more important. I would capture the very essence of what shotgunning is all about.

According to the Lefever's serial number it began life during the duck season of 1915. Market hunting of ducks was still in its prime, but I don't know if this gun's early days were spent on Chesapeake Bay potting ducks for the Baltimore restaurants, up Wisconsin way near one of Gordon MacQuarrie's old haunts, maybe even somewhere in the south – perhaps not that far from Old Beaver Dam itself. Ah, those were the days of shotgunning, as opposed to today's era of shotguns.

Somehow, some way, some year this Lefever found its way to Australia. That's where Chuck Webb found it for me. When Australia went overboard with its gun ban in the late 1990s, thousands of old shotguns left the country to come to the USA. In this case, this Lefever came back home. Webb picked this one out of a literal pile of Aussie shotgun returns. It was in pretty sad shape cosmetically, but Chuck says, "There's nothing I love better than bringing an old shotgun back to sparkling new life." As opposed to mere shotguns, this is what shotgunning is all about in Chuck's mind.

Chuck Webb, among other hats he wore, was the chief double gun restorer at Briley Manufacturing in Houston, Texas. He told me I could have shot this old Lefever right out of its shipping crate, for the action was still nice and tight and the bores were plenty good enough. But that wouldn't have been good enough for Chuck, and a gun in that condition wasn't good enough to me. You've already read Chuck's phrase above. We both wanted to bring this old Dan Lefever gun back to sparkling new life.

The others in the Owens blind that morning were taken aback a bit when I uncased this beauty. My old buddy Lamar Underwood was the one who was the most appreciative of what Chuck Webb had accomplished with the restoration. In fact, just the day before I started this rough draft Lamar reminded me of how much he had been impressed with the gun. He asked if I had sold it. I replied, "Would you sell your brother?" Lamar's mention of the old gun yesterday has prompted me to start penning these words about the difference between mere shotguns and shooting ducks with a piece of history like this Lefever, e.g., shotgunning.

The barrels were not just re-blued, they were rust blued, the bluing process that was used originally on these guns at the Lefever factory. The gun is an H grade, which means a case-hardened receiver. This Lefever receiver was case hardened by Briley the old fashioned way – using charcoal. The barrel bores were polished to a mirror shine, then Webb threaded the muzzles for Briley's unique square-thread screw-in chokes, so this Old Timer has the modern touch of screw-in chokes. The walnut finish was removed, then replaced with hand-rubbed oil. But before that the checkering was re-cut. The perfect finishing touch was the addition of a leather-covered recoil pad, the price of which will give just about anyone a heart attack.

The barrels are 30-inches, further indication that waterfowlers used this gun year after year. It weighs 7 pounds 9 ounces and balances beautifully right at the hinge. The rib is wide and solid. Two-thirds of the way down that rib is a small area where the gun received a bump, maybe from a fall in the blind. Chuck Webb didn't remove or restore that bump, for he believes in leaving such a part of the gun's history intact. This is a two-trigger Lefever.

The receiver lock-up is unique. The design hasn't been seen before or since. The barrels don't pivot on a hinge. Instead there's a ball and socket joint between the barrels and the front of the receiver. The ball portion is actually built on a screw. If the action loosens up – just back the screw out a hair – to restore original tightness. What a simple, straightforward idea.

Another part of the lock-up system is the top lug that's an extension of the barrels that fits into the matched, milled-out recess in the top of the receiver. Via a tapered screw in the barrel's lug extension you can tighten this part of the action as well.

Shooting this gun is a hoot, whether we're talking an orange domed clay target or a greenhead with big orange feet. Because of that leather-covered recoil pad this gun never hangs up on clothing during the mount. Despite the expense, I am now certain that a leather-covered pad is the best route to go to ensure no hang-ups on clothing. Those gunsmiths of yesteryear who first came up with the leather-covered pad concept really had something.

The chambers are only 2¾ inches, but

that's plenty enough shell for me firing non-toxic Bismuth or Kent's Tungsten-Matrix loads. Out to 35 yards, the Improved Cylinder chokes I usually have in place will smoke clay targets with lead loads, as well as flip ducks into somersaults if I do my part with Bismuth or Tungsten-Matrix shells.

This old Lefever also greeted several duck dawns in northwest Tennessee last season. Kelly Powers, one of my guides on that trip, fell in love with the Lefever so hard that he has given up his well-used auto-loader for a double gun he has had sitting in the rack for too many years. My old gun has that effect on some waterfowlers I've shown it to. This Lefever makes true shotgunners look closely at this marriage of metal and wood, and I can see a dream-like look in their eyes. I think they are forgetting about shotguns and they start dreaming about something more important, more basic – shotgunning. They want to replace the shotguns in their waterfowling with shotgunning, and they're seeing the difference.

Maybe the concept of a shotgun is that we're seeking a tool that will help us be ever more successful, make days of limiting out easier, more predictable. With the concept of shotgunning, success is still important, but limiting out is no longer all-important. A treasured shotgun, like treasured friends, becomes much more important than the bag, and believe me I'm still interested in the bag. But when this old Lefever accompanies me on a duck hunt, there's certainly a lot added to the pleasure.

This old Lefever is relatively new to me. But I look forward to carrying it into many a duck blind in the years to come. While this gun has already given me great pleasure, I'm certain that holding it and shooting it will be giving me a lot more fulfillment in the future.

The contact for old double gun restoration is Briley Manufacturing, 1230 Lumpkin, Houston, TX 77043. Phone 800-331-5718 – on the web its www.briley.com.

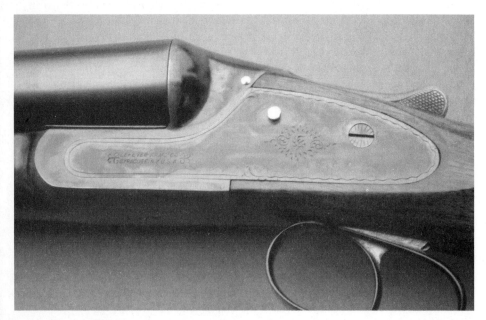

Check out the classic lines of this old Lefever receiver.

Leather-covered pads are expensive but worth it.

A classic blind on Beaver Dam with distinctive rounded shooting ports, not unlike those Nash Buckingham hunted out of.

If you have a license plate like this, folks know where you hunt.

The author, on the right, shows off his old LeFever to host Will Owen.

CHAPTER FIVE

SPORTING CLAYS

O f all the clay target disciplines, sporting clays most mimics the act of wingshooting for flying (and in the case of the rabbit, running) game. A typical sporting clays course might consist of 10 or more stations, some have less. At each station, the shooter steps in and might shoot 4 to 10 targets. One or more might be singles targets, but in most circumstances this is a doubles game. The rest of the squad shoots from that same station, and then everyone moves on to a second station. The person who shot second at the previous station shoots first at the next station. With every new station, the shooter who shot second previously now leads off the squad. Before actually shooting, shooters get an exposure to how each bird at that station will fly. Normally there are two traps at each that throw the clays station.

Doubles can be of several sorts, and the type of doubles to be thrown is often posted on a sign at each station. A "Report Pair" means that the second bird is thrown upon the report of the shotgun shooting the first clay. A "Following Pair" is slightly different with the second bird being tossed follow- ing the first. A "True Pair" is pretty obvious in that both traps fire a target at the same time. In most competitions only doubles are thrown. In non-tournament type situations you might see one or three single targets, and then the doubles. A typical scenario might be a single bird, then a following or report pair, finally a true pair, adding up to five targets for the station. On many sporting clays courses, shooters are only going to get doubles, including all of the double varieties already described. You could shoot alone, but a typical squad consists of three to five shooters.

The variety of target presentations can be endless, and this is one of the aspects that make this game so challenging, interesting and mimicking real hunting scenarios. On any given station it might be possible to get a straightaway, a quartering shot from the right, a quartering shot from the left, a crosser from either right or left, a straight incomer, a quartering incoming, various overhead angles – the list goes on. Those who set the targets can make doubles shoot- ing easier or more difficult – in some cases depending upon where the shot causes the muzzle to end up after the first shot. An easier second shot might mean very little muzzle movement to get to the second bird. One type of very tough second shot might mean significant movement required to get toward the second bird. Individual targets can be very tough regardless of the move needed.

There are five types of clay targets that you can see on any given station. All the targets are harder than the clays used in trap and skeet, simply because sporting targets must have the capability of being thrown harder/faster. The Standard bird has the same dimensions/size as the skeet and trap target. The Midi is slightly smaller and lighter, thus capable of faster speed. The Mini is very tiny so it can be tossed faster. Because of its small size the Mini might call for a tighter choke. A fourth target type is the Battue. This is a very flat type target, and it does not fly straight, but curls. Typically, a battue first presents itself "edge on." This makes it very tough to see as well as requiring a very tight choke to break it at this stage. But the battue then turns so the shooter will see the bird fully face on. Typically, however, that's the moment the battue drops, and it does so very severely and quickly. And don't forget the Rabbit targets that bounce along the ground so they have to be strong enough to take that. A target thrown upside down is called a chandelle. They tend to be thrown in an arc. If you don't shoot them on the way up most chandelles tend to drop quickly.

The targets can be all orange, orange domed with a black rim, even all black. Typically the mini, the battue and the rabbit clays are all one color – black or orange. Obviously, a black target against a dark background can be very hard to see. So black targets are usually thrown where there is a good background – like the sky.

The best way to find out more about shooting clays is to simply find a gun club that offers it, and then just go out and try it. Any gun and gauge is suitable. If you're a novice, a semi-auto will probably be preferred. Over/unders are seen maybe 50 – 1 over side-by-sides, but there are side-by-side only events at some competitions.

Sporting clays is fun but challenging. You may or may not shoot up to your expectations on your first or second try, but you can improve, and my sections on shooting instruction will help, though not nearly as much as personal instruction by a professional. For the novice or even the not-so-novice shooter, there are a number of fundamentals a person can quickly incorporate into their shooting that will certainly improve performance. At most sporting courses you have the option of shooting 50 or 100 birds. Further, most layouts offer an easier course for the less experienced, a tougher bird course for those who definitely want challenging birds. For more information, visit www.nssa-nsca.com.

A slightly quartering going-away sporting clays shot with an orange target flying in the background.

The guy or gal who pulls the sporting clays targets for you is generally a certified NSCA Instructor. He or she is able to give you concrete advice on the how-to of hitting targets.

*Loading up, which is **only** done when on the station and preparing to actually shoot.*

Clay target shooting is definitely a family sport.

Now we're ready to call for the bird.

Electric carts are popular in sporting. Some courses rent golf carts. Some serious shooters have their own.

CHAPTER SIX

SKEET

keet is a clay target game that was originally envisioned by a group of New England grouse hunters. Obviously, they wanted to improve their shooting on this difficult thick-cover bird. Their first course was set up in a full circle with shooting stations around the circumference. This didn't last long until the originators laid out a course in a half circle. (See the accompanying graphic.)

There are seven skeet stations around that semi-circle with the final (eighth) station in the middle. There is also a High and a Low House, the High on the left, the Low on the

right. Birds are thrown over a center stake that's a bit outside Station Eight. The whole idea from those New England hunters was to present all the shots that were possible in the grouse woods.

Station One is right under the window of the High House and the first shot is a clay going straightaway from overhead. The second shot is thrown from the Low House, so this clay comes into the shooter as a slight quartering incomer. Next both birds are shot – a double – taking the High bird first.

The shooter moves to Station Two, but only after all members of the squad have

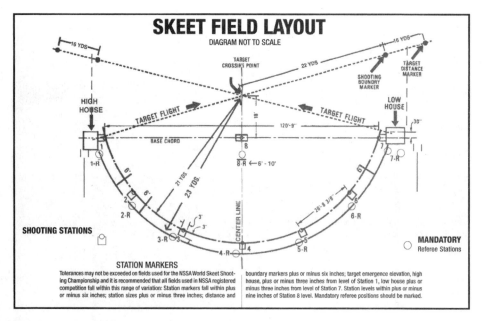

This is what a skeet field looks like.

shot at Station One. The first bird at Station Two is thrown from the High House at the shooter's call of "pull." Thus this one is a quartering away bird – and quick. Next comes the Low bird – a quartering incomer – but more of an angle than the Low One clay. This singles shooting is followed by doubles – taking the High House first.

On to Station Three. Only single birds here and the next two stations. The High is somewhat between quartering away and a crosser, perhaps more of the latter. The Low is somewhat of in incoming quartering clay but more of a crosser. On to Station Four both birds are full crossers. At Station Five, the High – a bit of a quartering incomer – comes first. The Low is a quick quartering away bird.

At Six, it's back to a four-shot station. First is the High House – a quartering incomer, then the Low a quartering away bird and quick. Next is doubles, but note the change here – the Low House is shot first. Now on to Station Seven where the shooter stands just to the left of the Low House window from which the clay is tossed. First the High House incomer, thus less of a quartering shot than the High Six. Next it's the Low House – a straightaway over the center stake (which is where all the birds are supposed to go, but seldom do). Next it's doubles here, shooting the Low House target first.

All that's left is Station Eight in the middle (between the High and Low House and just inside the center stake). The squad shoots the High first, and then everyone turns around to shoot the Low House. In case you've been counting that makes 24 shots. A box of shotshells contains 25. Where do you shoot the 25th shell? If you've not missed a target in the first 24 shots, you take the 25th shot as another Low Eight. In

Champion skeet shooter Paul Giambrone III shoots a Low Four skeet target with a Kolar Max Skeet.

skeet lingo this one is called The Option. Most tyros are going to miss before that so they take their option – shooting the first bird they have missed over again.

Skeet has changed over the years, but what I've just described is how the game has evolved today. This game started with a low gun position, no gun movement allowed until the target appeared, but for decades now shooters have been permitted to call for the bird with the gun fully mounted. Sporting clays also once required a low gun position before calling, but that rule has also been relaxed. F.T.A.S.A.C. requires a very specific low gun position, which I will cover when that game is discussed.

A more recent development is Skeet Doubles. Here doubles are shot at all seven stations (no shooting at Station Eight). In the first round the doubles are shot at Stations One through Seven (14 shells). Then the shooters reverse, coming back through Stations Six through Two. That makes 24 shells. On the next doubles round, after coming back and shooting Station Two the second time the squad finishes up by going to shoot the pair at Station One – making 26 birds. Normally four doubles rounds are shot – making a total of 100 birds or four boxes of shells. Skeet is always shot with the Standard clay targets. For additional information, go to www.nssa-nsca.com.

Skeet is a game of intense concentration.

Skeet shoot-offs are a thrill for any shotgunner.

The shoot-offs are over and now it's picture taking time.

Clay target awards can take on many forms.

CHAPTER SEVEN

TRAP

Trap is the original clay target game, and it continues to be the most popular evidenced by the sheer number of participants. Live pigeons were originally used, followed by the tossing of glass balls. When clay targets made largely of pitch were developed this probably made such shooting cheaper, thus more affordable by the shooting masses, and gun clubs were able spread all over the country, the world really. American Trap is largely an American game. In other countries International Trap is more popular.

With American Trap there are five stations in a semi-circle behind the trap-tossing machine, usually placed in a concrete bunker, accommodating up to five shooters on a squad. (See the accompanying graphic.) The targets are thrown from a trap that continually swings right and left. Theoretically, the shooter does not know which angle, possibly varying about 45 degrees right and left as the

This trap shooter looks like he's shooting a straightaway.

trap oscillates, but in years past experienced shooters could judge when the trap was going to throw an easier, more straightway bird – and they timed their calls of "pull." Modern traps, however, have interrupters of the oscillating trap motion that makes it much more difficult to anticipate the trap.

The shooter on Station One begins the shooting, followed by shooters at Two, Three, Four and Five. The shooter at Station One then calls for his second shot, and so on down the line. Each shooter takes five shots at their first station, and then they all move to the next station with the shooter on Station Five moving to Station One. This latter move takes slightly more time than moving to just one station to the right, so as the shooter who has moved to Station One gets there he usually makes a head movement indicating he's ready or actually says "ready."

All shooters fire five targets at each of the five stations for a total of one box. Round over. Time to start another. Trap is a fast game, faster than any other clay bird game. It's easy for a squad to shoot at 125 targets in 10 - 15 minutes. Skeet is not as fast, taking about 90 minutes for a five-man squad to each shoot 100 targets in a tournament scenario. Sporting clays takes longer – a 5-man squad shooting their 500 targets taking over several hours, much of this time involved is walking to the next station. Sometimes a squad has to wait at the next station for the squad shooting there to finish.

A second trap game is called Handicap, and this one separates the figurative men from the boys. In regular American Trap, the five shooting positions are 16 yards behind the trap itself. In Handicap Trap shooters move back from that 16 yard position, and the better shooter they are the farther they move back. The novice will shoot from 18

Most trap shooters want very high ribs. These guns shoot quite high so the shooter can still see the clay bird as they pull the trigger.

yards back, the best shooters from 27 yards back. That's the maximum. It might not sound like much of a difference – breaking targets from the 16 yard line compared to breaking that bird from the 27 yard line, but the difference is huge.

Most trap shooters gun with very tight chokes, especially when shooting Handicap. But a third trap game is Doubles. Shot from the same five 16-yard stations, both birds are fired simultaneously. Some trap shooters use a bit more open choke for the first doubles shot (which many of them shoot very fast), then a tight choke for the second bird, as-

suming they are shooting an over/under with a choice of two chokes. There's a typical scenario of which bird is shot first from which of the five trap stations, but let's not get into that. Try 16-yard trap for starters. More information on American Trap can be found at www.shootata.com.

International or Bunker Trap is a super tough game, and one that is very expensive because 15 traps are required – and they are more expensive traps because they not only oscillate right and left but also up and down. There are relatively few gun clubs in the USA that have a full Bunker Trap layout.

Loading the gun and getting ready to shoot a trap target. (Photo courtesy of Browning.)

This shooter engages the target with good form.

CHAPTER EIGHT

5-STAND

A s you can guess, for 5-Stand shooting there are five shooting stations in a row numbered 1, 2, 3, 4, and 5. As a rule, targets might be thrown from six to eight traps with all manner of target presentations possible from so many traps. Usually there's a rabbit and a springing teal, as well as an overhead from a trap sitting above on a roof or similar elevated spot behind the stations. Expect crossers from both the left and the right, as well as quartering incomers and out goers and about any other target the course owner can come up with.

A typical scenario might mean one single, next a following or report pair, finally a true pair – a total of five targets – and then all the shooters move to the next station to the right with the guy or gal who has shot at Station Five moving to Station One. An easier presentation might mean three singles – each station finalized by a double of some sort. The target presentations are placarded at each station and at each station different targets are shot.

5-Stand is a very fast game – about as fast as trap. Relatively speaking someone is shooting almost all the time. Moving from one station to the next takes very little time. Figure on shooting 25 targets in about 20 minutes. That means 125 targets for a squad of five, and the cost is often considerably more than for trap. No wonder. The owner has to invest in six to eight traps, instead of one target machine for trap shooting. There are 5-Stand competitions, plus this game is good practice for sporting clays and F.I.T.A.S.C.

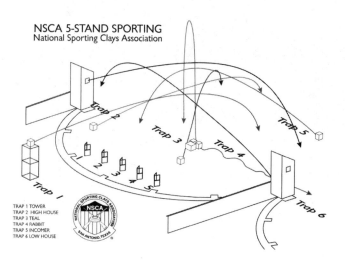

NSCA 5-STAND SPORTING
National Sporting Clays Association

TRAP 1 TOWER
TRAP 2 HIGH HOUSE
TRAP 3 TEAL
TRAP 4 RABBIT
TRAP 5 INCOMER
TRAP 6 LOW HOUSE

This is one way a 5-Stand layout can be setup by using a skeet field overtop a trap field and using the two skeet and the one trap thrower. Three to five additional trap machines will be needed for this type of 5-Stand layout. If the targets from the skeet machines and the trap throwers are not used then six to eight new trap throwing machines will be needed.

A big group gathers at the clubhouse prior to some clay target busting fun.

Golf carts are used to get the shooters to their stations.

CHAPTER NINE

F.I.T.A.S.C.

F.I.T.A.S.C. are the initials for the sport's French sponsoring organization – Federation International de Tir aux Armes Sportive de Chasse. Along with Bunker Trap this is one of clay shooting's most difficult games. The station is a hula hoop, and there will be many stations in a F.I.T.A.S.C. layout. A specific low-gun position is required. All manner of targets can and will be thrown, but if there's anything that's guaranteed in this game it's a concentration of very long targets. For more information, go to www.fitasc.com.

Typically a hula-hoop, where this shooter is standing, is used as a F.I.T.A.S.C. shooting station. The gun remains down until the bird appears.

The popularity of clay target shooting

In case you are wondering about the importance of clay target shooting here in the USA, Phil Murray of White Flyer Targets told me that over 8,000,000 clay birds are shot every year. That's a huge financial impact on our economy, especially when you add the financial impact of the shotshells fired, reloading equipment purchased, reloading components purchased, the guns used for this shooting (none of which are $500 guns), cost of shooting these targets – all money collected by the thousands of guns clubs across the country. All these costs are but the tip of the financial iceberg when it comes to the total impact of clay target shooting

CHAPTER TEN

SHOTGUNS FOR CLAY TARGET WORK

CAESAR GUERINI ELLIPSE EVO SPORTING

It was at the Barnsley Resort in northwest Georgia that I first met up with the Caesar Guerini Ellipse EVO Sporting. There were a number of other Guerini sporting clays and hunting guns to shoot and drool over on that trip, but I remember liking the looks of this new EVO Sporting. I did shoot it well, or at least better than the other over/unders I tried that trip. Consequently, I couldn't wait to put this newest EVO to the test in my own figurative backyard.

The first Ellipse EVO over/unders were hunting guns, 20- and 28-gauge easy swinging, lightweight smoothbores that would be ideal in the woodcock bottoms, for grouse in the grapevines, quail in the pines and sedge.

These new EVO models from Caesar Guerini have taken a different approach with a round-body receiver. To most of us a round-body receiver has a most appealing look. This is all eye candy of course, for a round body doesn't make the gun shoot any better. More than a century ago the world was introduced to the round-body action. Scottish maker Dickson is most often referred to as the round-body innovator in classic side-by-sides, but I think there were a number of side-by-side manufacturers in Scotland who also made such receiver contours – Dickson was probably the most prominent.

Wes Lang at Caesar Guerini USA tells me that a lot more has gone into the EVO receivers than merely grinding away metal at the action bottom edges. While the locking system remains the same as with all other Guerini O/Us with the barrels pivoting on trunnions and a receiver-wide bolt moving forward from the bottom of the receiver to engage lugs milled in the bottom rear of the monobloc, though the main lock-up strength comes from the recoil lug on the bottom of the monobloc. But other innards had to be redesigned. The EVO receivers are actually a bit wider. Consequently, barrels from other Guerini O/Us will not interchange.

It's not merely the round-body receiver that gives the EVO models their eye candy. The engraving will catch the eye at first look, even before the round body. This engraving is extremely well done, there's one heck of a lot of it, the engraving pattern is different than any you've ever seen before and the engraving is a combination of deep relief and tight – not scroll, but what I'll call tight bouquets, although the look of those tiny, intricate florals is not the same as traditionally engraved bouquets we've been accustomed to seeing in years past. Intricate engraving covers the top tang and the fences just behind the barrels, plus there's deep relief engraving on the opening lever. The trigger guard is engraved as well.

With that background in mind let's take a

look at the 12-gauge EVO Sporting that I've been putting through my testing. Compared with the Caesar Guerini Impact and its very high-adjustable rib, the EVO Sporter comes back to a traditional rib, plus a traditional look incorporating the round body and a special engraving pattern that wraps around the receiver. Thus there's a constant engraving flow from receiver sides to receiver bottom. On receivers built in the standard manner, the engraving on the side stops. Engraving on the bottom is then separate and often different than the engraving pattern on the receiver sides. Lang told me that he and Italy sweated this detail to get it right. The first few tries didn't work to their scrutinizing eyes.

My test gun wore 32-inch barrels, but 30-inchers are also available. It appears 32-inch barrels in sporting clays guns are far outselling the 30-inchers. These barrels I found overbored – both tubes measuring .733 on my Baker Barrel Reader. Six screw-in chokes are included in the EVO impact plastic case, though my test gun came only with the Skeet .727 and an Improved Cylinder .723 already screwed into the barrels. The screw-ins were blued and long at 3⅛ inches. They were knurled, but unless I tightened them with the wrench provided those chokes would loosen slightly. In measuring the amount of choke I could tell that there were long taper sections as well as long parallel sections. With many of the screw-in chokes I check these days there's no parallel section at all. These Guerini chokes have the constriction laser engraved on the knurled portion.

The barrels only weighed 3 pounds 5 ounces despite their 32-inch length. I've been told that all Guerini competition shotguns balance just ahead of the hinge area, and this was true of my test gun. My shooting took place on all very hot days, and those barrels did seem to get heated quickly and stay hot. I could even feel the heat through the forend. Maybe this has something to do with the barrels lightness and resulting thinness. Most if not all 30-inch O/U barrels I weigh heft more than 3 pounds 5 ounces, and, of course, most 32-inch barrels weigh even more. The rib between the barrels is solid, and there's a solid rib on top. Unusual for a target gun there is no mid bead; only a white bead at the muzzle. I measured the rib as tapering from .350 at the breech to .295 at the muzzle. Top serrations run the full rib length guarding against distracting glare.

The forend is rounded off at the front and weighed 11.7 ounces on my digital postal scale. Like most of the Guerini O/Us the forend removes by depressing the button at the front. The gun weighs 8 pounds 10 ounces, and that includes the company's Kinetic Balancer that was installed in the butt stock. The walnut wears an oil finish, and there's beautiful straight grain on both the butt stock and the forend. The recoil pad is non-vented, and a thin black spacer separates the pad from the stock. The checkering, always well done on Italian shotguns because of their laser engraving procedures, is also very fine line at 32-lines-to-the-inch. If there's a grip swell it's a tiny one. The grip is also quite open compared to many grip styles we see on sporting clays guns these days, many of which have significant re-curves.

I shot a variety of loads through the gun, all with nary a hiccup. Like all Guerini over/unders (the company does not make side-by-sides, pumps or semi-autos), the triggers are of the inertia variety. Trigger pulls were nice and crisp, a little too light to my liking, but I'm betting the pulls will suit most of you. On my Lyman Digital Trigger Pull Scale pulls averaged just a hair over 3 pounds. The trigger itself appears to be of stainless steel. It can be moved back and forth, enabling you to select your perfect grip-to-trigger distance. A small hex-head wrench is provided

to make this minor adjustment. The barrel selector is part of the top tang safety.

To further check out the EVO Sporting go to the www.gueriniusa Website. I measured the stock dimensions – found them to be 14.75-inches length of pull, 1.5-inches drop at comb and 2.25-inches drop at heel. I particularly enjoyed shooting this one. You will, too. And then there's the eye candy of the round body action and that distinctive, super well done engraving.

SPECIFICATIONS

Action: Over/Under
Gauge: 12 gauge only
Weight: 8 pounds, 10 ounces
Barrels: 32-inch tested. 30-inch also available
Chokes: Screw-ins, extended. Six supplied.
Stock: 14.75 length of pull, 1.5 drop at comb, 2.25 drop at heel
Suggested Retail: $6,120
Manufacturer: Manufactured by Caesar Guerini in Italy. Imported by Caesar Guerini USA in Maryland. www.gueriniusa.com.

This EVO Sporting receiver, with the unique round body, has super engraving.

The Invictus incorporates an innovative lock-up system using the new Invictus Cams and Block.

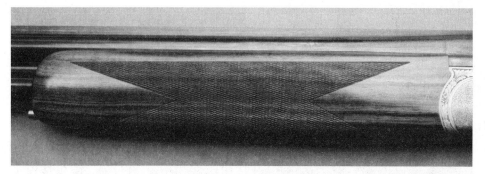

The rounded-off look of the EVO forend. The checkering is perfectly executed and at 32-lines-to-the-inch.

The bottom of the round-bodied receiver. Notice how the flow of the engraving goes uninterrupted from sides to bottom.

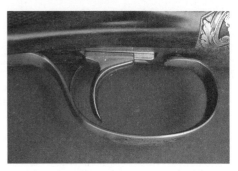

The trigger can be moved to gain your perfect grip-to-trigger distance.

The grip is fairly open. Note the tight 32-lines-to-the-inch checkering.

Note the straight grain of the test gun's butt stock. The finish is traditional oil.

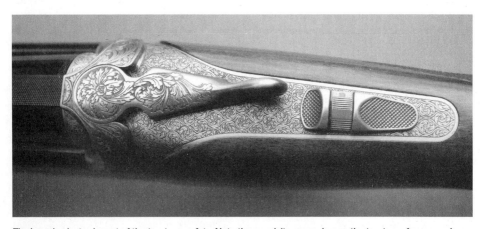

The barrel selector is part of the top tang safety. Note the exquisite engraving on the top tang, fences and opening lever.

These are some of the shells Sisley put through the Ellipse EVO Sporting.

CAESAR GUERINI INVICTUS

I have a Caesar Guerini Summit Sporting. Yes I have a few other shotguns, but I'm not telling my wife how many. How about you? These different shotguns have differing locking systems. My Summit Sporting, like many of today's over/unders, have barrels that pivot on trunnions and a bolt extends forward from the base of the receiver to engage matching lugs milled into the bottom of the monobloc. I always thought these two features, trunnions and the bolt from the bottom of the receiver were the major strength factors that keep this O/U shooting for thousands and thousands of rounds. Did you think similarly?

Wes Lang at Caesar Guerini straightened me out on my misconception. While the bolt and trunnions do have some bearing on strength, these are not responsible for the strength that allows double guns to be

shot thousands and thousands of times. That strength comes from the recoil lugs built into the bottom of the monobloc that fit into recesses milled into the base of the receiver. With Browning over/unders, recoil lugs at the bottom of the monobloc go all the way through the base of the receiver. The same with the original Ruger Red Label and no doubt a few others. With the Perazzi MX8, MX2000 and some other guns of that ilk, the strength design is built into the sides of the receiver matching up with areas in the monobloc sides when the gun is closed.

You can replace trunnions with slightly larger ones to tighten up the action a bit. You can replace the tapered bolt at the base of the receiver with a slightly larger one, or replace the locking bolts of a Perazzi, Beretta, et al to tighten up the action. But what happens if after many thousands of rounds those recoil lugs at the base of the monobloc wear to the point that they are no longer tight to their opposing areas that have been milled out in the base of the receiver? When that happens the barrels are no longer tight to the receiver, which is called "off face." When this happens the gun is worn out. There's not much you can do about it, outside of maybe a very expensive fix.

This is where the new Invictus has the answer, and it's an inexpensive one. The Invictus does not have trunnions, but a new concept called Invictus Cams. Attached to the monobloc, this part matches up with opposing surfaces inside the receiver, creating an system where barrels can pivot.

The new Invictus Block is in the base of the receiver. A recoil lug milled into the bottom of the monobloc nestles into the area just behind the Invictus Block.

Also note the two screws in the Invictus Block, as well as two screws in the Invictus Cam where the barrels will pivot. Thus these two parts are easily removable and replaceable. Let's say you shoot such a gun 400,000 rounds, (I know one trap shooter who shot 117,000 registered targets in one year.) Eventually wear will occur on the recoil lug on the monobloc, and/or the Invictus Cams where the barrels pivot. Send the gun back to Caesar Guerini USA, they replace the Invictus Block and the Invictus Cam, and then your gun is good for who knows how many thousands of rounds that it takes to again have the barrels no longer tight to the breech face. This can be done a third time, a fourth time, more. Conceivably the gun can be shot millions of times. No matter how many times you fire any Caesar Guerini, these shotguns are guaranteed for life. Most of us aren't going to shoot any one gun we own a million times or more, but it has to be comforting to know we can – with the Invictus.

The Invictus itself is designed to last even longer than the other Guerini shotguns,

the Invictus Block not withstanding. The receiver has been made wider and thicker, which probably means added durability, but also maybe an ounce or two of weight added between the hands. Guerini did a number of things to improve handling qualities even more in designing the Invictus. The wider, thicker receiver is one of them. The receiver sides also have a deeper sculptured look. The fence area is distinctive and elegant. A lot of metal has been milled away and such milling is costly. Don't be scared off thinking the Invictus is going to sell as a five-figure shotgun. Suggested retail is to be $6,700!

Invictus Turkish walnut will be upgraded to Magnus-quality wood. The finish is in traditional oil. Length of pull will be 14.75. Drop at comb 1.375, drop at heel 2.25. There are vented side panels, but no vents under the forend. Internally the trigger has been redesigned with different hammers and sears. Internal parts are now coated with a new substance that increases lubricity, the result a more velvety feel to the triggers. Checkering remains 32 lines-to-the-inch. My test gun was one of the first to go to a gun writer, and Lang says this engraving pattern will be improved upon. Bottega Giovanelli was working on it in Brescia, Italy. There is also engraving on the opening lever, the top tang and the trigger guard.

Barrel length choices will be 30, 32 and 34 inch. My test gun's barrels are deeply blued. measuring 30 inches that heft 3 pounds 8.5 ounces on my digital postal scale. The forend is rounded in front, its shape somewhat like the Browning Lightning forend, but the Invictus forend is slimmer and weighs 10.6 ounces. The trigger is moveable back and forth. The recoil pad is rounded all around the edges and set off from the stock with a black spacer.

This trigger-plate action gun will come in an impact resistant case. The Invictus

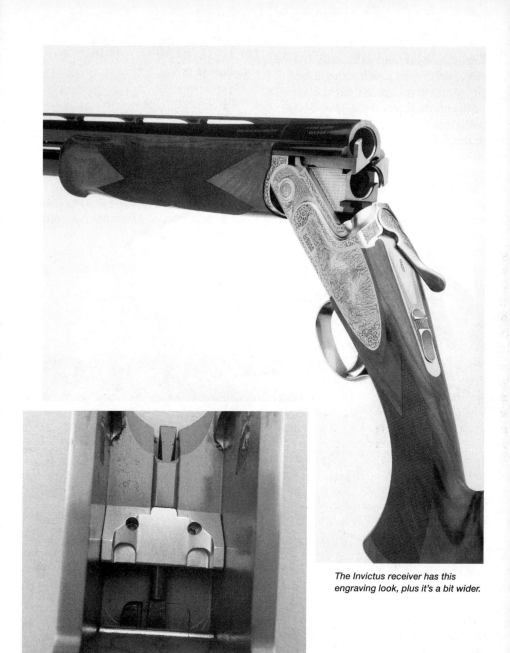

The Invictus receiver has this engraving look, plus it's a bit wider.

If the barrels ever become lose to the breech face just replace the Invictus Block – the bright and shiny part in the photo – easily via removal of two.

forend opens the same as the other Guerini over/unders – with a push button at the forend tip, but the Invictus forend contains a vibration dampener. So you may be able to feel less vibration, but forend tightness should remain even longer. Metal parts including the receiver have the Invisalloy coating for wear and corrosion resistance. My test gun has a bright receiver, but blued receivers could be available.

SPECIFICATIONS

Gauge: 12 Gauge
Action: Over/under
Weight: 8 pounds 5.5 ounces
Barrels: 30, 32 and 34 inch
Chokes: Six screw-in chokes
Stock: 14.75 length of pull. 1.375 drop at comb, 2.25 drop at heel
Suggested Retail: $6,700
Manufacturer/Importer: Made in Italy by Caesar Guerini. Imported by Caesar Guerini USA in Cambridge, Maryland. www.gueriniusa.com.

On a cold winter day Sisley puts the new Invictus through its clay target paces.

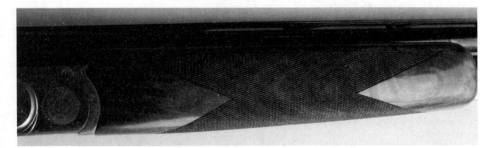

The rounded shape of the Invictus forend.

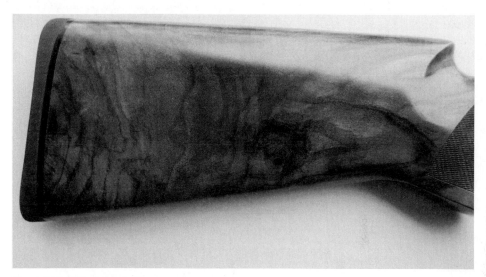

The oil finished Turkish walnut is an upgrade on the Invictus.

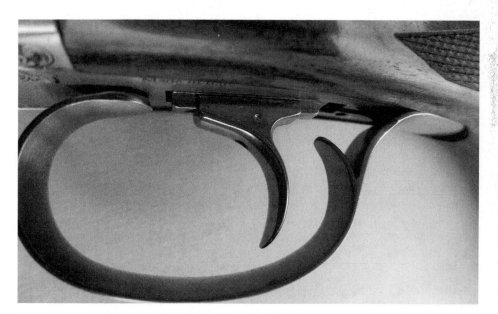

The trigger can be moved forward and back, as an adjustment.

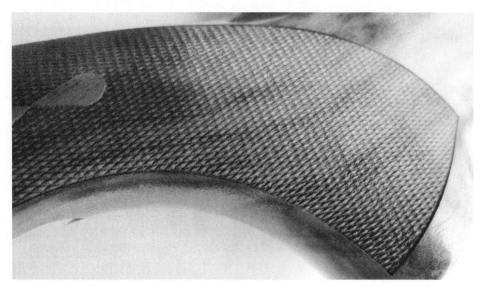

The checkering is at 32 lines-to-the-inch on both the pistol grip and the forend.

The new sculpturing around the Invictus fence area.

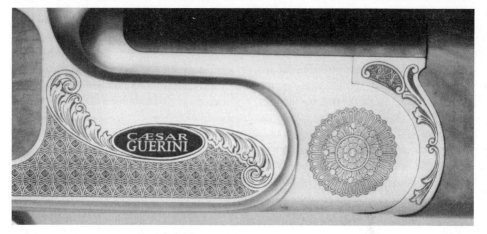

This is the receiver engraving on the prototype. Compare this with the new engraving on the now-for-sale models.

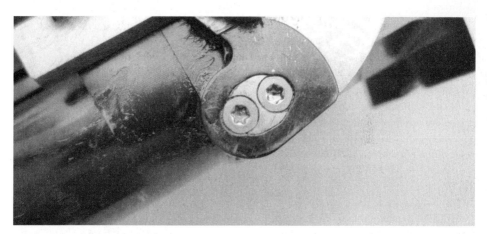

This is the look of the Invictus Cam. The two screws are easily removed and the cam replaced with a slightly larger one if the Invictus ever starts to shoot loose after who knows how many thousands of rounds.

CAESAR GUERINI SUMMIT ASCENT

Some may think that Caesar Guerini might be under the figurative radar a bit when it comes to a top-notch sporting over/under. Maybe that's because so many of the big hitters in this sport shoot a sponsored O/U from the likes of Krieghoff, Kolar, Perazzi, Zoli, Blaser or a few others. But when it comes to sales numbers it's my bet that Guerini would make some eyes widen if those they were known, especially when compared to the sales numbers of the shotgun names specified just above.

All of the above gun companies have their version of the hottest models in the sport; Krieghoff with the Pro Sporter, Kolar with the MAX Sport and ACC, Perazzi with the 2000/3 and 2000S/3, Zoli with the VCS and Blaser with the SuperSport. But Caesar Guerini was one of the first with one of these high adjustable rib/high adjustable comb over/unders matched to a major ad campaign. This over/under was their Impact model.

Interestingly, prior to the Impact model, Guerini's best-selling sporting clays gun was the Summit Sporting. The 12 gauge was the biggest seller in this model, but the Summit Sporting is available in 20, 28 and .410, the latter three on the same but smaller 20-gauge frame. It was the Summit Sporting that was used by Caesar Guerini to come out with that first high adjustable rib/high adjustable comb model.

Many sporting clays enthusiasts have switched to these high rib guns as they see the big hitters in the game are winning and winning with these types. But there are also plenty of sporting clays buffs who look at these modern guns as maybe being on the ugly side, or mainly that they are not traditional looking. Thus Caesar Guerini has come out with the Summit Ascent model.

The Ascent is definitely a more traditional looking shotgun. The gun's main appeal is an elevated rib in conjunction with an adjustable comb stock that also has that step down at the top rear – a la all the Krieghoff Pro Sporter, Kolar MAX Sport and others of this ilk.

Not long after the first Caesar Guerini shotguns hit the market I was invited to shoot many of the company's models in Georgia. A 28-gauge Summit Sporting with 32-inch barrels impressed me so much that I bought it. It's a bit unusual for a gun writer to buy a gun. That Summit has been taken on several high-volume dove trips to South America. I later had a set of 20-gauge 32-inch barrels wedded to the receiver. That's the gun and barrels I took to Uruguay and Argentina for several more recent trips. Further, not only have I shot this gun extensively at clay targets for several years, this Summit has been my main pest pigeon gun. Even in 28 gauge, properly choked, I've enjoyed some banner 28-gauge Summit

Sporting days with the pigeons.

While the current Summit Ascent is in 12 gauge, the receiver is essentially the same, save for size, as the 28-gauge Summit Sporting receiver I bought several years ago. Lock-up is via a bolt that extends forward from the bottom of the receiver. Upon closing the gun, it snugs into milled out recesses in the bottom of the monobloc. The barrels pivot on trunnions. Recoil lugs at the base of the monobloc nestle into matching milled-out areas in the base of the receiver. This has proven to be a very strong locking system, and it's a system used by a number of other over/under manufacturers.

The adjustable comb needs little more said about it as the adjustments are up, down, right and left, plus the back of the adjustable part can be raised a bit higher than the front of the comb. This offers the possibility of a nearly level comb stock, which is one that tends to recoil past the face rather than up and into the face. Relatively speaking, no matter where you put your face on a level comb, further forward or further back, you are experiencing the same amount of drop at comb.

The elevated rib tapers from .400 at the breech to .320 at the muzzle. The first four and one-half inches at the rear of the rib there are six thin straight lines on top. From that point to the muzzle there is a very thin straight line with no cross hatching, but the rib is cross-hatched on both sides of that centerline to eliminate distracting glare. There's a metal mid-bead and a white front bead.

The elevated rib is the main difference. It's hard to measure the rib height, but I come up with .400. Using the same "eye-balling with a micrometer" technique on my Summit Sporting, I come up with a rib height of .300. That's only a difference of .100, which does not seem like much, but it is. I think you will agree that the difference is noteworthy.

So what's the advantage of this elevated rib? By matching up the height of the adjustable comb with the height of the slightly higher rib on the Ascent, so you have the pattern printing exactly where you want, you are going to experience some of the advantages of those new shotguns with the high adjustable ribs/high adjustable combs. Why? Because your head is going to be slightly higher to accommodate the slightly higher rib/comb, thus recoil is going to tend to go more past your face rather than up into your cheek. The barrels are going to be further below your line of sight, effectively taking them out of your sight picture, or at least putting the barrels somewhat further down and thus away from where you are looking. Sure, we all recognize that we should never look at the barrel/rib, but with traditional shotguns the barrel/rib has to be in our peripheral vision. If the sight of the barrel is more out of the way (lower) that leaves only the rib to be seen, a much more narrow peripheral reference point and a reason many claim for the high adjustable rib/high adjustable comb guns to be more effective breaking targets.

My test Ascent wears a richly blued receiver, but it is covered with Guerini's own Invisalloy finish. The result is a very shiny blue. The 32-inch barrels have a slightly muted matte finish, like they were bead blasted very minimally. This slightly muted matte barrel finish does effectively work against distracting glare. The engraving pattern on the Ascent is the same as on the Summit Sporting, but on the former there's just a little more of it. Caesar Guerini is in gold on both sides of the receiver, and Summit is in gold on the receiver bottom. The trigger guard and top tang are also engraved. The same barrel selector and safety is on the top tang. The recoil pad is beveled all around, about one-half inch thick, and set off from the stock by a black spacer. The pistol grip has more of a re-curve than on my 28 gauge Summit Sporting. The forend is rounded, reminiscent of the Browning Lightning forend. The checkering is done at 26 lines-to-the-inch – and done well, probably by laser machinery.

Measurement wise the gun weighed 8 pounds 12 ounces, the forend 10.8 ounces and the 32-inch barrels 3 pounds 7.5 ounces. While many manufacturers include five screw-in chokes with their sporting clays models Guerini includes six. They were; a Cylinder at .723, a Skeet at .724, two Improved Cylinders – both at .720, a Light Modified at .717 and a Modified at .713. The barrels are of the DuoCon variety, which my Baker Barrel Reader reads at .739 just in front of the chamber creating 5-inch forcing cones, but .735 just behind the screw choke portion. Both barrels measured the same internally.

Some additional features of the Summit Ascent include: hand-rubbed oil finish to the wood, 2¾-inch chambers, a trigger that can be moved back and forth (release triggers are an option) and a left-hand stock is available for $215 extra. The gun comes in an impact plastic soft-lined case.

SPECIFICATIONS

Gauge: 12 gauge
Action: Over/under
Weight: 8 pounds 12 ounces
Barrels: 32-inch. 30-inch also available
Chokes: Six included
Stock: Length of pull 14¾, pitch 5 degrees, adjustable comb
Suggested Retail Price: $4,295
Manufacturer/Importer: Made in Italy by Caesar Guerini. Imported by Caesar Guerini USA in Cambridge, Maryland. www.gueriniusa.com.

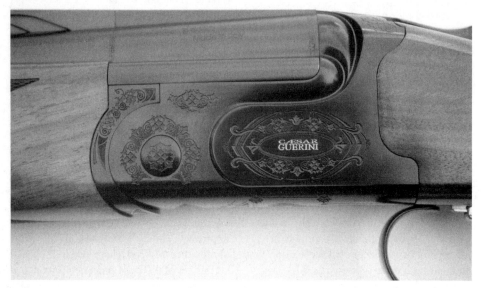

Close up of the Summit Ascent receiver. The bluing is bright and shiny due to the protective Invisalloy coating.

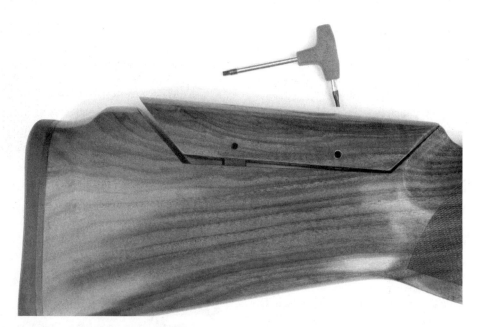

Here's a look at the straight-grain stock. Note that the back of the adjustable comb can be raised slightly higher than the front resulting in a near level comb stock.

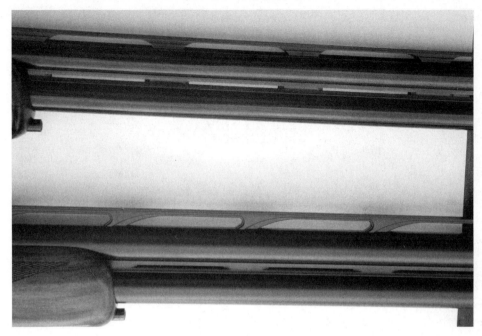

The elevated rib of the new Summit Ascent (bottom) as compared to the standard Summit Sporting (top).

Note the rounded forend of the Ascent. The Summit Sporting comes with a Schnabel-shaped forend.

The gold-plated trigger can be adjusted forward and back.

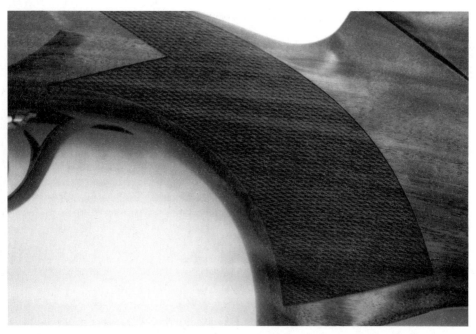

The checkering is finely done at 26-lines-to-the-inch, and there's a bit of re-curve to the pistol grip.

The bottom of the Ascent receiver. This model has the same engraving as the Summit Sporting – there's just more of it.

The Summit Ascent comes with six screw-in chokes.

CZ-USA STANDARD SPORTER

From a cost standpoint some amazing shotguns are coming out of Turkey these days. I missed the SHOT Show the first year Turkish shotguns were introduced at Matt Guzeldere's ARMSCO booth in Las Vegas, but I heard about these over/unders and side-by-sides as that year progressed. Honestly, the ARMSCO booth was the first one I headed for the second year the company had their Turkish shotguns on display. I was thoroughly impressed with the guns they had on exhibit, one of which was a 28-gauge side-by-side that, paradoxically, I bought several years later.

Those initial Turkish guns certainly would not compete with the Purdeys, Hollands and Fabbris of the world, but the price points on these guns secured one heck of a lot of attention. What I've seen over the last decade is that Turkish shotguns in general are improving significantly in both quality and reliability, all the while with price-points still remarkably low. Early reliability problems probably revolved around the triggers, but it appears those issues are behind most Turkish makers. It's important to point out that there are now several gun makers in that country that borders Iran, Iraq and Syria – all three involved in momentous political upheaval; plus there is political upheaval in Turkey so who knows what may await Turkey and thus Turkish shotguns in the coming years.

Not only are side-by-side and over/unders made in Turkey gaining more and more market share, an increasing number of American-based gun companies are importing Turkish-made gas-operated semi-autos, and those guns are becoming a significant part of these companies' bottom lines.

CZ-USA, no doubt because of their extensive distribution and marketing clout in the rifle and handgun realm, eventually took over marketing the shotguns originally introduced by Guzeldere's ARMSCO. Again, steady improvement in both quality and durability has been an integral part of the CZ-USA connection.

For a couple of years now CZ-USA has been selling two sporting clays models; the intro-priced Redhead Target with Monte Carlo-style stock and wide step rib atop its 30-inch barrel, sold with a quintet of screw-in chokes. These guns come with an attractive bright receiver, and, as is the case on all CZ double guns, the barrel interiors are chrome lined. The Redhead Target originally priced at $1,348.

The CZ Sporter is a definite step up. Originally priced at $2,509, this one features a Grade III Turkish walnut adjustable stock, black chromed receiver and chromed barrels. The engraving and the checkering is done by hand, and the trigger is built for demanding competition-type shooters.

I am impressed with the newer CZ Standard Sporter. Looking at the company Website, the photo of the new Standard Sporter shows a red hue to the walnut. In the gun I have for testing the wood is totally different in shade, with more of a blonde look. The oil-finished butt stock, reportedly Grade II, is attractively figured, and the pores are very well filled in; ditto for the forend.

Again, the checkering is hand done, not machine cut. There's minimal engraving, but, it too is hand done – a bit on the receiver, more surrounding the stubs or outside of the trunnions, the opening lever and the trigger guard. These guns are not blued, so the metal parts do not have that blued look of traditional firearms we have been accustomed to viewing all our lives. Instead the metal finish is black chrome. Since chrome is involved, I'm betting corrosion and wear resistance is going to be a lot better than standard bluing. Assuming this is true, will more and more guns made worldwide have their metal parts black chromed in the future

instead of with traditionally blued?

Same goes for the chrome-lined barrels these guns come with . Are we destined to see more and more of those from gun manufacturers everywhere? Already there are barrels made outside of Turkey which are chrome lined, or the chambers are chromed. Many shotgun aficionados don't like chrome-lined barrels because those choke areas cannot be hand-honed easily. However, these days the vast majority of shotgun barrels come with screw-in chokes, making traditional non-chrome-lined barrels perhaps a moot point.

Barrel length options for this new Standard Sporter are 30 and 32 inch. Champion sporting clays shooter Tom Mack is on the CZ-USA shooting team, so he shoots one of these over/unders. Interestingly, another of Tom's sponsors, Kicks Chokes, supplies six Tom Mack-selected Kicks screw-ins for this new CZ Standard Sporter. Instead of the usual Cylinder, Skeet, Improved Cylinder, Improved Modified, Modified and Full selections, Tom maybe has a better two-barrel choke idea – one set of chokes for close range, another set for medium-range clays and a third pair option for the longer birds. Of course, if a sporting station offers two shots of varying range, the choke selection can be varied – perhaps one choke for a long range clay, a second choke for a close bird – not unusual for many sporting clays stations.

All these Kicks chokes are well extended – 3-inches total with $1\frac{3}{8}$ inches outside the barrel, so there are long taper and parallel sections. The chokes for closer birds have one ring in the extended/knurled section. These are marked .726. Barrels measured internally were .730, so that's .004 constriction for these one-ring chokes. The two chokes with two rings in the knurled section went .715 equaling .015 constriction. The two chokes with three rings went .705 for .025 constriction. Tom Mack no doubt feels these choke constriction selections make choke choice easier and more straight forward.

The 30-inch barrels on the test gun went 3 pounds 2 ounces – fairly light for 30-inchers in my experience. The 9½-inch forend weighed 11.1 ounces; the gun: 8 pounds 3 ounces, thus making for a lively package. There's an adjustable comb stock. Side panels between the barrels are vented with no venting between the barrels under the forend. A thin rubber recoil pad is separated from the stock via a black spacer. The pad itself feels a bit sticky. Sporting clays buffs who always shoot with a mounted gun will not doubt like this sticky feel as the stock is going to stay in place with no movement for the second shot. Personally, I prefer the recoil pad on the several CZ guns I purchased previously with a plastic insert at the top to help prevent gun hang ups on mounting. These pads also have a more slippery feel. Of course it's always easy to change recoil pads to one of your particular liking.

The pistol grip shows a bit of re-curve. There's a grip swell on the right side. Priced in between the Redhead Sporter and the CZ Sporter, retail for this new Standard Sporter is $1,799. Length of pull is 14.75 inches. There's a Monte Carlo look to the stock with that bit of step down at the top rear. Stock width is fairly wide, which won't make Gil Ash happy, but the adjustable part of the stock can be offset to the right to mitigate against the wide stock feel for any shooters who are so inclined.

It's interesting to note that where these shotguns are made in Turkey there are no restaurants, no movie theaters, no Internet cafes, but the town does have sporting, trap and skeet ranges. I guess those town folks have their priorities straight.

SPECIFICATIONS

Gauge: 12 gauge only
Action: Over/under
Weight: 8 pounds 3 ounces
Barrels: 30 and 32 inches
Chokes: 6 Kicks Chokes included
Stock: Adjustable comb stock; 14¾-inch length of pull
Suggested retail: $1,799
Manufacturer/Importer: Made in Turkey for CZ-USA. www.cz-usa.com.

The sculptured look of the CZ Standard Sporter receiver shows some obvious similarities with the Perazzi receiver look.

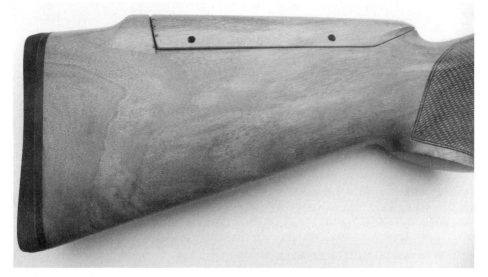

The CZ Standard Sporter butt stock shows fine figure, as well as the adjustable comb feature.

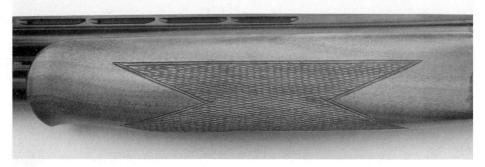

The Schnabel look of the gun's forend with hand-done checkering.

CZ sponsored shooter Tom Mack has selected 6 screw-in chokes from Kicks Industries for this CZ Standard Sporter.

These Kicks chokes are long and extend from the barrel more than most extended chokes.

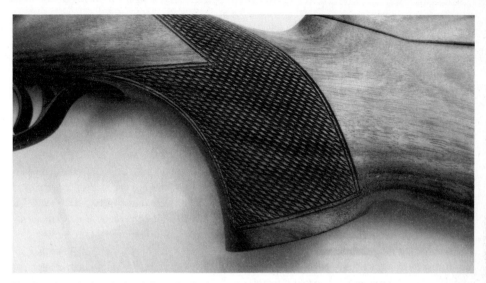

Here's a closer look at the hand-done checkering on the pistol grip, which also shows the amount of re-curve to the grip.

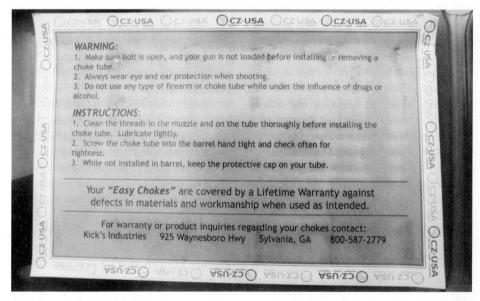

WARNING:
1. Make sure bolt is open, and your gun is not loaded before installing or removing a choke tube.
2. Always wear eye and ear protection when shooting.
3. Do not use any type of firearm or choke tube while under the influence of drugs or alcohol.

INSTRUCTIONS:
1. Clean the threads in the muzzle and on the tube thoroughly before installing the choke tube. Lubricate lightly.
2. Screw the choke tube into the barrel hand tight and check often for tightness.
3. While not installed in barrel, keep the protective cap on your tube.

Your *"Easy Chokes"* are covered by a Lifetime Warranty against defects in materials and workmanship when used as intended.

For warranty or product inquiries regarding your chokes contact:
Kick's Industries   925 Waynesboro Hwy   Sylvania, GA   800-587-2779

Kick's choke selection instructions are on the inside of the choke container.

BROWNING CITORI

The story of the Browning Citori over/under has to start somewhere, but it's a matter of conjecture where to begin this saga. Its predecessor, the Superposed, was on the drawing boards for several years before the first one was produced in Belgium at Fabrique Nationale. That could have been in 1929, but was probably a year or so later.

The first wholesale negotiated price by

Browning was $30 a gun. Thirty years later, I remember when a department store in Pittsburgh – The Joseph Horne Company – was divesting itself of the gun business. I could buy any Grade I Superposed for $300. But in those years I couldn't scrape up $30 for a used single barrel let along a new Superposed.

Superposed prices continued to escalate through the 1960s, no doubt each price increase related to increasing labor costs in Belgium, but U.S. dollar devaluation may have also be a factor. The so-called "salt wood debacle" might have been the wound that would stab the Superposed in the heart. Superposed sales were fairly high in the mid-1960s, and Browning was experiencing increasing difficulty obtaining good quality walnut. This problem was especially true with regard to very high-grade walnut, and plenty of high-grade Brownings were being ordered during those years, examples being the Pigeon, the Pointer, the Diana and the Midas Grades.

A large quantity of Claro walnut was discovered in California. The quality of this wood was excellent, so Browning ordered a huge quantity. With how-to advice from the University of California Davis, the kiln drying process was started on this wood. But this particular drying process took a long time, plus if even slightly over-done, wood cracks would appear.

To help solve this drying problem Browning bought a process from Morton Salt Company that reduced the amount of drying time. Morton had used this salt drying process successfully with furniture wood, and Browning conducted its own tests, hopefully ensuring no problems. Satisfied, Browning covered the Claro walnut blanks that had previously been stacked with salt. The idea was that the salt would leach out moisture in the wood to dry the walnut more quickly.

But guess what happens when salt in wood touches metal? An estimated 90 percent of the Superposed over/unders produced between 1967 and 1969 had salt wood problems that reacted with the metal. The Superposed bore a lifetime warranty, so any original owner could return the gun to Browning for re-stocking. The cost of doing this had to be huge, and that's why I suggest that maybe the salt wood debacle was the actual beginning of the Superposed's demise.

In 1969, total Superposed sales were over 13,000, but were down to 10,500 in 1970 – a decline of about 25 percent. By 1971, sales were down to little more 10,000, but by 1972 sales were closer to 7,500 – another 25 percent drop. Why the sales decline? Prices of Superposed shotguns were going up. Labor costs kept escalating, the U.S. dollar kept falling in value to European currencies (sound familiar even today?), plus there was a four-month crippling strike at Fabrique Nationale in 1973 that was yet another dagger in the heart of the Superposed.

In 1972, Browning had imported its first shotguns from Japan – a side-by-side called the BSS – an acronym for Browning Side-by-side. So with all the problems of the salt wood, increasing Superposed prices, decreasing sales, increasing labor costs, devaluation of the dollar, coupled with the Browning's discovery of how good Japanese workmanship was in the BSS, the Citori was born.

The Citori is a very close cousin of the Superposed. Both rely on the strong hinge pin for the barrel to pivot upon, as well as the huge under-locking bolting system. The bolt moves forward upon the gun's closing to engage a massive lug built into the bottom of the barrels. The bolt can move forward as the gun is shot extensively, keeping the action solid and tight. As has been discussed previously there are also the dual recoil lugs milled into the bottom of the monobloc that dovetail into square cutouts in the base of the receiver, all ensuring one of the strongest lock ups offered by any shotgun.

The cost of a 1973 Citori, compared to a 1973 Superposed, was very low - $325 for the Citori compared to $735 for the Superposed. By 1976, the Superposed was up to $1,100. However, those were years when the perception of goods made in Japan was inferior to those made in many other parts of the world. Since a Citori's price was less than half the price of a Superposed, that furthered the thought that Citori shotguns were not close to the quality of the Superposed. Time has proven that this is certainly not the case. The Citori is a very high-quality shotgun for the price, and they have proven to hold up extremely well, no matter how much they are shot.

In March of 2008, I visited the factory in Japan where the Citori and several other Browning firearms are made. There's no question that two things were most impressive on that two-day factory tour. First to impress was the high quality of workmanship that goes into these over/unders. There are no shortcuts. For the most part the Citori is a handmade shotgun. Second to impress was how fast the Japanese worked – and I mean worked fast performing very specialized and intricate tasks. I've visited many gun makers here in America, and it's a fact, we just do not work as fast.

Over the years, the Citori has evolved into many different models, though all are based on the already described action. Perhaps the best selling and most appealing Citori is the Lightning model. Interestingly, there was a Superposed Lightning, and from that model the Citori stole the rounded style of the forend, as well as the pistol grip that I think is reminiscent of the Prince of Wales grip found on a number of side-by-side shotguns, mainly made in England a century ago.

The Lightning model is still in the Citori line, is the least expensive Citori, and, to my eye, the most elegant. Over the years, there have been a number of Trap model Citoris. The trap model that has survived to this day is dubbed the Citori XT Trap, with a slightly elevated rib. Plus this model is offered with either a trap stock or an adjustable comb trap stock.

Skeet shooters have not been forgotten, despite sporting clays shotgun sales being vastly better for many years now. The current Citori skeet gun is an excellent one – the XS Skeet model with finger groove forend – in 12 and 20 gauge and either 28- or 30-inch barrel in both. With the same above options, there's also an XS Skeet with adjustable comb. There is a satin finish to the wood, and all these 12- and 20-gauge Citoris come with backbored barrels, lengthened forcing cones and screw-in chokes.

One of the early and successful Citori sporting clays models was the 325. Initially this 325 was sold to the European market, maybe because shotgunners over there had discovered sporting clays before we did here in the USA. However, when the 325 was introduced in Europe, sporting clays had already become popular on our shores. USA-based sporting enthusiasts who went to Europe started bringing the 325 back here with them. Those shooters were that impressed. If I had to put my finger on why so many were impressed with the 325 it would be the dynamic feel these over/unders had. Paul Thompson at Browning told me that he thought the barrels on the 325 were a bit lighter, which explains my feelings about the 325's improved dynamics. So many 325s were brought back from Europe that Browning began offering this model here in the USA.

But that only lasted for a relatively short time because Browning updated the 325 with its next model aimed at sporting clays shooters – the 425. That was in 1995. The 425 differed from the 325 with a new engraving pattern, but most importantly the 425 was

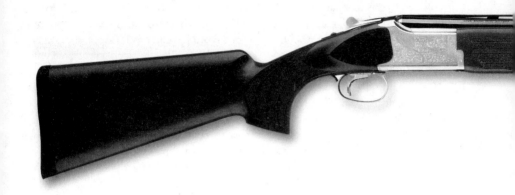

the first Citori with monobloc construction. Miroku, the Japanese company that makes the Citori and other Browning guns, must have had enough chopper lump barrels in stock to include that type of barrel construction until 1998 – when all Citori models were made with monobloc construction.

The change to the next sporting clays model was the 525 replacing the 425 in 2002. It had a redesigned trigger that was crisper and with less over travel, new European-style checkering, a more pronounced pistol grip with palm swell, a new rib design with forward angle posts, and new slim line barrels for a bit less weight. The 525 was also supplied with five Midas Grade extended Invector-Plus choke tubes. Next came the 625 Citori sporting model. The 625 featured Vector Pro™ lengthened forcing cones to go with the overbored barrels and Diamond Grade Invector-Plus screw-ins that are ported.

Keep in mind that these sporting models were not the only ones Browning produced. Earlier sporting models included the Golden Clays, the Ultra, the Grand Lightning, the Grand Prix Sporter and no doubt a few others. More recently it has been that 25 series of sporting over/unders that have resulted in Browning being a shotgun to be truly reckoned with in the top sporting clays circles. The latest 25 rendition is the 725 series –

covered elsewhere in this book.

In addition to the standard Lightning model with engraved and blued receiver there is a White Lightning model. It is the same Citori overall, wearing just a bright nitrided receiver for extra corrosion protection. I've always thought that bright receivers showed off engraving better than a blued receiver, but I'm still stuck (e.g., in love with) the blued Lightning receiver. I asked Browning for several years to bring out the standard Lightning with 30-inch barrels. Previously only 26 and 28-inch barrels have been available in the Lightning. I thought both sporting clays enthusiasts and hunters will love the idea of these 30-inch barrels, and they would be used as crossover guns in hunting, sporting, 5-Stand, FITASC, even skeet and trap. It was sporting clays that showed shotgunners that longer barrels can be a definite benefit. Of course, trap shooters spoke similarly for many years before that. Skeet shooters swung 26-inch barreled over/unders in the 1960s, and went to 28-inch barrels in the 1970s and 1980s, but many have since gone to 30-inch barrels, some even to 32-inchers. I hoped Browning could get these new 30-inch Lightning models into the pipeline en masse because not only are longer barrels the wave of the future, the Lightning is the lowest priced Citori, and, as

The Citori Sporting Model 625.

I've already stated, I think the Lightning is the most elegant Citori. Alas, the Lightning with 30-inch barrels was short lived.

While we're speaking of elegance Browning has always offered the Citori in higher grades. Early on there was the Grade III and the Grade VI. New engraving patterns on these special Citoris have changed that Roman numeral designation to Grade IV and Grade VII. The engraving is intricate with game birds in game scenes, all hand chased to finish up. The Grade VII and previously the Grade VI add gold birds to these specially engraved Lightnings. Recently I returned a .410 Grade VII Lightning to Browning, a beautiful gun that I sincerely considered buying, but I'm to the point in life where I'm selling guns rather than buying them.

Another facet to the Superposed/Citori relationship centers on barrel construction. All the Superposed shotguns were of "chopper lump" construction, which essentially means the barrels and the chambers came from one piece of steel. Most of today's over/unders have barrel/chambers of monobloc construction – the barrels and the chamber area are not made from the same piece of steel. Original Citori over/unders were also of the chopper lump style, but in 1998 Browning changed the Citori over the monobloc construction.

We can't forget the BT-99 – the Citori with a single top barrel that trap shooters have bought by the tens of thousands. In addition to having only one barrel, the BT-99 also has no ejectors. Of course, all a trap shooter needs is the gun's extractor, as many trap buffs save their empties for reloading. Further, most trap and skeet clubs have signs posted suggesting or requiring that spent shells be picked up. The BT-99 is without question a very, very popular trap gun.

The Citori story will always be somehow wrapped around the Superposed – for without the Superposed first the Citori would never have been born.

The 425 Sporter was introduced in 1995.

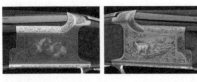

12 Gauge

This is the blued receiver version of the Grade VII Lightning.

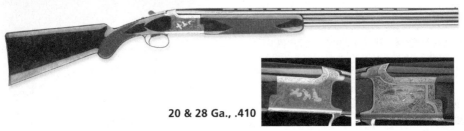

20 & 28 Ga., .410

The author like this .410 Grade VII Lightning test gun so much he almost bought it.

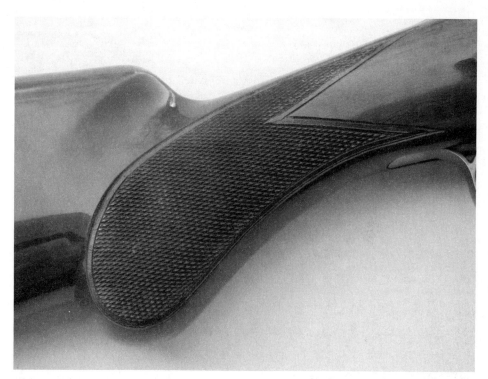

The author is very partial to this grip style on the Lightning Citori, which has a bit of an open grip with a rounded-off base.

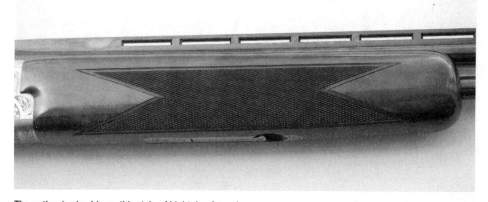

The author is also big on this style of Lightning forend.

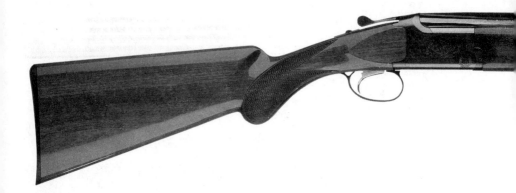

Luck with South Dakota pheasants shooting the Citori Lighting.

BROWNING'S MAXUS GOLDEN CLAYS SPORTING

The Maxus gas-operated semi-auto was introduced in field configuration in 2009. This was a semi full of considerable innovation. New in 2013, was a new Sporter version of the Maxus, officially dubbed the Maxus Sporting Golden Clays. This Sporter is replete with all the original innovation, along with cosmetics that take this shotgun to a new level of attractiveness.

First let's take a look at all the innovation that makes the Maxus tick, before we get into the specifics of this new "Golden" Sporter rendition. There has been considerable trouble with gas systems working consistently over the last several decades, so gun companies that make them have had to do a lot of gas-system tweaking to improve reliability of performance. Browning has done that with the Maxus via their Power Drive Gas System. One improvement is larger port holes that dump powder gases more quickly when higher powered shells are fired.

The Achilles heel of many a gas system can be powder gas fouling getting on the several working mechanisms inside, and especially the outside of the magazine tube. Browning has largely reduced this possibility by better sealing out such non-burned propellants. Consequently, the Maxus stays cleaner, and that results in more functional reliability over a longer period. All shotguns need their periodic cleaning, gas semis more often than other shotgun types. So don't assume you will never have to clean your Maxus just because a lot of crud and residue is sealed off. I put 200 rounds through the

Full length view of the Citori Lightning.

Starting the swing on a fast flushing South Dakota rooster.

Maxus Sporting Golden Clays with no cleaning and not one malfunction. Eventually, however, like any semi, the Maxus should be cleaned. But a lot of this cleaning is easy. Remove the forend and barrel, wipe of the magazine tube and clean out the gas valve (which slides back and forth on the mag tube). That should be all the cleaning required for several more hundred rounds.

A second new feature of the Maxus I like is the new Lightning Trigger System. Perhaps the fastest in the semi-auto world,

lock time is .0052 of a second. The Sporting Golden Clays trigger has minimal creep, but is a bit heavy at nearly six pounds on my Lyman Digital Trigger Pull Gauge. However, I am not trigger critical unless the trigger is too light. A less than six-pound pull suited me fine on the clay pigeons I shot. I would assume a gunsmith knowledgeable about triggers could lighten these pulls. Tap two retaining pins out of the receiver for easy removal of the trigger assembly.

Locking and unlocking the forend is

unique. There's no tightening nut, but a lever under the front part of the forend. Drop the lever down and pull the forend off. To replace, push the forend all the way against the receiver and lock that lever down. This is both quick and easy. Browning, in fact, calls it the Speed Lock Forearm. The magazine plug is probably the easiest to work that you've ever seen. With the forend off use a door or car key to turn the retaining cap on the mag tube to remove or install the magazine plug.

With the bolt back, just slide a shell into the magazine slot and automatically that shell is fed into the chamber. Similarly, unload the magazine by depressing the latch on the inner right side of the receiver. Shells in the magazine pop out into your hand, one at a time. Pretty slick.

The receiver is relatively long at nearly 9 inches, leaving plenty of room for the engraved eye candy. In gold on the left side is a flushing duck in a five-gold-sequence that emerges into a clay target. On the right side of the receiver there's a flushing quail for starters, and in four-gold-sequence changes into a clay target. The floral engraving is equally attractive, and Browning has done an excellent job with the shadow effect on this unique engraving. Further, this floral stuff is highlighted with encircling gold lines, plus Sporting Clays is in gold on both sides of the receiver.

But there's more. At the top of the receiver there's a gold target – right and left – with the engraved hint that the gold pigeon is spinning. Also there's more floral engraving on top – four sections of it – all encircled with gold line. The trigger guard features the standard gold Browning stag's head logo. Also note that the entire receiver, as well as the forend iron, is in a bright but soft patina that includes corrosion resisting silver nitride coating. Finally, there's a deep line at the top of both receiver sides that sort of sets the whole package off. For the money this is probably one of the most attractive semi-auto receivers in a sporting clays specific model.

The walnut finish is traditional Browning, very glossy with a length of pull to the center of the recoil pad at 14.5 inches. The forend wood is a good match to the butt stock wood on my sample test gun. Said forend is just over 12 inches long and a bit wider at the base than near the top. Weight was 8.9 ounces. The checkering is very well done, pretty fine line, probably by machine, and you will have to look very closely for any flaws.

You'll see significant re-curve on the pistol grip, which most sporting clays enthusiasts demand these days. The recoil pad is hi-tech. Called the Inflex Pad, the material is very soft, but that's not all that contributes to less felt recoil. This pad is built so that the butt stock does not come up into your face upon recoil. Further, the pad is rounded all around the edges mitigating possible hang up on clothing. The pad is ¾-inch thick at its mid point. There is no spacer between the pad and the butt stock.

Browning has maintained the lightness in the Maxus Golden Sporting Clays model as the gun went 7 pounds 3 ounces on my digital postal scale. It's probably a fact that many competitors and just-for-fun sporting clays shooters like the light weight of most newer semi-autos designed for the game, and the very light recoil of the gas operation. During more than one of my target busting test sessions, I shot this Golden Sporting Clays semi-auto and a light over/under. Despite shooting 1-ounce, 12-gauge loads the recoil difference between those two guns was more than significant. End result this unique Maxus, I thought, was very light on recoil yet it still functioned perfectly with my low-power loads.

The 30-inch barrel is a dark, dark blue.

The rib tapers from .340 at the breech to .250 at the muzzle. There's a white mid bead, a glow sight at the muzzle, and Browning provides several additional glow sights of different colors so they are interchangeable. Backboring was to .739 with lengthened forcing cones – what Browning calls Vector Pro. Five screw-in chokes were included in the lockable plastic carrying case: Full, Improved Modified, Modified, Improved Cylinder and Skeet. Check out www.browning.com.

SPECIFICATIONS:

Action: Semi-auto with Power Drive Gas System
Gauge: 12
Weight: 7 pounds 3 ounces
Barrel: 30-inch Vector Pro
Chokes: Five screw-ins supplied: Full, Improved Modified, Modified, Improved Cylinder and Skeet
Stock: 14.25 x 1.75 x 2
Suggested Retail: $2,000
Manufacture: Browning Arms in Morgan, Utah. www.browning.com

The Maxus Golden Sporting Clays stock is well shaped and features Browning's high gloss finish.

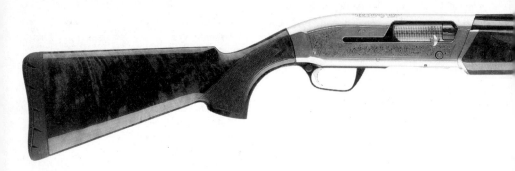

The Maxus Golden Sporting Clays receiver shows lots of eye candy.

Full-length view of the Maxus Sporting.

The gun's forend is easily installed and removed via a system Browning calls the Speed Lock Forearm.

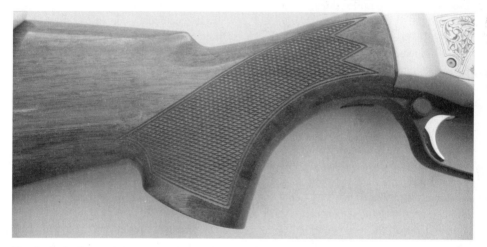

The checkering is so well done that it's tough to find a flaw. Note the re-curve shape of the pistol grip.

BROWNING 725 OVER/UNDER

When you read shotgun test reports, the torture such guns are put through normally involves shooting 150 to 250 cartridges. Of course, there are other aspects about such shotgun testing that I and others report on, but normally there is only so much gun writers can do from a test standpoint to determine how that particular smoothbore functions. In other words, the gun cannot be shot for years, nor can thousands and thousands of rounds be put through it. It's just not economically feasible.

This was not true for the 725 over/under because Browning Arms took five shooters and five new pre-production model 725 O/Us to the Cordoba area of Argentina. Most all of you know this is where the eared dove reigns supreme, all to the dismay and disgust of the local small grain farmers. Consequently, these five new Brownings were fired literally tens of thousands of times down there, all to determine if they were figuratively up to snuff, and, if not, what was needed to make these pre-production 725s run even more perfectly.

The basis of all the 25 Brownings is the time-tested Citori action, with a receiver-wide hinge pin that the barrels pivot upon, as well as the receiver-wide horizontal bolt that moves forward upon closing to engage a receiver wide lug under the bottom barrel. And don't forget what is probably most important to strength – the recoil lugs milled into the base of the monobloc that upon closing dovetail into milled out areas in the bottom of the receiver. So all the over/unders in the "25" series are still Citoris. Over a million of them have been sold, and there's hardly a shotgunner around who doesn't recognize this one as being among the most reliable and most bullet proof, especially in their price range.

So what makes the 725 new and different? Writer Layne Simpson, Browning honcho Scott Grange and I shot mainly the Field version of the 725, while sporting clays stalwarts Robbie Purser and Rick Camuglia shot the Sporter rendition. Our Field 725s wore 28-inch barrels, while the Sporting guns wore 32-inch barrels. Further, the field gun had the standard Citori rib while the longer-barreled Sporting versions had a tapered wide top rib – $\frac{5}{16}$ths to $\frac{7}{16}$ths – as well as vented side panels between those barrels. The 725 Sporting barrels were also ported.

Perhaps the most important new feature is the 725 has been fitted with mechanical triggers. As most of you know the standard Citori and all the previous specialized Citoris have always come with inertia-style triggers. Why go to mechanical? One reason is if the first barrel does not go off in a hunting situation, just pull the trigger again. No recoil is required to set that second trigger. This can be important in the field and an over/under with mechanical triggers allowed me to make an easy shot on a grouse after I'd missed one, opened the gun to eject the empty and there was no time to reload for that second flushing grouse. So I simply closed the gun, pulled the first trigger where I knew there was no shell, but then hit the second trigger and added another little bump to help fill the pouch in the back of my old hunting coat.

Why mechanical triggers for a sporting clays gun? Other over/under manufacturers are going this route so maybe it's a "Keep up with the Joneses" type thing. Beyond that a number of sporting enthusiasts are having their 12-gauge competition over/unders fitted with sub-gauge tubes – in 20, 28 and .410 – from the likes of Briley in Houston, Texas and Kolar in Racine, Wisconsin – as sub-gauge sporting continues to increase in popularity. A shotgun with inertia triggers has to be converted over, so the second trigger can be set for the light recoiling 28 and .410.

These mechanical triggers on the 725 do have hammers, not the strikers that were designed for the Browning Cynergy over/under that also has mechanical triggers. Further, Browning has achieved a slightly lower profile with the 725 compared to other Citori models. The lower profile may be a result of smaller, sturdier hammers. We all found these 725s to have not only crisp triggers, but also light triggers. Back at home I measured the let off on my 725 Field at 3 pounds 10 ounces when the bottom barrel was fired first.

A third new aspect of the 725 is the new choke system. Called Invector DS (the DS for Double Seal), Browning had heard requests for a choking system that allowed less crud to creep past the outside of the screw-in and to the inside of the barrel under the choke. Browning accomplished this by putting a band of softer brass on the bottom outside of the screw in. I checked after each several hundred rounds of shooting and do feel that the system works as designed with less powder residue and plastic wad crud crept in on the outside of the choke and the inside of the barrel threads.

The length of pull is 14.25 inches but that's easily lengthened because a set of plastic spacers comes with the gun that fit quickly and easily between the recoil pad and the butt stock. Each spacer is .275. The drop at comb for the Field model is 1.625 x 2.5 drop at heel. Stock dimensions for the Sporting versions are 1.563 drop at comb, 2.5 drop at heel. The forend on the both models is Schnabel in shape. Like most recent Citori models, the barrels are overbored and the forcing cones are quite long – about 5 inches. Browning calls this Vector Pro.

Then there is the engraving, all new and different for the Field model compared to the Sporting 725. Both receivers wear a bright and protective nickeled finish. On the Field model inside the scroll on the left side are two flushing pheasants. On the right side it is two flushing ducks. On the bottom there's a bit of engraving, a dog's head and "Field 725 Model."

My test Field gun wore an attractive piece of walnut, and recoil is reduced by the company's Inflex recoil pad. The checker-

ing is well done and very sharp. I decided to wear shooting gloves in Argentina, the checkering is that sharp. And shoot those 725 Brownings we did. Some on the trip (not me) were shooting over 2,000 doves a day. I did not get a total on the number of shells fired on that trip, but I'm sure it was nearly 20,000, if not more. I did not experience one 725 hiccup, and I didn't hear that any of the other four shooters experienced anything negative about the new O/U.

Because the idea behind this South America shoot was gun testing I doubt that Browning had any significant number of 725s made up other than those we took. That's because – if we did encounter problems – which we didn't – there would be time for fixes.

SPECIFICATIONS

Gauge: 12 gauge only
Action: Over/under
Weight: 7 pounds 6 ounces
Barrels: Field model - 26 and 28 inch; Sporting – 28, 30 and 32 inch
Chokes: Invector DS – 3 supplied with the Field, 5 supplied with the Sporting
Stock: 14.25 x 1.625 x 2.5 for the Field, 14.25 x 1.563 x 2.5 for the Sporting
Suggested Retail: Field $2470, Sporting $3140
Manufacturer/Importer: Browning Arms, Route One, Morgan, UT 84050 – www.browning.com

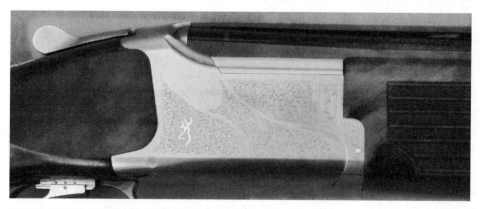

Close up of the standard grade 725 Sporting receiver.

The 12-gauge 725 gets put through some torture tests in Argentina.

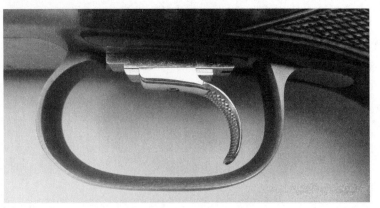

The trigger can be moved forward and back to obtain your perfect grip-to-trigger distance.

Close up of the bottom of the 725 receiver.

Note the band of brass at the base of this Invector Pro DS screw-in choke. This brass band prevents powder fowling, plastic and other crud from entering the choke and barrel threads.

BROWNING 725 SPORTING CITORI 20 GAUGE

Browning's 12-gauge 725 Citori Sporting has been a big hit, as has the Field version of the 725. The latest in the 725 lineup is the 20 gauge Sporting rendition. That's the one I've been putting through its paces of late on clay targets. Obviously, the new 20 gauge is built on a smaller 20-gauge frame. Surprisingly, the total weight of my test gun with 30-inch barrels was only 6 pounds 11 ounces on my digital postal scale. I found the gun thus plenty lively and quick on hard crossers, but with no tendency to over swing, which can be a problem with a whippy smoothbore of extreme light weight. By comparison the 12-gauge 725 Trap I recently had for testing weighed 8 pounds 11 ounces with 32-inch barrels, while the 725 Field I brought back from Argentina hefted 7 pounds 6 ounces with 28-inch barrels. I've also tested the 12 gauge 725 Feather, this model with the aircraft aluminum frame that weighed 6 pounds 7 ounces. All these weights are given to offer a little weight perspective. For a really light upland hunting gun many of us are wondering if Browning will bring out a 20-gauge 725 Feather sometime in the future. If they do it could be a 6 pounder, or even a tad less.

The 725 Citori is still a Citori – barrels pivot on a receiver-wide hinge pin and a lock bolt extends forward from the bottom of the receiver to engage lugs milled into the bottom of the monobloc. But the real strength part of the Citori are those recoil lugs milled into the base of the monobloc which extend all the way through milled out recesses in the base of the receiver. These days there are a number of shotguns that easily last through hundreds of thousands of rounds, but the Citori and its Superposed predecessor have been enjoying that type of longevity for over 80 years. Yes, this is a very strong action design.

But the 725 is also a bit different from the standard Citori. One main difference would be the 725's mechanical trigger system. All other Citori model triggers are inertia driven. Is this a big deal? Maybe not, as a good trigger is a good trigger no matter inertia or mechanical. Maybe Browning was guided by popular opinion to develop these new mechanical triggers. The Fire Lite Mechanical Trigger System is a good trigger, as it is has been on all the previous 725s I tested. This current 20-bore 725 has triggers that are crisp and go off at just a hair over 4 pounds on my Lyman Digital Trigger-Pull Scale. Barrel inner diameters were both .628 – traditionally 20-gauge barrel internal diameters have been .615, so these barrels are well overbored beyond traditional bores. My test barrels were 30-inches. In the Sporting version there are also 28- and 32-inch barrel options. There is also a Field version of the new 20 gauge 725 with barrel length choices of 26 and 28 inches. Forcing cones appear to be about one-inch.

There's a HI-VIZ sight at the muzzle and a white mid-bead over the vented top rib. The top of the rib is scored horizontally on each side with the mid portion of the rib scored longitudinally. Does this provide a natural pathway to the target? Probably in theory. There are vents between the barrels, a portion of the barrels under the forend is open. Both barrels are ported, the top barrel with five slots on top of each side and four below. The bottom barrel has 10 slots on top and four below. I shot mostly doubles with this gun, and I have to say those abundant porting holes in the bottom barrel did seem to keep the muzzles down after the first shot.

Barrels went 2 pounds 13 ounces.

The screw-in chokes are the Invector DS which were a new design with the 12-gauge 725 models. A ring of brass encircles the base of the screw choke. The idea is for this ring of brass to prevent powder and plastic crud from entering the thread area. I shot with the same chokes for over 200 rounds. Removed, they looked about the same as when I installed them cleanly wiped and oiled.

Five Invector DS screw-ins were supplied. The Skeet went .624 for .004 constriction over the .628 bore; the Improved Cylinder went .620 for .008 constriction; the Modified went .614 for .014 constriction; the Improved Modified went .606 for .022 constriction and the Full went .596 for .032 constriction. Total screw-choke length was just a bit over 3 ½-inches – plenty of length for the significant taper and parallel sections.

Regarding the gun's eye candy two areas stand out. The receiver engraving is just about 100 percent coverage of tiny ovals on both sides of the receiver. "725" is also part of the engraving on both receiver sides. On the bottom there is no oval engraving, just but "Browning 725 Sporting." The forend also has the tiny engraved ovals, as well as a small Browning stag logo in gold. There's the same logo in gold on the trigger guard. The trigger itself is gold plated, plus the trigger can be moved back and forth so you can easily attain your perfect grip-to-trigger distance. All metal parts are silver nitride coated – an excellent guard against corrosion. It's also noteworthy that all the metal parts have been finely polished, as poor polishing would show up easily on any bright non-engraved area.

The other area of eye candy would be the stock. The 725 20-gauge Sporting gets upgraded to III/IV walnut with a low gloss oil finish, different from the shiny finish put on traditional Citori Lightning model stocks. Checkering on the forend and pistol grip is 20 lines-to-the-inch. From the grip photo you can judge the amount of re-curve. Pores were not entirely filled in. That could offer good eye appeal to some.

A very big part of the low recoil package has to be the recoil pad. Dubbed the Inflex II, there's good compressibility. More importantly, I like the pad's design. It's rounded to eliminate gun hang ups during the mount, plus there's a smooth plastic insert at the top to further mitigate hang-ups on clothing.

Stock dimensions are 1.25x 1.5 x 2.375. The forend is slim at 1.68-inches, what I'd call a semi-Schnabel look. Total length along the bottom at 10-inches. The forend snaps on and off easily, and there's no wiggle once in place. Forend weight was 12.1 ounces.

While all of the foregoing has been most positive, I have to say further that this is one special shotgun. I'm not the only one with this claim as the 725 20-bore was put in the hands of five other shotgunners, and they were all of the same opinion. We all liked this 725, but the opinions run deeper. The ease of the way the gun handled, how it moved so effortlessly, how it stayed steady during the swing, the positive balance, its lack of recoil, and especially the way it smoked targets were all factors.

Scott Grange at Browning not only wears a public relations cap at this Morgan, Utah-based company, Scott is also a friend. I knew he had recently bought a 725 20-gauge Sport-ing with 32-inch barrels, and I wanted to get his input on that experience. Scott told me, "Many folks find themselves shooting behind a lot of targets with 32-inch 12-gauge barrels. I have struggled with this problem myself, so I started shooting a 30-inch 12-gauge gun. I've found my new 32-inch 725 20-gauge is such a race horse I have to be careful not to shoot in front. The longer sighting plane is a plus, and I love the sleek lines. The low profile receiver places my hands more in line with the bores. I am once again shooting 32-inch barrels with tremendous confidence."

It's obvious that Browning has hit a home run with the 725 Citori series. The two newest versions, the 20-gauge Sporting and Field, both promise to add significantly to the 725 line. And who knows what the next 725 offering will be. I bet a new 25 is on the Browning drawing board right now.

SPECIFICATIONS

Action: Over/under
Gauge: 20 gauge
Weight: 6 pounds 11 ounces
Barrels: 30 inch. 28 and 32 also offered
Chokes: Five screw-in: Skeet, Improved Cylinder, Modified, Improved Modified and Full
Stock: Grade III/IV walnut with low gloss oil finish – 14.25 x 1.5 x 2.375
Suggested Retail: $3,340
Manufacturer: Browning Arms, Morgan, Utah. www.browning.com.

Close up of the 725 engraving shows 100-percent coverage in tiny ovals on both sides of the receiver. Note the oval engraving and Gold Stag Logo on the forend iron.

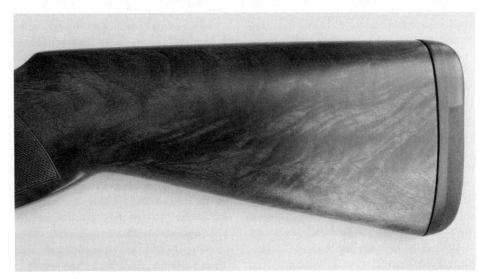

A second factor in the 725 eye candy is the oil-finished walnut upgraded to III/IV.

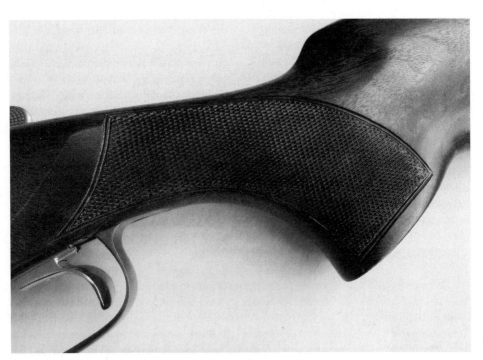

The shape of the 725 pistol grip with excellent checkering at 20 lines-to-the-inch.

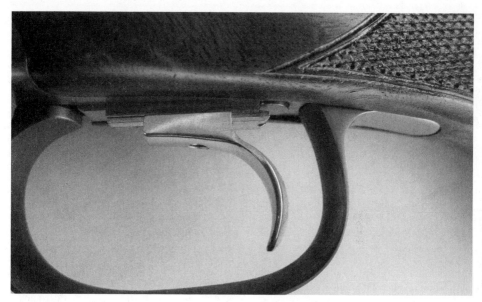

Two additional, differently shaped triggers are included in the package.

Five Invector HP chokes are included. At the base of the choke note the ring of brass that keeps powder fouling, plastic crud and other dirt from entering into the choke threads.

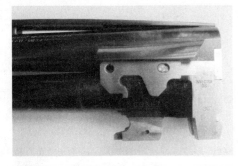

The extreme strength of the Citori system comes thanks to lugs at the bottom of the monobloc which mesh into milled-out areas in the bottom of the receiver. Additionally, there's the receiver-wide hinge pin and the locking bolt that extends forward from the base of the receiver to engage the lugs milled into the base of the monobloc. The total package means one super strong locking arrangement.

BROWNING 725 TRAP

"Nick, I not only like this 725 as a trap gun. I could shoot it at sporting clays, skeet and 5-Stand." It was trap shooter Joe Peters pontificating. We were shooting at the Pony Farm Trap & Gun Club. Joe had just finished banging away with Browning's new Citori 725 Trap with the adjustable comb that I had on consignment. I thought to myself, "He's right. Is this an all-around over/under?" If that were true I'd have to try breaking targets with it, other than those from a trap bunker.

A week previous I had traveled to the Harrisville Trap Club. I wanted to have one of my best friends try the 725 Trap. Dr. Donald Lavely shoots trap four and five days a week so I knew he'd give the gun a good look-see. While there, I had another guy shoot the gun. Owen is semi-retired, but started two gun shops in our area, both of

which are now run by his son. Owen liked the 725 Trap so much that he vowed to order several for those gun shops.

The day after Joe Peters shot the 725, I went to the Tarentum District Sportsman's Club and tried the 725 Trap on 25 skeet birds. All the screw-in chokes were plenty tight. (No open chokes came with the 725 Trap, but, of course, they are available from Browning.) I remember shooting the Low House from Skeet Station One with the Full screwed in. WOW! What an ink ball. Joe Peters was correct. The 725 Trap did just fine on the skeet field.

The next day I took the gun to Vandergrift Sportsman to put the new gun to work at their 5-Stand. The targets weren't long ones, so I didn't need the Improved Modified and Full screw-in chokes I had in the gun, but as long as I did my part it was one ink ball after another. So, yes, this is a trap gun but it does just fine with other clay target disciplines.

The shotgunning public was introduced to the 725 at the 2012 SHOT Show in Las Vegas. A Trap version of the 725, however, was yet to come. In 2013, four Trap versions of the 725 became available. My test 725 Trap came with the adjustable comb stock, while a second model has a raised cheek rest stock, plus left-handed versions are available in both.

The 725 Trap is a Citori, but it is also different. The height of the receiver is lower than all the other Citoris in the 25 line, as well as all the other specialty Citori over/unders. Previous Citori models come with inertia triggers; the 725 comes with mechanical triggers. And they are good ones, nice and crisp – and light. According to my Lyman Digital Trigger Pull Scale, when the bottom barrel is fired first let off is at 4 pounds 3 ounces, top barrel at 4 pounds 6 ounces. Browning calls these triggers FireLite.

The lock-up is the same – barrels pivoting on a receiver-wide hinge pin with additional lock-up via a tapered bolt that moves forward upon closing which engages milled out lugs in the bottom of the monobloc. Plus there's steel dovetailing into the bottom of the receiver. This is a super strong system and that strength is why Brownings are so well known for being very durable.

The other new aspect to the Trap 725 is the very high rib. I measure the rib post closest to the receiver at ½ inch. The rib is also ⅛ of an inch thick, so there's plenty of strength. I always worry about thin, high ribs and how much of a ding it will take to dent them. No worries on this issue with this 725 Trap rib. The rib is tapered - .340 at the breech, .285 at the muzzle.

On top is a white mid-bead and a HiViz green glow sight at the muzzle. Additional HiViz sights of varying colors are packed with the gun and are easily changed. Above the receiver there is a pretty huge step up to the high rib. Vent ribs are between the barrels. The top of the rib has very fine cross hatching – preventing distracting glare.

The 32-inch barrels (30-inches also available) are overbored and weighed 3 pounds 10.5 ounces. With my Baker Barrel Reader the bores went .738 and with a long forcing cone in front of the chambers measuring approximately 5 inches. The screw-in chokes are new with the 725 series called Invector-DS. The DS is for the band of brass at the base of these screw-ins. Screw-in chokes are noted for allowing plastic build up, powder fouling and other crud to creep in – between the outside of the choke and the inner barrel. The brass band helps to prevent this. In Argentina, we constantly monitored how this was working. Very little crud was seen creeping in to this area despite the firing of many, many thousands of rounds.

The receiver wears a bright silver-nitride finish. The engraving on the receiver sides consists of a series of tiny ovals that Browning calls Gold Enhanced, though the gold in this case is a small gold stag head logo on the forend iron. Maybe the tiny ovals simulate clay target; the oval shape perhaps how a real clay target looks from trap stations one through five. On the bottom of the receiver there is "Browning 725 Trap." The top tang, opening lever and trigger guard also wear the corrosion resistant silver nitride finish. The trigger guard also has the stag logo in gold. The trigger itself is gold-plated, as is the base above. Importantly, the trigger can be moved back and forth so the shooter can attain his or her perfect grip-to-trigger distance.

Another plus in the 725's favor is a walnut upgrade to what Browning calls Grade III/IV. The high gloss finish is typical Browning. The company is convinced their customers prefer this high gloss look.

The adjustable stock works a bit differently. Loosen the nut reached through the recoil pad. Move the adjustable portion up, down, left or right – until you have it where you think you want it. Re-tighten the lock nut through the recoil pad. Make it tight enough. When Joe Peters shot this gun with his tight cheek position, I didn't have the lock nut properly tightened and the adjustable portion moved on him.

There is a significant re-curve to the pistol grip. One shooter complained that upon recoil the trigger guard was banging against his middle finger. I did not experience this with my shooting of the 725 Trap, nor did others. The cut checkering on the grip and on the forend is very well done at 20 lines-to-the-inch.

The forend has finger grooves, is about 10-inches in length and 1.94-inches at its widest area. Weight was 12.8 ounces on my digital postal scale. The opening lever is well checkered or serrated, offering a firm thumb grasp for opening. Three screw-in chokes were provided; a Modified that went .732 for .006 constriction over the .738 barrels; an Improved Modified measuring .725 for .013 constriction, and a Full was .702 for .036

constriction. Total gun weight was 8 pounds 11.5 ounces.

The recoil pad is vented – ¾-inch thick and separated from the stock via a thin black spacer. The back of the pad wears sort of a stippled or rough surface so the pad stayed in place on the shoulder during doubles shooting. Two spare triggers of differing shape are also included and easily interchanged. The 725 Trap is going to be a welcome addition to the many Citori variations that were and still are available.

SPECIFICATIONS

Gauge: 12 gauge
Action: Over/under
Weight: 8 pounds 11.5 ounces
Stock: Adjustable comb. LOP: 14.375 inches
Barrels: 32 inch. 30 inch available
Chokes: Three Invector-DS included: Modified, Improved Modified and Full
Suggested Retail: $3,530
Maker: Browning Arms. Morgan, Utah. www.browning.com

Dr. Donald Lavely checks out the 725 Trap at the Harrisville Trap Club.

Joe Peters puts the 725 Trap through its paces at the Pony Farm Trap and Gun Club.

The 725 Trap receiver with bright silver nitride finish, gold stag logo and tiny oval engraving that Browning calls Gold Enhanced Engraving.

Dr. Lavely on the trap line at Harrisville, putting the 725 Trap through its paces.

The re-curve to the 725 Trap pistol grip. The checkering is very well done and at 20 lines-to-the-inch.

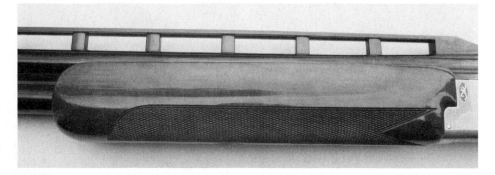

The shape of the 725 forend with finger grooves.

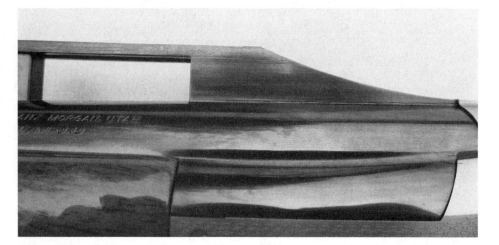

The sharp step up to the high vent rib starts just above the receiver.

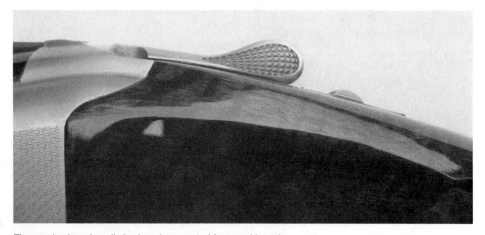

The opening lever is well checkered or serrated for a positive grip.

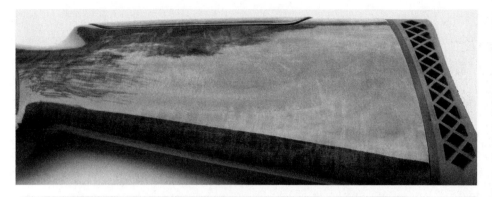

The high gloss well figured Grade III/IV 725 Trap adjustable comb stock.

Two extra triggers of differing shape are packed with the 725 Trap. Also note the brass band around the Investor-DS screw choke.

BROWNING SPECIAL SPORTING CLAYS

The year was 1989 when Browning brought out their Special Sporting Clays Edition. Since then, the many sporting clays models Browning has announced may need more than two hands to count. But Tom Nichols, Dave Hartsell and Dan Goodsell at Guns Unlimited (GU) in Omaha, Nebraska, had always thought highly of this classic clays gun, and wondered if they could bring back the Special Sporting at a price considerably lower than the current sporting clays guns Browning and others are now offering.

Working through both Browning and their factory in Japan, Guns Unlimited has pulled it off. Further, GU will be the only dealer where you will be able to find this new/old rendition. Guns Unlimited contracted to have 900 of these over/unders made. When they're gone, they're gone – unless, of course, these Special Sporting guns sell so rapidly that GU contracts for another order.

With only a couple of exceptions, these new Special Sporting Clays rendition guns are the same as the originals – with the raised rib. In 12 gauge, these guns will have the newer longer forcing cones and over-bored barrels, plus the 12- and 20-gauge barrels will be fitted with Invector Plus chokes, and those barrels will be ported. But GU hasn't forgotten the small-gauge crowd as both 28-gauge and .410 Special Sporting guns are also available with standard Invector chokes. In fact, I've been shooting one of the 28-gauge guns extensively. No short barrels this time. Sporting clays buffs want the longer tubes, so your choice here will be for either 30 or 32 inchers.

Dan Goodsell remarked to me, "Many sporting clays guns, including those from Browning and others, are selling for $3000 and more. We thought there was a market for a gun priced considerably less, and this Special Sporting is priced less, a lot less."

Full retail on both the 12- and 20-gauge Special Sporting will be $1,995. The little 28s and .410s will be $100 more. An adjustable comb (by Grayco) is available for $175 – pretty cheap for an adjustable comb installation these days. Stock dimensions are 14.375 length of pull, 1.5 inches drop at comb, 2 inches drop at heel. The 12-gauge rib tapers from ⅜ to ¼. The smaller gauge ribs are .355 at the breech and .355 at the muzzle, so no taper.

My test gun wears the 32-inch barrels with the slightly tapered ramp to the raised rib. This raised rib is one of the factors that made the Special Sporting Clays Edition so popular two decades ago, and now look at the popularity of those relatively new extra-high adjustable rib shotguns. Of course, this over/under is a Citori through and through. I visited the Browning factory in Japan a few years ago, and it was very enlightening. A Citori, in fact all the Browning O/Us, are virtually handmade guns. Sure there's lots of metal milling that goes on, but don't forget that Citoris were born in Japan 40 years ago. Those made 40 years ago are pretty much dead ringers for those made today. While I'm certain the factory has made a lot of progress in parts making and parts fitting over the last 40 years, today's gun is still the same as yesteryear's hand-fitted Citori. What I saw during my visit was that there was hand-fitting galore, and along most every step of the way. What really impressed me were the Japanese workers and their ability to work so quickly while performing very intricate and low metal tolerance tasks. Along those lines, Guns Unlimited's head honcho Tom Nichols commented, "It's the fun part of the business to work with Browning and do something special, in this case quality, price and new features on a classic shotgun."

The rounded forend on the Special Sporting Clays is the same as on the Browning Lightning model – a forend shape that is my personal favorite. The pistol grip is more traditional with not as tight a re-curve as we are tending to see on some modern-day competition over/unders.

Invector and Invector Plus chokes have already been mentioned. Three Invectors were included with my test gun; a Skeet I measured at .550 – the same dimension as both 28 gauge bores. The Improved Cylinder went .547, so .003 constriction. The Modified went .544 at .006 constriction. Of course, Invector and Invector Plus screw-ins are available from a myriad of aftermarket makers, including Guns Unlimited.

The recoil pad has relatively sharp edges. On my test gun that rubber pad is about

⅜-inches thick, offset from the butt stock with a ¼-inch black spacer. The receiver, barrels and forend are richly blued – a task that I've found Browning to be very good at over the years. On both sides of the receiver there is "Special Sporting Clays Edition" in gold. In gold at the bottom of the receiver is "Browning Sporting Clays." The Browning stag logo is in gold on the trigger guard. The trigger is both gold-plated and moveable back and forth, making it easy to select your perfect grip-to-trigger distance. Further, in addition to the trigger on the gun as it comes out of the box two additional triggers are packed inside. These additional triggers are, of course, of differing shapes. My suggestion is to try all three to determine which one you like best. Taking these triggers on and off is easy, and a thin hex-head wrench is provided for this. Trigger let off was at 5 pounds with minimal creep.

The same tried-and-true Browning safety and selector is on the top tang. Same tried-and-true Citori lock-up. Incidentally, the original Citoris were not made with the monobloc system, but came with true chopper lump barrels. I was told the year this change over to a monobloc system took place was 1998.

This 28 gauge with 32-inch barrels weighed 7 pounds 12 ounces on my digital postal scale. This is a nice weight for a small gauge sporting gun. The barrels went 3 pounds 4.5 ounces; the forend 12.1 ounces.

On the adjustable comb stock I was able to raise the back of that comb a bit higher than the front of the comb which made for a nearly level-comb stock if such an arrangement appeals to you. It does to me. That comb, of course, can be raised and lowered, as well as moved from side to side. Just take the comb piece off and look at the posts in the top of the stock which have marked increments. Loosen the set screws, move

the posts left or right to where you think you would like them, retighten the screws and try the new dimensions out. It's easy to make further changes or return those posts to their original positions.

The walnut on my test gun is straight grain, which bodes well for strength. Some folks are nuts for magnificent wood. Grain that's built for strength is more important. The checkering is at 18-lines-to-the-inch and very well done, and I'm not sure it was done by machine.

I shot this gun a lot simply because it was fun. All but the new 725 model Browning Citoris have inertia triggers, so I put the Special Sporting inertia triggers to the test on my 28-gauge gun shooting pipsqueak ¾ ounce reloads at a measly 1,120 feet per second. I always loaded two shells, and the second barrel's trigger never failed to set despite the low-powered shells. Of course, I shoot those shells to both test an inertia trigger gun's mettle as well as not face hard recoil issues.

While this Special Sporting Clays Edition is available in all four gauges most serious shotgunners are at least a bit enthralled with the small gauges. I've certainly been enthralled with this one from Guns Unlimited. I hate to send it back.

SPECIFICATIONS

Action: Over/under
Gauge: 12, 20, 28 and .410
Dimensions: 14 14.375 length of pull; adjustable comb
Price: $1,995 for the 12 and 20 gauges; $2,095 for the 28 and .410. Add $175 for the adjustable comb
Maker/Importer: Made at the Browning factory in Japan. Imported for Guns Unlimited, 4325 South 120th Street, Omaha, NE 68137. www.gunsunlimitedomaha.com.

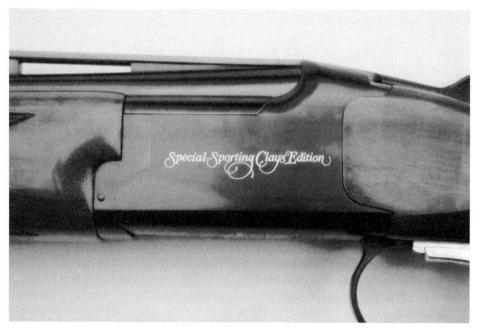

The receiver is engraved on the Gun Unlimited Special Sporting Clays Edition.

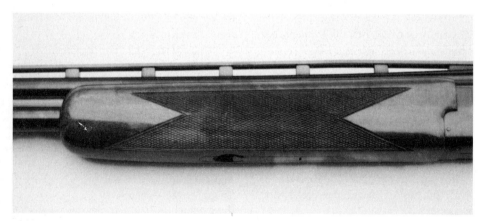

The rounded forend on the Special Sporting is much the same as the forend on the Citori Lightning model.

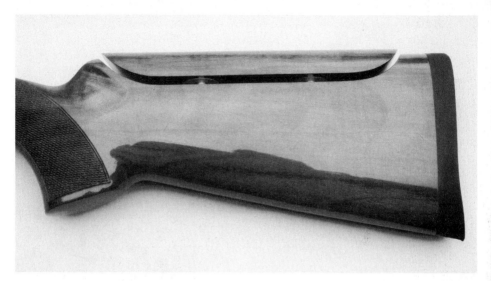

The stock features walnut and adjustable comb.

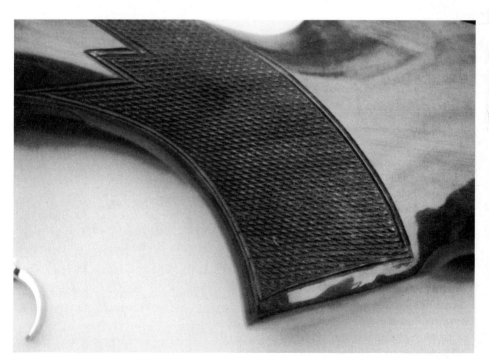

The grip shape is more "traditional" compared to the re-curve style grips on some of today's sporting guns.

Two extra triggers are packed with the gun. With the choice of three triggers you are bound to find the one you like best. Note also that the trigger position is adjustable forward and back.

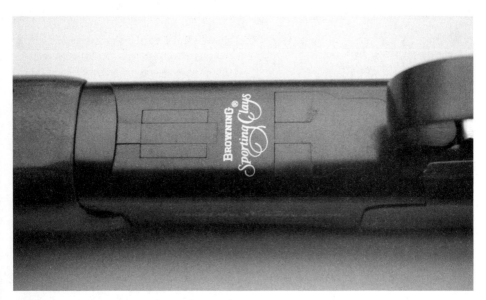

The bottom of the receiver on the Special Sporting Clays.

Another view of the Special Sporting Clays Edition receiver – with the gun's manual.

CZ-USA HAMMER CLASSIC

Early shotguns used external hammers to cock the trigger springs. It wasn't until near the end of the 1800s that design ingenuity permitted trigger springs to be cocked internally. But even long after so-called "hammerless" shotguns were readily available, many, many astute shotgunners still preferred a smoothbore with outside hammers and ordered their "bespoke" side-by-side shotguns with those hammers. I'm guessing at the date, but somewhere around the early 1980s thousands of these older hammer guns were brought in from England where they had been made and the importers found a ready market for these storied masterpieces here in the USA. One of the movers and shakers in this scenario was Houston's Cyril Adams. There were others, of course, but Adams certainly had a lot to do with this

importation of hammer guns, and with making them popular.

In old western movies you have probably seen some side-by-side hammer guns in action. The hammers were cranked back in a dire situation, the noise for added emphasis on the silver screen. Usually called "coach guns," that name was probably for their use in defending stagecoaches against bandits. These were short-barreled hammer guns and more intended as people killers rather than waterfowl and upland bird killers. If there have been any longer-barreled hammer guns produced for the average American hunter over the last several decades I'm not aware of any.

That is until now. CZ-USA, more noted for their outstanding bolt-action rifles, has been importing shotguns from Turkey for several years now. Early on one of these imports was a so-called "coach gun," this one with the exposed hammers and very short side-by-side barrels. The shotgun maker is Huglu in Turkey, and 30-inch barrels have been added to their "coach gun" and voila, we now have a shotgun that has a lot in common with the English hammer guns of yesteryear – well, a little in common anyway.

I remember shooting a vintage hammer gun in Uruguay. It belonged to a collector from the USA, and he kept urging me to come over to his stand and try shooting it. That was maybe 15 years ago. I recall that old gun to be marvelously balanced, quite light, and it swung like the extension of one's body. I had no problem adapting to cocking those hammers when it was apparent yet another flock of doves were approaching the stand.

The new CZ-USA hammer gun, dubbed the Hammer Classic, isn't quite of the same ilk as those old English vintage hammer guns that now bring five figures in U.S. dollars, but the new arrival is nonetheless a fun gun to shoot. Cocking those hammers prior to each shot is going to take many of you back to the English countryside of yesteryear where you can imagine yourself standing next to the likes of Lord Wallsingham and/or Lord Ripon, both of whom were adamant hammer gun users. Further, they shot more game than had ever been shot in the world – at least up until that time – and with hammer guns.

I see the CZ Hammer Classic as a fun gun for waterfowl. As a clay bird gun, I found that even light 12-gauge loads got to my sensitive shoulder after about 50 birds. For ducks and geese this new side-by-side has these-days-required 3-inch chambers. The CZ is plenty heavy enough, but it has a steel butt plate which absorbs zero recoil. The stock dimensions read 1.5 inches drop at comb (pretty good in my book, though 1.35 would probably be better for me), but 2.3-inches drop at heel perhaps a factor in contributing to recoil. Most won't feel the bump this gun gives, so I admit to being very recoil sensitive.

Looking into the barrels it is obvious this Hammer Classic has very short forcing cones. Longer cones could dampen recoil slightly and probably treat pellets on the outside of the shotstring more gently, thus providing fewer pellet flyers and more even patterns down range. The barrels measure .732. So these barrels are overbored, and that should help with recoil dampening as well as help reduce the number of pellet flyers.

The other modern innovation with the Hammer Classic is that the gun comes with screw-in chokes – Full, Improved Modified, Modified, Improved Cylinder and Cylinder. I measure these screw-ins at Full .686 for .046 of constriction, Improved Modified at .692 for .040 constriction, the Modified at .707 for .025 constriction, the Improved Cylinder at .713 for .019 constriction and the Cylinder at .725 for .007 constriction. So these screw- ins provide some quite tight

choke constrictions. The .007 constricted Cylinder bore smoked targets hard at 25 yards. Understandably, the Improved Cylinder screw in with .019 constriction smoked those 25-yarders even harder.

On the Website (www.cz-usa.com), the information says this gun weighs 7.3 pounds, but the one I was consigned for testing went 7 pounds 13 ounces on my digital postal scale. The forend hefted 9.3 ounces; the 30-inch barrels with two screw-in chokes in place went 3 pounds 1.5 ounces. The Website says the length of pull is 14.5-inches. I measured this distance at 14.75 from the front trigger. So now you finally know this is a twin trigger side-by-side. When initially received the triggers were very heavy. I sent the gun back to CZ in Kansas City for trigger revamping. The company now claims triggers will come through more like the one mine has been adjusted to which was under five pounds for the front trigger, just over five pounds for the rear trigger (left barrel).

The receiver and trigger guard are case color hardened, which was typical of the old English hammer guns. There's a bit of engraving, and it's hand done. "Hammer Classic" is on the bottom of the receiver. The hammers are nicely contoured, and there's an audible click when you move them back into the "fire" position. The safety is the non-automatic type, so after firing in the field make certain you engage that safety.

I can't find any polishing marks on the barrels which are hard black chromed. Inside the barrels there's chrome plating for added corrosion resistance. The forend is fairly small, almost a true splinter type. There's hand checkering on the forend and the pistol grip. The walnut on my test gun does not have a lot of figure, which bodes well for strength, and the cost of this one is only $915 at full retail, so there's no reason to expect spectacular wood. The wood-to-metal fit is nice and tight, particularly at the top and bottom tang areas and the sideplates. The steel butt plate is not serrated. The rib between the barrels is raised slightly, plus that rib is lightly serrated for glare control and there's a metal bead at the muzzle. The forend comes on and off easily, and once installed it is tight with no wiggle.

Lock up is typical for many side-by-side models the barrels pivoting on a hinge pin. Two bolts protrude forward from the bottom of the receiver upon closing to engage two lugs milled into the bottom of the monobloc. Further, a lug built into the base of the monobloc snugs into a matching recess in the base of the receiver.

Interestingly, Rick Staples won the 2010 Vintage World Championship with the CZ-USA Hammer Classic, so you can bet Rick did not object to this gun's recoil. In addition to being a fun gun for clay birds and waterfowl the Hammer Classic should also feel very at home on pheasant forays. This one might not be a classic English Purdey hammer gun, but it doesn't wear a $20,000 price tag either.

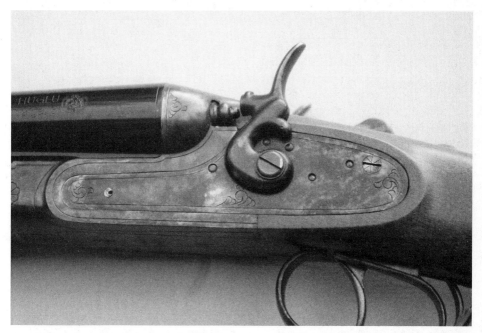

The CZ-USA Hammer Classic has a color case hardened frame. Note the nicely contoured hammers.

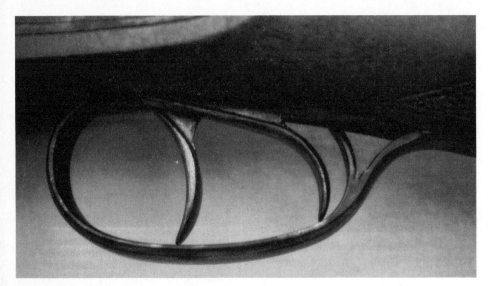

The Hammer Gun wears traditional twin triggers.

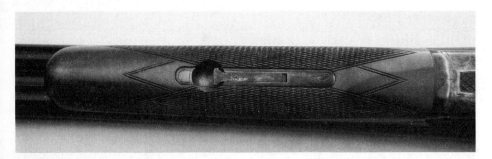

The forend is small, almost splinter-like and is hand checkered.

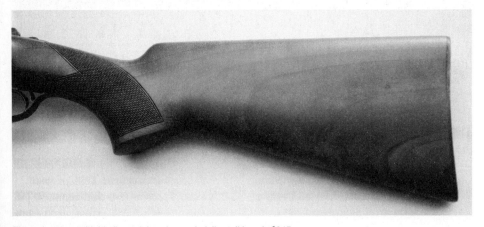

The walnut is not highly figured, but the gun's full retail is only $915.

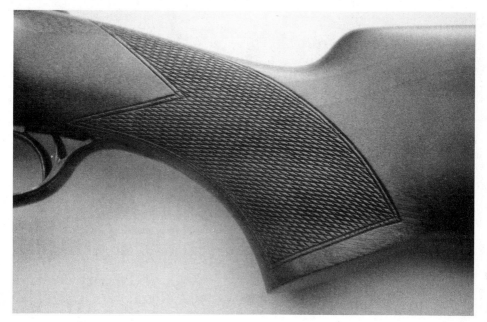

The grip is hand checkered.

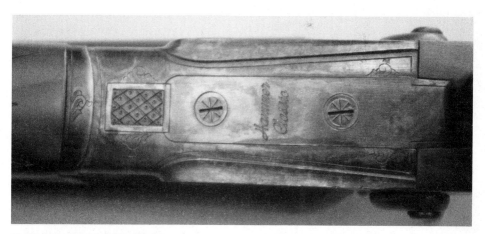

The Hammer Classic receiver bottom.

The Hammer Classic wears a steel butt plate with the color case-hardened finish.

The Hammer Classic comes with five screw-in chokes.

BENELLI 12-GAUGE VINCI SUPERSPORT

There are few readers who are not familiar with Benelli's Vinci semi-auto. That's because the Vinci was introduced with magnum-style fanfare. The gun's announcement was made at the January 2009 SHOT Show, but only via proclamation that a very special new gun was coming. No photos, no literature, and definitely no gun were seen at that SHOT Show. But there was a late March date promise when the world would get their first look at this gun. The first look for most everyone was via the Internet and the www. benelliusa.com Website. Thus for better than two months that Website kept telling shotgunners about the totally new concept in semi-autos Benelli would introduce. They really hyped it up.

The first non-Benelli folks to see the new gun were a group of gun writers Benelli had gathered at Pica Zuro Lodge near Cordoba Argentina. I was lucky enough to be in that group. After an afternoon arrival, cocktails and dinner the writers sat down to a great Power Point slide presentation about the new gun. Immediately thereafter Benelli folks opened box after box of these new Vinci shotguns we would shoot over and over for the next three days. Even Internet viewers didn't see their first Vinci until several days later – and that was via photo on the Website. At the end of that dove-shooting bonanza we were told 30,000 shotshells had been fired at Cordoba's endless supply of doves. The Vinci guns performed flawlessly.

One new aspect the Vinci brought to the shotgun table is its three-unit design. One unit is the stock, which Benelli now calls the ComforTech® Plus. In large part that stock was born a few years earlier on another Benelli semi. The stock features 11 compressible chevrons plus a 12th longer, larger chevron. These help take out recoil sting. Benelli autoloaders are not gas operated.

There's a recoil pad that's also high tech in its recoil-absorbing qualities. Further, there's a soft gel-like comb pad that relieves the shooter's face from recoil punishment. All these features bode well for clay target work.

A second unit is the barrel that has an extension that's actually the receiver part of the Vinci, including the bolt. The barrel goes through Benelli's deep freeze treatment that they call Crio. Surface metal stress relief is claimed for this procedure. The new Vinci SuperSport barrel has a stepped vent rib. Of course, screw-in chokes are supplied, and they, too, receive the company's Crio deep-freeze treatment. The bolt is rotary in performance, lugs at the front of the bolt turning into recesses milled in to the barrel extension. The bolt has a spring that's very important to the Vinci's very reliable function. Benelli calls their operating system Inertia Driven. This inertia spring behind the bolt is everything when it comes to ejecting the just-fired shell and loading a new shell from the carrier into the chamber. Shotguns with gas-operating systems have a number of other parts that control function. The inertia system is a very simple one and no doubt a major reason why Benelli shotguns have such a good reputation for being reliable no matter what shells their guns are fed.

The third Vinci unit is the forend, magazine and trigger group. The trigger group can easily be knocked out for thorough cleaning. Before moving on to more about this third unit, realize now that the three units simply snap together. Line up specific marks on the barrel/receiver with a mark at the front of the butt stock, push together and twist. Those two units click into place. Line up specific marks near the bolt and the forend and simply rotate the forend portion until you hear the click. The three units are now together. Not one tool and no screw threads have been used. The forend has no cap screw to keep tight. That forend stays

solidly attached until you want to remove it by simply depressing the button on the bottom of the forend and then twisting the forend.

Benelli has replaced standard checkering with a corrugated look to the grip and forend of the SuperSport. There's an appreciable re-curve to the pistol grip, a feature many sporting clays enthusiasts prefer. There's a non-slip finish to these areas as well. The carbon fiber finish to the black synthetic stock and forend makes the stock distinctive.

They call this new stock the QuadraFit because it's adjustable in so many ways. A set of shims that are placed between the front of the stock and the rear of the receiver offer easy change of drop at comb and cast. But that's not all. Three different AirCell recoil pads are available for the SuperSport, all of differing length to help you attain your perfect length of pull. Again the pads are easy to change – just pop one pad off and then shove another into place. The pad stays in place despite the ease of changing. Further this Vinci can be had with three different gel comb pads, each of differing height, which allows you even more options for changing drop at comb height. To reduce muzzle jump the barrel of this sporting clays specialist is ported.

New is their In-Line Inertia-Driven operating system with the new SpeedBolt. That bolt has a tungsten inset for added strength, plus the system is designed for both faster cycling and for handling light loads – Benelli says is a light as ⅞ ounce.

My 12-gauge test gun with 30-inch barrel balances right at the rear of the chamber. A 28-inch barrel is also available. The safety switch is positioned in front of the trigger guard. There's a tapered "step" rib on the barrel – with steel mid-bead and a red-glow front bead. The rib measures .385 just in front of the "step," and .320 out at the muzzle. The trigger had a bit of creep, but not objectionable and went off at just under 5 pounds. The recoil pad is well rounded with a significant taper at the top mitigating against the possibility of hang ups on clothing during the mount. Additionally, horizontal striations on the back of the pad help keep the gun in place for the next shot. A toggle on the right side of the receiver closes the bolt. To have the bolt stay back when opening there's a toggle to press on the bottom of the receiver just in front of the trigger guard. On my digital postal scale my test gun went 7 pounds 6 ounces. Catalog hype claims 7 pounds even. I found with the 30-inch barrel and the light weight – the Vinci SuperSport was a quick swinger.

Five extended screw-in chokes (again Crio) are included that measure 3.5-inches. The bore was .723, so this one is not overbored. The Cylinder choke went .725, the Improved Cylinder at .710, Modified at

.700, Improved Modified at .692 and the Full measured .682. That's .051 of constriction – a lot. I shot a variety of both steel and lead loads out of the gun with not one malfunction. The steel loads were factory fodder, the lead loads my 1 ounce 1150 feet per second reloads shot out of the Federal paper case.

SPECIFICATIONS

Action: Semi-auto using the In-Line Inertia-Driven System

Gauge: 12 gauge

Weight: 7 pounds 6 ounces

Barrel: 30 and 28 inch.

Chokes: Five supplied: Cylinder, Improved Cylinder, Modified, Improved Modified and Full

Stock: Adjustable

Suggested Retail: $2,119

Manufacturer/Importer: Made by Benelli in Italy. Imported by Benelli USA. www.benelliusa.com.

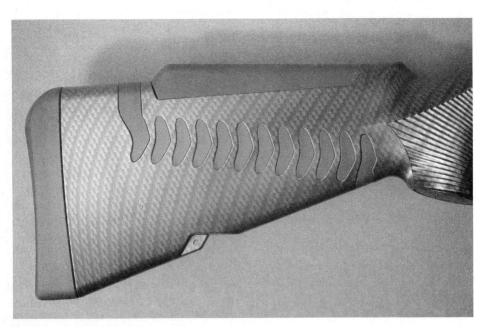

The SuperSport butt stock with the recoil absorbing chevrons, gel cheek pad and carbon fiber finish.

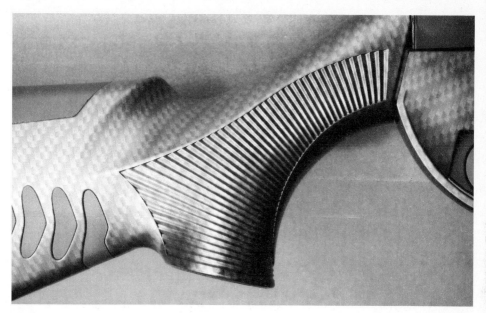

Note the corrugated look to the Vinci SuperSport grip area. Similar corrugations are molded in to the forend area. Also note the significant re-curve to the grip.

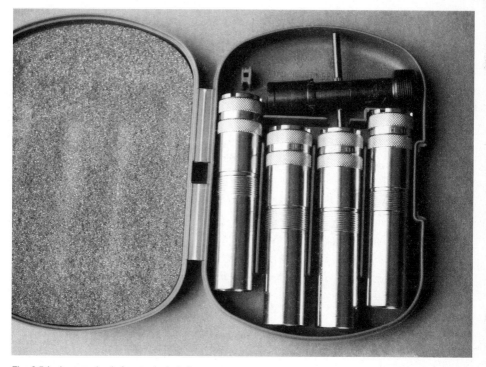

Five 3.5-inch screw-in chokes are included.

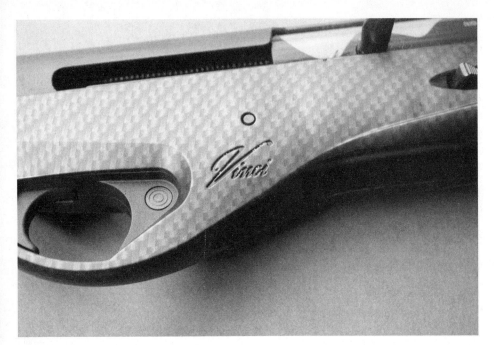

View of the safety position.

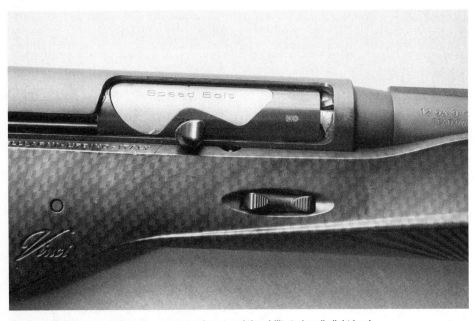

The SpeedBolt is new and features a tungsten insert and the ability to handle light loads.

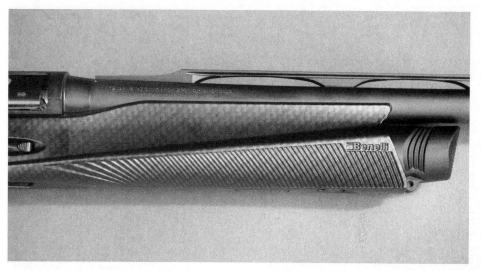

The rakish look to the forend.

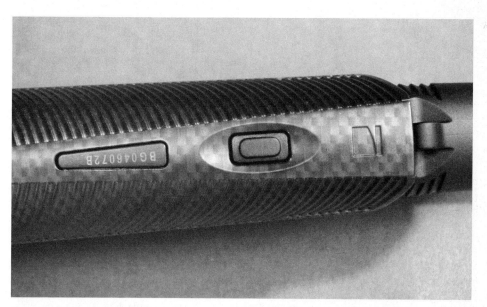

To remove the forend, magazine and trigger group just press this button and twist the forend.

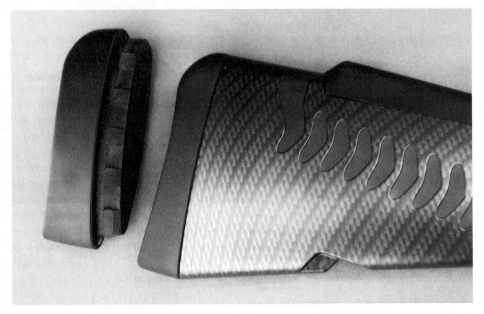

Benelli includes recoil pads of differing length in this package.

There's a sling attachment at the base of the stock.

The forend is not a screw cap. It locks into place when you twist the entire forend a quarter turn. Also note the sling attachment spot.

BENELLI ETHOS

Ethos. Where does that name come from for a shotgun? Ethos is sort of the opposite of pathos – the latter meaning to arouse feelings of pity, sorrow, sympathy, compassion. In contrast ethos means the universal or objective elements of a work of art. Both words are of Greek origin. One look at the Benelli Ethos conjures up a feeling that you are viewing a work of art. Compared to previous and other current Benelli autoloaders the Ethos has the best looks yet, hands down. The contour of the receiver is different – in my view a look of sleek elegance – a tough feat to pull off in a semi-auto.

Further, while many of Benelli's most popular and best selling semis come with composite stocks in black or camo, the Ethos reverts to walnut which traditionalists will find appealing. The stock lines provide more eye candy, plus the lines of the forend are new, different and also appealing. Further yet, the engraving on the highly polished aluminum receiver is yet another new twist for Benelli. That engraving is very intricate with a zillion tiny floral-like curlicues on the nickel-plated receiver. There is also a black anodized Ethos receiver available.

My test gun, at only 6 pounds 8.5 ounces, is not going to take over with Master Class shooters. They will obviously stick with their Krieghoffs, Kolars, Zolis, Guerinis, Perazzis, Berettas et al. While I look at the Ethos as mainly a hunting gun it could also make a good clay target gun for those of smaller stature who might get too fatigued swinging an 8 pound plus over/under for 100 or more targets. From Master Class on down, however, the Ethos is going to be ideal on our nation's Great Plains for pheasants, sharptails, Hungarian partridge and the like. Even in grouse and woodcock thickets this Benelli is light enough for hour after hour carrying in a "ready" position.

Internally the Ethos is the same as the other Benelli autoloaders. The system, dubbed "Inertia Driven," is noted for its reliability of function. This system is neither gas nor recoil driven (recoil driven referring to the barrel coming back into the receiver to eject the just-fired shell and slam a new one in the chamber). The Inertia Driven system does not work that way. Instead, upon firing the bolt moves rearward against a strong spring behind the bolt. When the bolt reaches its maximum rearward travel the bolt slams forward, chambering the next round. Not only is Inertia Driven reliable in function, it's also very fast.

My test gun came with a 26-inch barrel but a 28-incher is available. To save further weight, the rib on top of the barrel is of carbon fiber which is feather light. Reportedly, differing configured ribs are available so they are interchangeable. On the rib top is a steel mid-bead with a glow sight at the muzzle. The forend contour slants a bit upward from the receiver side and slants downward toward the forend cap screw. That cap

threads into the front of the forend, which is a bit of a different twist compared to most forend caps. Also the forend cap screws into detents that ensure that cap won't loosen with firing. Overall the total forend look is also sleek and elegant.

The butt stock is topped with a black insert made of a proprietary synthetic visio-elastic urethane polymer. That insert does not feel "soft," but there must be high technology in its composition as I found recoil did not beat up my face. Maybe the slickness of this material allows the face to slide easily as the gun comes back with recoil.

The Inertia Driven system does not suck up recoil like a gas-operated semi-auto. Benelli's ComforTech® recoil reduction system on the Super Black Eagle, Vinci and other Benelli models works only with their specially designed composite stocks. The company had to come up with a new recoil reduction system for the walnut-stocked Ethos. Dubbed Progressive Comfort, it is made up of many leaves that individually compress upon firing to help dampen recoil sting. Since these individual leaves compress, it stands to reason that the compression allows the stock to move rearward – at least a bit, and perhaps that's the reason for the slick black insert on the butt stock's comb.

I like the recoil pad itself. It's rounded all around and very well rounded at the top – all of which mitigates gun hang ups during the mount. The back of the pad is checkered to help keep the stock in place once the mount is completed. The pad is set off from the stock via a black spacer. While the gun is supplied with a 14.375 length of pull. Benelli supplies a set of spacers that allow the shooter to increase the length of pull to 15-inches or reduce the length of pull to 13.75 inches. In that same insert package shooters will also find spacers that permit changing the amount of drop and cast.

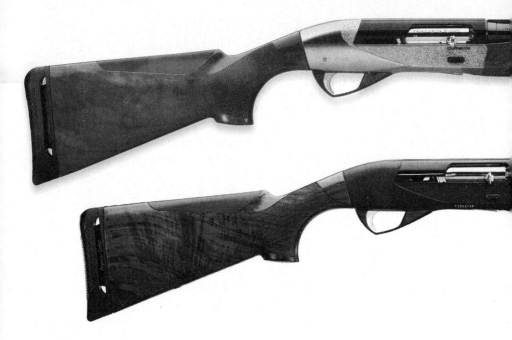

The checkering on the forend and the pistol grip is well done it's tough to find a flaw even under a 2X loupe. The barrel and top of the receiver are a deep black. Double check the receiver close up again. Note how the rear portion of that receiver is all polished aluminum with no engraving. This is true on both receiver sides. I genuinely like the look of the engraving, and I think engraving always stands out better on a "bright" receiver compared to a blued or case colored receiver.

The trigger group removes by knocking out only one retaining pin. Both the bolt and opening lever are bright chromed, and the opening lever has been increased in size. The bolt lugs rotate into recesses built into the rear of the barrel ensuring a very tight lock up. Further, new technology ensures this rotating bolt lock up no matter how easily the bolt is closed. The closing button on the right side of the receiver is black and plenty big enough. The safety is behind the trigger guard, the trigger is gold plated. There's a bit of creep though not objectionable to me. Trigger let off is at about 5 pounds.

The 26-inch, 3-inch-chambered barrel measured .725 internally with my Baker Barrel Reader. Five screw-in chokes were included – each with "notches." The 5 notch choke went .528 – so .003 bigger than the bore. The 4 notch went .718, the 3 notch .705, the 2 notch .697 and the 1 notch .685. The forend went 6.1 ounces (very light as forends go) and is a bit over 12-inches in length. The 26-inch barrel weighed 1 pound 15 ounces – as previously stated the gun went 6 pounds 8.5 ounces. The barrels and the chokes receive Benelli's "Crio" treatment that reportedly relieves metal stress.

The Ethos is said to function with $\frac{7}{8}$-ounce loads, but my guess is those loads need to be zipping out to at least 1,200 feet per second. My 1 ounce reloads at 1,140 feet per second functioned with Remington STS hulls, but not with 1 ounce Federal paper hulls at 1,115 feet per second.

While Ethos might be an unusual name for a shotgun, Benelli has come up with a good moniker for this smoothbore. It does reek of an art form in the shotgun realm.

Engraved nickel-plated Ethos.

Black anodized Ethos receiver.

SPECIFICATIONS

Gauge: 12 gauge

Action: Benelli's proprietary Inertia Driven® semi-auto system.

Barrel: 26 or 28 inches

Chokes: Five flush mounted screw-ins supplied

Chambers: 3 inch

Stock Dimensions: 14.375, (but adjustable from 13¾ to 15-inches) x 1.5 x 2.25

Weight: 6 pounds 8.5 ounces with 26-inch barrel

Suggested Retail: $2,000 for the black anodized receiver model; $2,200 for the nickel-plated receiver model

Maker: Made by Benelli in Italy. Imported by Benelli USA in Accokeek, Maryland. www.benelliusa.com.

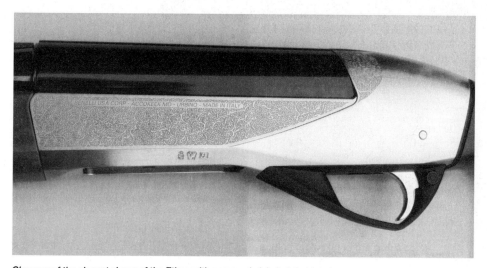

Close up of the elegant shape of the Ethos with engraved nickel-plated receiver.

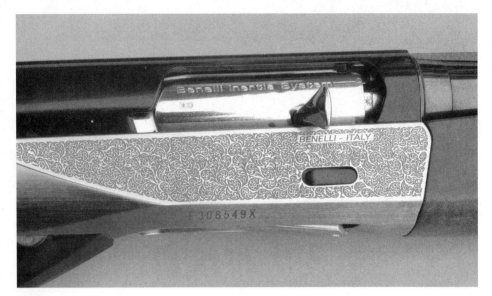

Right side of the Ethos nickel-plated well engraved receiver also showing the chrome-plated bolt and slightly enlarged opening lever.

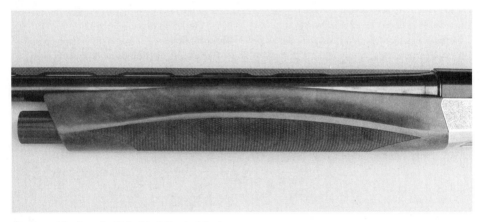

Close up of the forend with its futuristic, sleek look.

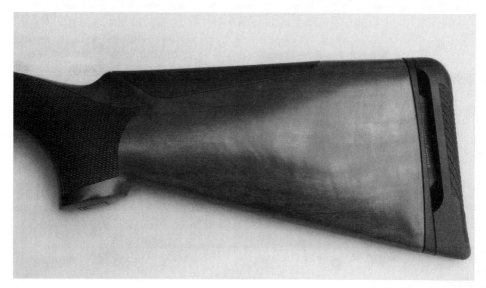

The walnut on the Ethos means upgraded AA quality wood.

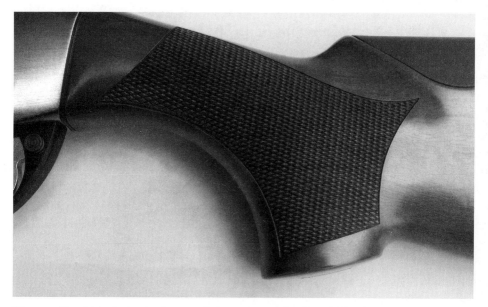

Close up of the pistol grip showing the amount of re-curve as well as the excellent checkering.

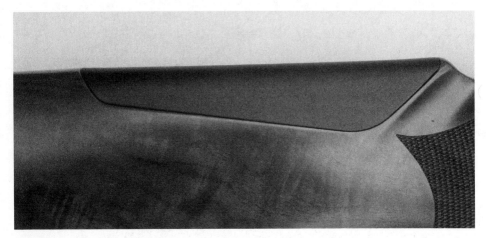

Note the insert at the comb of the butt stock. Made of a proprietary synthetic visioelastic urethane polymer, there's a slippery feel that treats one's face tenderly upon recoil.

The Progressive Comfort recoil reducer is built into the butt stock. Note the many tiny leaves that individually compress upon recoil, taking the sting out.

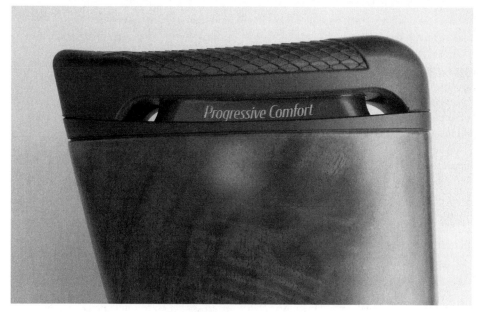

The recoil pad is rounded all around and especially at the top

CONNECTICUT SHOTGUN 20-GAUGE INVERNESS

I knew it was going to be a good day when I opened a certain package from Connecticut Shotgun. WOW – was my first look/reaction. I blinked my eyes in surprise at the beauty. I expected a good looking over/under, but this one went far beyond what I had anticipated. The new model is the Inverness in 20 gauge from Connecticut Shotgun. It is a hunting gun, but I promise you it will break plenty of clay targets.

Here's how to get a $9,000 over/under shotgun that Tony Galazan at Connecticut Shotgun makes right here in the good old USA for $3,000. The first 500 20-gauge guns are priced at $5,000. However, if you are a previous Connecticut Shotgun customer you could take $1,000 off the $5,000 price. Further, if you paid up front, take another $1,000 off, thus the $3,000 price of the gun I had just opened. Galazan said the guns will be priced at $9,000 after the first 500

are completed. And after looking, fondling and shooting mine $9,000 still looks like a good price.

No doubt Galazan used the $5,000 entry level price and the up-front payment as a way to get the ball rolling with the new over/under Inverness. That monetary initiative allowed investment in final design, tooling and all the other costs involved in bringing a new shotgun to the market. He used a similar game plan to introduce and bring to production his 20-gauge round-body side-by-side – the RBL (for Round Body Launch) – now offered in all gauges.

I had waited almost a full year after putting that $3,000 dent in my Discover plastic, but now I see it was worth it. How so you ask? I have the Inverness sitting on my lap so I can better tell you all about it as I type away at my computer keyboard. The first eye candy upon package opening was the wood. I don't know if you're going to get a piece of walnut this startling if you order an Inverness, but my stock and forend are figuratively to die for.

The second quick eye candy aspect centers on the over/under's receiver. I have never been much of a fan of case-colored receivers, mainly because they are done with a chemical process that is a poor excuse for old fashioned charcoal bone case hardening. The latter is a very expensive process these days and being done by fewer and fewer gun shops. Connecticut Shotgun uses bone charcoal case hardening, and their final product comes out looking just great. There are blues, oranges and other color variations all over my Inverness receiver.

The second receiver aspect that pops out is the engraving. I don't know how you feel about engraving, but I've never looked at gold inlays with special favor. Obviously well-done gold inlays by hand do make a shotgun more valuable. I have one Krieghoff model 32 engraved by Brian Rishel, who worked for Briley at the time with three types of engraving, rose and scroll, bolino and Germanic deep relief. It is a great piece of art.

I'm becoming more of a fan for tight rose and scroll and a lot of it, not too deeply engraved with the engraving tool, but full coverage. I had become a fan of this engraving style before the Inverness arrived, plus I had seen photos of the Inverness engraving when I ordered the gun.

That's how the engraving is done on the Inverness, very tight rose and bouquet, lightly done by the engraver's touch, but full coverage – both receiver sides, the bottom, the forend iron that rides against the front of the receiver, the trigger guard, the metal grip cap, the top tang and the opening lever. As with how the case hardening is done, that's proprietary. But this engraving is not rolled or etched, yet it is magnificently done. But there's more eye candy, and this relates to the round body receiver. More and

more double gun makers are offering round actions. In some cases companies achieve round actions simply by machining roundness to the bottom of the receiver. This looks good, but that process doesn't make it a true round body action. To accomplish that design changes have to be made internally and that means more money.

The 20-gauge Inverness is built around a true round action, and that style adds significantly to the rose and bouquet engraving. Why? Because that intricate and tight engraving has no stop to it that engraving just keeps going. There are no engraving breaks at the bottom of each receiver side as with a standard receiver having squared off lines at the side/bottom edge. Unfortunately it is difficult to get a photo that really captures the Inverness action of round body, case hardening and engraving. I've tried but I'm not satisfied the digital captures the real thing.

And yet there's more. The checkering is not only well done, there's plenty of it – classic two-point on both sides of the grip and all around the forend. Again, don't know how Connecticut does the checkering, but they are doing it superbly and at 24 lines-to- the inch. The forend release is a push button in front, and the forend comes off and on easily. Once in place there is no wiggle. In front of the forend, there's a side panel between the barrels, and there are unique-to-me barrel side ribs that match up with the forend.

These are special order guns as already covered. Standard stock dimensions are 14.375 x 1.375 x 2.5. If those stock dimensions don't fit you, I'm sure Connecticut can fix you up at additional cost. As previously stated this is a hunting gun, though I'm betting most of them are going to be used from time to time on all manner of clay target fields. That said, barrel length choices are 28 and 30 inches. Mine are 28. Barrels are Tuff-Bore coated, plus Crio treated making them super hard and suitable for steel shot.

Five Trulock screw-in chokes are included, also suitable for steel. The rib is file cut and tapered from .330 at the breech to .240 at the muzzle.

It's the same price for a straight grip or semi-pistol with engraved grip cap. The Galazan recoil pad is separated from the stock via the traditional black spacer. The trigger is black, blued or black chromed – I don't know. The barrel selector is a part of the automatic top tang safety. Triggers are excellent and go off at 3¾ pounds – plenty light enough for a hunting gun.

Back to the receiver, or rather the top and bottom tangs. Note how the top tang is classically sculptured. Obviously one can't pull the stock off by pulling straight back. The bottom tang on my gun extends all the way back to the metal grip cap. The rather open grip is traditional for a hunting gun. Auto ejectors are a part of the Inverness package,

and mine have worked flawlessly. Additional upgrade options include a leather-covered pad and several wood upgrades.

As you can tell by now I'm extremely high on my new Inverness, so much so that I've already ordered their A-10 American Rose & Scroll Special Edition model. That one will be another 20-gauge and built on a 20-gauge frame.

SPECIFICATIONS

Gauge: 20 gauge
Action: Over/under
Weight: 6 pounds 8 ounces
Barrels: 28 inches. 30-inches available.
Chokes: Five flush-mounted Trulock Chokes
Stock: 14.75 x 1.375 x 2.5
Suggested Retail Price: $9,000, but $3000 if you pay up front and are an existing Connecticut Shotgun customer.
Manufacturer: Connecticut Shotgun. www. connecticutshotgun.com

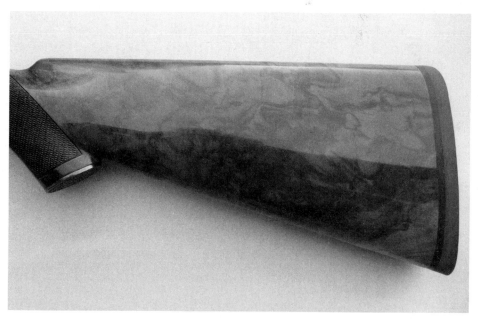

The Connecticut Inverness package displays a spectacular piece of walnut. (From Conn. Shotgun)

This bone charcoal case-colored receiver exhibits blues, oranges and other colors. And don't forget the rose and bouquet engraving in full coverage and around the round-body receiver.

The bottom of the round body receiver and engraving.

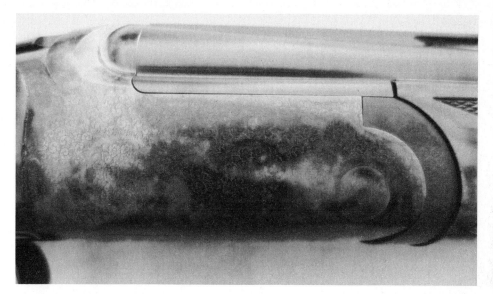

The right side of the Inverness receiver.

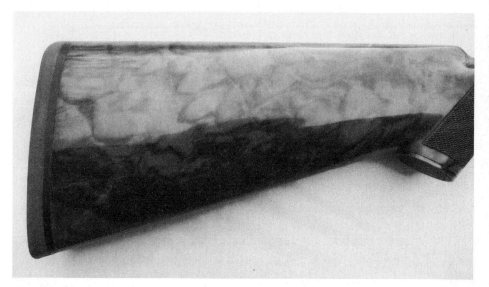

The right side of the butt stock.

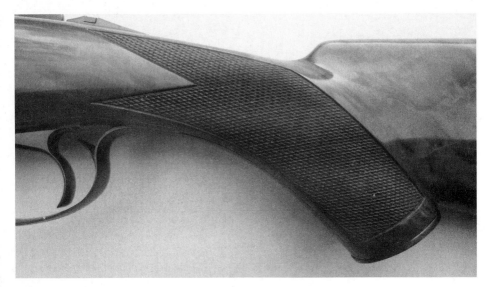

The checkering on the hunting gun pistol grip is exceptionally well done.

The shape of the Inverness forend with exceptional checkering and full wrap around.

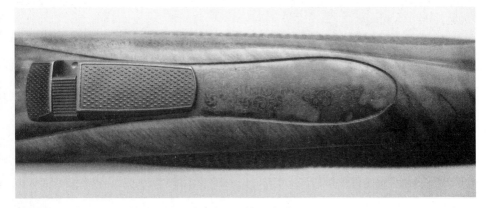

The sculptured look of the top tang. Note the safety and barrel selector.

Full side panels are between the barrels.

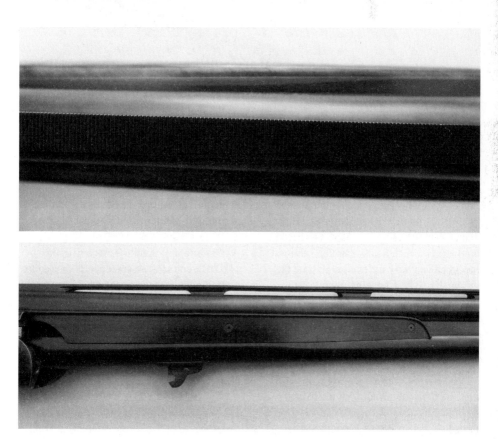

The side panel on the barrels matches up nicely with the forend.

Five Trulock screw-in chokes made of stainless steel, flush mounted for traditional good looks and suitable for steel shot are included.

BERETTA 20-GAUGE A400 XPLOR

Beretta hit a home run with the 12-gauge A400 Xplor. That 12 is ideal as a competition or a hunting gun, depending upon model, but the new 20 gauge is a different animal. The 12 gauge was/is somewhat light, but I remember that gas-operated semi-auto model having very little recoil despite the minimal weight. Checking my previous notes that gun weighed 7 pounds 13 ounces on my digital postal scale. It was the Sporter version of the A400. There was a Light version in 12 gauge, so it was probably lighter, but I have not tested that one.

The Beretta Website claims 5 pounds for this new 20-gauge A400, but my test 20 goes 6 pounds 1 ounce. However, that Website projected weight is without the Kick-Off system installed in the stock, and my test 20-bore A400 does have that Kick-Off installed. Actually, I think it was the Kick-Off installed in my original 12 gauge test gun that turned the gun's recoil into just about

nothing. As I recall, I was shooting 12-gauge Federal paper reloads delivering 1 ounce at about 1,140 feet per second. This 20 gauge is lighter yet, but the recoil sting is still next to nothing shooting ⅞-ounce loads at about 1,180 feet per second. With my 12-gauge A400 write up, I think I said something like, "Beretta really has reduction in recoil figured out." And the company accomplishes very light recoil in very light shotguns, all the added bonus.

Of course, clay target shooters usually appreciate some extra gun weight, mainly because more heft means less recoil,– but also because a somewhat heavier gun can be instrumental in keeping the gun moving with a flying target. But these days Beretta has taken the recoil sting out – somewhat arguably – without any extra weight. I know that defies one of Newton's Laws, but I know he would even agree that what Beretta has done – it's that significant.

There are many ways to help reduce felt

recoil, and no doubt gas-operation of a semi-auto is one of the most significant ones. Remington led the way on this issue 50 years ago with their model 1100 built on a steel receiver. Beretta reduces recoil to maybe an even greater degree with an aluminum alloy receiver. How do they do that?

The Kick-Off has already been mentioned. You can tell when a Beretta has the Kick-Off installed by seeing the oversized (long), recoil pad. The pad also says "Kick-Off" marked on the side. I planned to take the recoil pad off to view the Kick-Off, take it out and report my findings, but the back of the Kick-Off says, "Do not remove!"

So I contacted Beretta's public relations person asking for a detailed description and a Kick-Off photo – here's what she said. "The Kick-Off is the only reduction system in the world that uses hydraulic dampeners – very similar to those used in automobile suspensions."

But the Kick-Off and the gas operation aren't the only special features of the A400 series. There's the unique compensating exhaust valve with its self-cleaning piston – the latter also no doubt a factor in the A400's functional reliability as it keeps the magazine tube free of dirt and crud. The A400 just keeps working ejecting just-fired shells and inserting the next shell into the chamber over and over and over. Most semi-autos have a breaking point in this procedure as most often the gun quits working because of excess dirt and crud on the mag tube.

Perhaps even more important regarding the gas valve is its involvement of the "Blink" system, which Beretta claims speeds up cycling significantly. Still another factor in recoil reduction is the recoil pad made of high tech Micro Core. It is very long and made of a high tech material. Finally, don't forget the overboring in the barrel, yet another recoil reducer. Dubbed Optima Bore HP – that high tech barrel geometry results

in delivering great patterns in addition to the reduction in recoil.

There's lots of eye candy on this little 20-gauge A400, in addition to the technical stuff that mitigates recoil. The receiver has a gray/brown look. Beretta calls it "Bronze Toned." My guess is that the brown tone has some corrosion inhibiting qualities, although corrosion resistance isn't nearly the problem on an aluminum alloy receiver compared to a blued steel receiver. The bolt is black and lugs built into the front of the bolt lock into recesses milled into the barrel extension resulting in added strength to the lock up.

This one has 3-inch chambers. It seems 2 ¾-inch chambers are a thing of the past on today's shotguns. But 3-inch 20-gauge shells are not for me, though if you want to take this one turkey hunting or waterfowling the bigger shell might be in order. In either of those hunting situations, I have other shotguns that will probably be more appropriate, and you probably do, too.

There's a magazine cut-off button on the left side of the receiver – a good idea when you just want to remove a shell from the chamber and not have a shell from the magazine pop on to the carrier. On the left side of the receiver there is also "A400 Xplor-20 ga" and below that "Action" below that "Made in Italy." On the right side of the receiver is the Beretta three-arrow logo and "Xplor Action." That receiver side also has the button for releasing the bolt closure. At the base of the receiver , just in front of the trigger guard is the small button to allow the bolt to stay back upon opening, and to allow a shell from the magazine tube to pop out on to the carrier. The safety is triangular in shape and positioned toward the front of the trigger guard. The trigger is chrome-plated. Trigger let off, according to my digital Lyman Trigger Scale is at 5 pounds with some creep, though not objectionable.

More eye candy. That's the stock and

forend. Beretta calls this "Xtra-Grain Technology with an Oil Finish." Check the accompanying photo of the butt stock and forend for the very nice figure this wood-enhancing technology produces. Unusual checkering patterns cover both the pistol grip and forend. Laser cut so it's very hard to find any imperfections, and with stylized lines that improve appearance. The result is a somewhat racy look. The bottom of the forend also has the Beretta Three-Arrow logo lasered in.

That forend hefts 4.1 ounces – very light despite is foot-long length. The 28-inch barrel weighed an even 2 pounds – pretty light as 20-gauge 28-inch barrels go. The vent rib measures .240 at the rear and .235 near the muzzle, so, essentially, no taper. The bore measured .626-inches –a little overbored as traditional 20-gauge barrels have gone .615-inches for many years. Three screw-in chokes are included; Cylinder at .626 (same as the bore), Modified at .611- a .015 constriction, and Full at .602 for .022 constriction. Stamped on the Full screw-in is "No Steel." These are flush-mounted chrome plated chokes that measure 2 ½-inches with some taper and parallel sections included.

As with most all Berettas the A400 comes with a set of stock spacers to fit between the front of the stock and rear of the receiver that allows the user to set up the gun with more or less drop and more or

less cast. Stock length of pull was 14 ¼ to the middle rear of the recoil pad. At the bottom of the pistol grip note the black plastic portion. This is where Beretta's Gun Pod can be added that can count the number of shells fired, plus the temperature is read. The Gun Pod is an extra on most Beretta A400 semi-autos.

The forend retains the familiar gas exhaust at the front bottom. The front forearm retaining screw has a swivel stud for sling attachment and there's a sling swivel stud at the base of the butt stock. Sling swivels are also provided and the A400 20 gauge comes in an impact resistant plastic case. All in all handling and shooting the new A400 Xplor 20 gauge has been a very positive experience. There was nothing to hunt while I had this Beretta on consignment, but I did put this A400 through its paces on clay targets. Shot the gun hundreds of times with nary a malfunction.

SPECIFICATIONS

Action: Gas-operated Semi-Auto
Gauge: 20 gauge
Weight: 6 pounds 1 ounce with Kick-Off
Barrel: 28-inch vent rib
Chokes: Three screw-ins provided
Stock: 14.5-inch length of pull
Suggested Retail: $1,525
Manufacturer/Importer: Made in Italy by Beretta. Imported by Beretta USA, Accokeek, Md. www.berettausa.com.

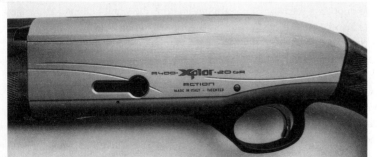

The left side of the 20-gauge A400 receiver.

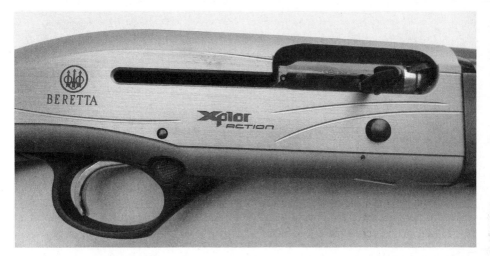

The right side of the A400 20-gauge receiver with the bronze tone coloring, which the author believes will also be corrosion resistant.

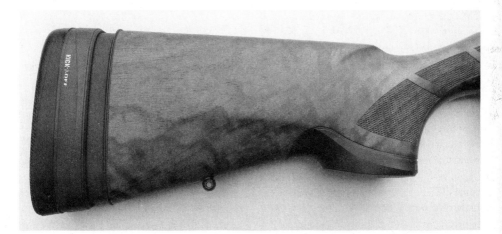

The walnut features a hand-rubbed oil finish as well as walnut enhancing Xtra-Grain.

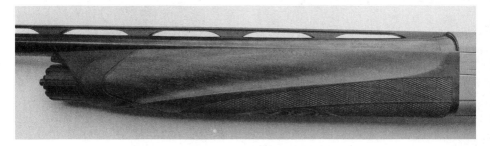

The 20-gauge Xplor forend is very light despite its one-foot length.

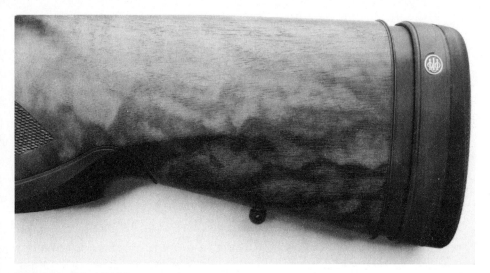

The left side of the A400 20-gauge stock.

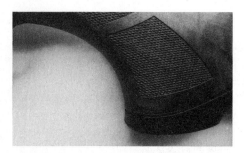

Close up of the pistol grip shows excellent checkering. Note the amount of re-curve.

This A400 20 gauge is fit with Kick-Off pad as shown, which is much, much longer compared to a typical recoil pad.

Swivel studs are at the base of the butt stock and a part of the forend tightening nut. Swivels are included in the package.

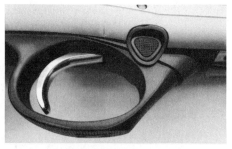

The trigger is chrome-plated.

Note the checkering pattern on the forend, as well as the checkered-in Beretta three-arrow logo.

BERETTA MODEL 692 OVER/UNDER

Beretta's staple competition gun since 1982 has been the venerable model 682. While the 692 retains many of the 682's features, what's mostly new about the 692 has been stolen from Beretta's DT11, that one with the crossbolt closure. The 692 retains the 682 lock up system with the barrels pivoting on trunnions, two bolts protruding from the upper back part of the receiver to engage milled-out areas on both sides of the upper barrel of this over/under. The recoil lugs on the 682 and the 692 are in the shoulders on each side of the receiver which match up with opposing surfaces on each side of the monobloc. This lock up has proven to be a very strong one for many 682s have lasted way beyond 100,000 rounds. While the 692 comes with many of the features of the DT11, the 692 comes at about half the price.

So what are some of the changes of the 692 over the 682? In cosmetic appearance there's not much. There are, however, two major internal differences. One would be the Steelium Plus barrels. The forcing cones are 5.5 times longer than the cones on even the

most recent the 682. Previous forcing cone lengths were 2.6-inches on a 30-inch barrel. Steelium Plus barrel forcing cones run to 14-inches on a 30-inch barrel. When I ran my Baker Barrel Reader into each of these 692 barrels I was surprised to see .750-inches diameter in front of the chamber, and taper didn't start until *way* down the barrels. Even then it was a very slow taper to .730 near the screw choke thread area.

I shot a box of Winchester AA TrAAcker shells the first time I tried the 692. These shells at 1 ⅛ ounce had been hard kickers to my jaw in previous over/unders I'd shot, but there was a big recoil reduction shooting the 692 with those shells, and my test 692 weighs several ounces less than the other O/Us I'd shot with that Winchester factory ammo. The test gun has no Kick-Off recoil reduction system, so I have to attribute recoil reduction to the new technology in these Steelium Plus barrels. Incidentally, the DT11 comes with Steelium Pro barrels, which have even longer forcing cones – 360mm in cone length for the 692 barrels, 480mm for the DT11 barrels.

Are these exceptionally long forcing

cones major issues in recoil reduction? I had two others shoot the 692 the first day I shot it, both commented about the lack of recoil, and both guys were shooting well-known competition over/unders – costing considerably more than the 692. Yes, I think these cones could be a major issue with recoil reduction. If others agree with me on this point will other O/U makers start revamping their forcing cones to something exceptionally long? If recoil reduction actually takes place why wouldn't they?

I've always been of the opinion that lengthening forcing cones by one or two inches has not been a recoil dampener – at least for me. What I have seen with cones lengthened by an inch or two is pattern improvement. Splotchy areas of too few or too many pellet hits seem to go away. I think I usually see less pattern centering as well, as forcing cones are lengthened only a bit, and thus there tend to be more pellets in the outer part of a 30-inch circle, at least I see this with patterns shot from relatively open chokes.

Of course, Beretta claims better patterns with this innovative Steelium Plus inner barrel work, even more than they claim recoil reduction. Most shells that Americans shoot have plastic wads that offer excellent gas-sealing qualities. In Europe, plastic wads are banned in many areas. So will fiber wads be suitable in a gun like the 692 and DT11, or will powder gases leak out around the fiber wads in these bigger bores? I don't know, and I solicit any input from those of you who do shoot shells with fiber wading in guns with super long forcing cones of the DT11 and 692. If there is gas leakage around fiber wads there could be velocity variations. I'm not talking negatively about this Steelium barrel technology because I haven't shot a fiber wad in decades, and I probably won't in the future.

The second big change with the 692, also similar to a change of the DT11 over the discontinued DT10, is the width of the receiver.

It's wider. The widening is only 1.3mm or .05-inches, so there is a minimal weight increase. I'm guessing maybe an ounce. The idea, however, is to put that added weight between the hands, which theoretically makes most any gun handle better. That's what the very slightly wider receiver does. Of course, there has to be added strength as well – which adds durability in a competition gun.

Note 682 barrels cannot be fit to a 692 receiver. For the same reason DT10 barrels cannot be fit to a DT11 receiver, all because of the slightly wider action.

My test gun has 30-inch barrels. I assume 32-inchers are available, but the Website doesn't say so, or maybe I'm just looking in the wrong places. I've already talked about the barrel innards, but the 30-inchers went 3 pounds 3.5 ounces on my digital postal scale. This is about as light as 30-inch competition barrels go in my experience. Chambers are 3 inches. There are vented side panels between the barrels and no panels under the forend. The top vent rib is tapered 10mm to 8mm with steel mid bead and white front bead.

The receiver wears a nice patina satin bright finish. Shape of the receiver sides are much like the 682 and the Perazzi, so classic in looks. The top of the receiver around and behind the fences is well stippled to help prevent glare. There's a slight change in the safety button. When firing the bottom barrel first (selector to the left) two dots show – a white one and a red one. The red dot is on the bottom – indicating the bottom barrel is ready to fire. If you want to fire the top barrel first move the selector to the right. Now the red dot is on the top (indicating the top barrel will fire first).

To go with the Steelium barrels you'll find five Optima-Choke HP screw-ins. Manufactured of high-strength steel they are also nickel-alloy coated. Bottom line, they are hard enough for steel shot use. Plenty long at

3½ inches, these extend beyond the muzzle just over ¾ inch. Interestingly in measuring constriction of these chokes (which have ample taper and parallel sections), the last ⅜-inch or so the chokes opened slightly. I wonder if this is another possible pattern improvement feature. The Cylinder screw-in was .730 (same as the bores near the choke threads), the Skeet went .723, the Improved Cylinder .719, the Modified .708, the Improved Modified .705.

The forend has a Schnabel flare, weighed 10.0 ounces, is just over 9-inches in length and 1.845-inches wide. Checkering is wrap-around and very well done. The pistol grip has a slight right-hand swell (left-hand versions of the 692 are available), and, again, very nice checkering. The trigger can be moved back and forth. Both sides of the receiver have "692" and "Beretta." The bottom of the receiver has "692" as well as the company's three-arrow logo.

The adjustable comb is called the B-Fast System. You're looking at a series of washers that can be added or removed to adjust comb fit. Though the 692 is adjusted for proper balance at the factory, up to four additional ⁷⁄₁₀ths ounce weights can be added to the butt stock.

Maybe Beretta really has something with this Steelium Plus barrel technology. When I did my test report on the DT11, I didn't notice recoil reduction as much as I did with the 692. That's because I was shooting the same shotshells in the DT11 and not a shell that I thought had plenty of recoil for me. But going into the first day of shooting the 692, I could easily recall how those shells bumped my shoulder and cheek when shooting previous O/Us. With those same shells in the 692, I immediately noticed a definite difference. Since then, I've shot plenty of 1-ounce Federal paper factory loads in the 692 which have turned this 12 gauge into a recoil pussy cat.

SPECIFICATIONS

Gauge: 12 Gauge
Action: Over/under
Weight: 8 pounds
Barrels: 30 inches
Chokes: 5 screw in
Stock: 14.5 x adjustable comb
Suggested Retail: $4,755
Maker/Importer: Made by Beretta is Brescia, Italy. Imported by Beretta USA in Accokeek, Md. www.berettausa.com.

The test gun's 692 stock has some nice straight grain.

The adjustable comb stock can be moved up and down with spacers provided. Of course that comb can also be moved right and left.

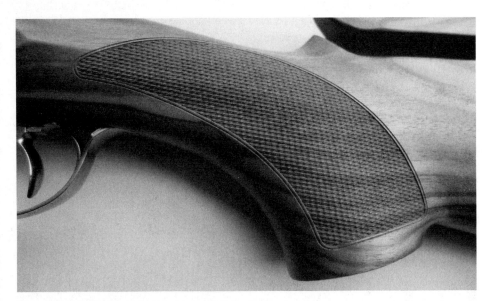

The look of the 692's pistol grip. Note the excellent checkering.

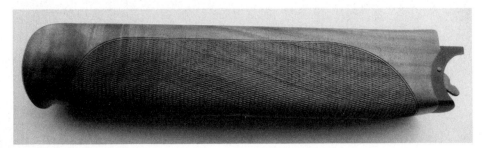

The 692 forend.

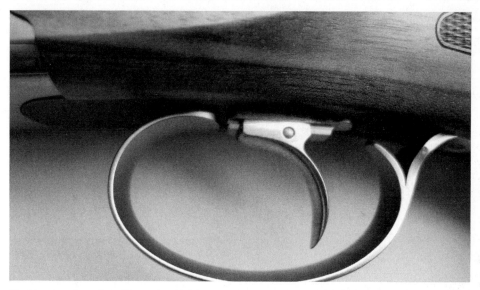

The trigger can be adjusted forward and back.

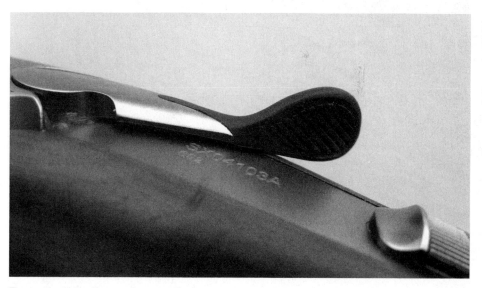

The opening lever offers a new ergonomic shape.

Note the two dots on the safety/barrel selector. When the red dot is on the bottom the bottom barrel fires first and vice versa.

The 692 comes with five Optima Bore HP screw-in chokes.

Four 7/10ths ounce weights can be added to the butt stock if the shooter wants to adjust the gun's balance.

BERETTA DT11

Back in 2002, Beretta introduced their DT10 competition over/under. Owners of the gun's predecessor – the ASE 90 – sometimes cried the figurative blues lamenting the fact that the ASE 90 they loved was gone – and probably fearing that their investment in this competition over/under was going to lose importance and value. Now owners of the DT10 may be quick to do the same thing as the DT10 is gone, replaced by the DT11. Neither DT10 nor ASE90 owners should have fretted. The ASE 90 has certainly retained its value as that O/U is still in demand on the used gun market. I expect the same is going to be true for the DT10, not only for the next decade but for decades to come.

But the DT11 is the competition over/under that's the subject of this report. That testing was done at Dover Furnace Sporting Clays and Ten Mile River Preserve – both about 90 miles directly north of New York City and in the Empire State. While the Ten Mile River Preserve is private and for members only, the Dover Furnace sporting facility is open to the public. Members of the shotgun media shot the new DT11 at both facilities.

Perhaps the most important new feature the DT11 brings to the competition gun table is its new inner-barrel philosophy. For many years gun makers have been extending their barrel's forcing cones. I'm certain most of you know all about this, but bear with me briefly while I explain this forcing cone thing to those who might not be as shotgun savvy as you. Before the advent of plastic wads, shotshells were put together with fiber or paper wadding above the powder. In a 12-gauge, the inner chamber area measures approximately .800. In those early days inner barrel diameters were running about .725. Consequently, there had to be a step down from the chamber to the barrel – i.e. from .800 to .725. Because fiber and paper wading didn't seal nearly as well as today's plastic shot cups that step down area from .800 to .725 had to be a very short one – often only about a quarter of an inch in those early days. Otherwise the powder gases would escape around the fiber or paper wadding, make its way into the shot column while still in the barrel and wreak all manner of havoc with that shot string all the way to barrel exit.

Several years ago longer forcing cones were introduced, yet many gun makers were reluctant to do this. Early forcing cone lengths were extended to maybe ½-inch, then ¾-inch, then 1-inch and later more. The DT11 takes this forcing-cone philosophy to a whole new level. From the 12-gauge chamber of about .800 the DT11 step down is to about .770, which is roughly the inner diameter of a 12-gauge shotgun shell with the just-fired crimp opened up. But this taper takes place for like 15 inches from the chamber to midway up the barrel – a very, very slow taper. From .770, the DT11 barrels taper again very, very slowly and slightly – almost to the muzzle – to .730.

As the shot string from a just-ignited shotshell is forced into a forcing cone from yesteryear, the shot compression resulted in such violence that pellets then on the outer part of the shot column were deformed, and deformed shot pellets quickly fly out of the effective pattern. By making forcing cones longer, there were fewer deformed pellets, thus fewer pellets flew out of the shot string. But with the Beretta 692 and the DT11 there are no forcing cones at all. The outer pellets simply ride the inner part of the barrel as that inner barrel diameter very slowly tapers from .800 to .730. Shortly thereafter comes the transition to the choke area.

Will Fennel, full-time shooting instructor and once a member of the Beretta Shooting Team, told me that on extra-long F.I.T.A.S.C. shots he was getting either much harder breaks or did not have to use as much choke with the DT11. In other words, with fewer deformed pellets in the DT11 he's getting better, tighter patterns with less choke. It has always been my contention that as forcing cones became longer patterns improved – not only with a higher percentage of pellets in the 30-inch circle that most use for such measurements, but also in the overall evenness of patterns shot with long forcing cones. Now that Beretta has taken long forcing cones to a new level – as the DT11 has no forcing cones –why wouldn't patterns improve? The barrel material is also totally new on the DT11, made of a super hard steel alloy Beretta is calling Steelium Pro.

Back in the late 1980s Stan Baker out in Seattle offered his Big Bore Barrels for Remington 1100 semi-autos. Stan's Big Bore went from .800 in the chamber and stayed at .800 all the way to the screw choke transition area. Baker's no-forcing-cone idea was no doubt ahead of its time.

Baker's Big Bore Barrel didn't only improve patterns; that philosophy significantly reduced recoil. All gun makers who have lengthened forcing cones have claimed recoil reduction as a bonus as well. Personally, I have found this recoil reduction hard to measure on my shoulder unless the cone is sort of eliminated as in the DT11 and 692. Does the DT11 with its new barrel philosophy have less recoil than its predecessor the DT10? To prove this was true, Beretta set up a test in Italy. They hung a DT10, fired a shell and then measured how far back the DT10 went before stopping. They did the same thing with the DT11, and Beretta personnel did claim the DT11 did not come back as far after firing, thus had less recoil.

But wait, there's more – as the many TV ads claim. The DT11's receiver has been widened by 3mm. That means DT10 barrels won't fit. The idea is slightly more weight, (probably only an ounce or two) is between the hands – philosophically the best place for added weight to be in any shotgun.

The opening lever has been redesigned, which Beretta claims enhances the gun's ergonomics. The look of the receiver is similar to the DT10, but the DT11 receiver shows a combination of high polish and the satin look. The finish is also nickel based for increased corrosion resistance. The DT11 lock up is the same as its predecessor, utilizing the super strong Kersten-style crossbolt – the same locking system also used on Beretta's best over/unders in their SO series. Of course, the DT in this series is for Drop-out Trigger, and the DT11 retains that feature.

The DT11 will be available in Sporting, Skeet and Trap versions. Barrel lengths offered for the Sporting model will be 71, 76 and 81 centimeters, which I think results in about 28, 30 and 32-inches. The gun comes in its own impact resistant plastic case, with a number of accessories included. The screw-in chokes, five included, are Optima-choke HP – and they are long at approximately 3-inches.

SPECIFICATIONS

Gauge: 12 gauge only
Action: Over/under
Weight: 8 pounds 8 ounces
Barrels: 28, 30 and 32 inches
Chokes: Five Optimachoke HP included
Stock: Drop at comb 35mm, drop at heel 56mm – or – drop at comb 38mm, drop at heel 60mm – or adjustable comb stock
Suggested Retail: $8,050
Manufacturer/Importer: Manufactured by Beretta in Italy. Imported by Beretta USA. www.berettausa.com.

The DT11 ready to go on the Dover Furnace Sporting Clays Range.

Sisley gets ready to put the new DT11 to work with instructor Mitchell Muncey behind.

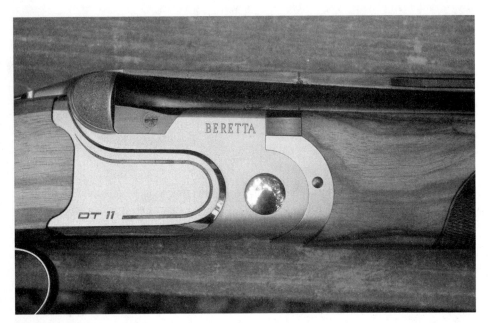

Close up of the DT11 receiver.

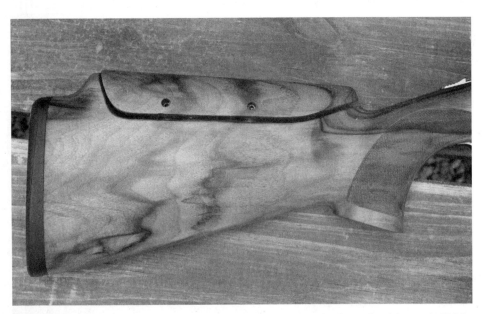

The DT11 can be had with a non-adjustable or an adjustable stock. Note also the quality of the wood which is Grade III Turkish walnut.

Full-length view of the new DT11.

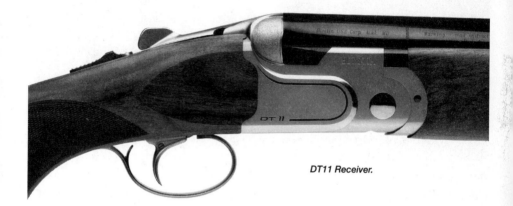

DT11 Receiver.

Receiver close-up showing the top lock locking system on the DT11.

Instructor Will Fennell was on hand to pass on shooting tips to the media folks who were introduced to the new DT11.

KRIEGHOFF PARCOURS MODEL

In competition clay target shooting – skeet, trap or sporting – a Krieghoff K-80 has stood with its owner on top of the championship podium many, many times. Skeet shooters fill their 12-gauge K-80s with sub-gauge skeet tubes from the likes of Kolar and Briley. Trap shooters go with a K-80, mostly for doubles, and match it to a K-80 single barrel – top single or un-single. Sporting clays shooters tend to go with a K-80 with 32-inch barrels, screw-in chokes and an adjustable comb stock – and in the Pro Sporter model couple that high adjustable stock with a high adjustable comb.

The company's latest introduction is none of the above. Dubbed the Parcours model, this latest K-80 is obviously designed especially for F.I.T.A.S.C. courses, which are also called parcours layouts. Evidently, what the parcours shooter wants is a somewhat lighter and faster handling Krieghoff. Neither the K-80 nor the model 32 predecessor are light weight over/unders.

But building a lighter gun involves a lot more than merely eliminating weight. This job requires the manufacturer to not only retain balance, but also to improve the gun's dynamics, as well as preserve and progress with all the subtle handling qualities that have made the original K-80 so popular, sought after and durable.

Speaking of the latter, this is one of this gun's most treasured, sought after and important qualities. The old Model 32 was possible to wear out – say after 100,000 or more rounds were poured through these old guns. That's when these 32s would have to go back to Krieghoff for a major and expensive re-do. When the K-80 came out, it was pretty much a dead ringer for the model 32. The main difference with the K-80 is that its receiver was hardened by an annealing process which made the surface areas harder and thus less prone to wear. To my knowledge Krieghoff is the only gun company that goes this extra mile to harden the metal surfaces. You cannot wear a K-80 out. Sure, you might have to replace trunnions, the sliding top lock, have Krieghoff weld up the ears that the top lock slides over, but that's about it. That receiver will simply take one heck of a pounding.

However, all shotguns need to go through an annual just like an airplane. A ballpark figure would be sending your over/under into the manufacturer every 10,000 rounds. There the gun will be intensely inspected; small springs will be replaced, perhaps other small parts. This you should do with not only a Krieghoff, but a Perazzi, Caesar Guerini, Blaser, Kolar, Zoli, Beretta, et al.

But let's get to the nitty-gritty about what makes the new Parcours a Parcours. F.I.T.A.S.C. is a game of many two-shot sequences. A high percentage of those doubles requires considerable gun movement – from the first bird to the second. This is only one of the requirements for a somewhat lighter, faster Parcours gun. Typically a standard K-80 will spin a scale needle well past 8 pounds, with nearly 9 pounds fairly common. Evidently, the demand by Parcours shooters was for a 12-gauge over/under in the 8-pound range instead. As already mentioned such a lighter Krieghoff had to maintain a number of other desirable qualities.

So what did Krieghoff do to make the Parcours different? "Parcours" will not be engraved anywhere on this new model. The receiver will still be the surface hardened K-80 with standard or various upgraded engraving. One area that has changed over recent decades has been the thickness of the butt stock on most competition guns. OPS principal Gil Ash has been harping on such stocks for a long time, and he has reasons why he does not favor these butt stocks that are overly wide. So that's one obvious change that Krieghoff made – the Parcours butt stock is much trimmer in width. The company did retain their adjustable comb on the Parcours stock. I think virtually all K-80

stocks, no matter the model, are coming with adjustable combs these days. Of course, removing a bit of the Parcours stock thickness meant a few ounces less overall weight.

The Parcours forend, though shaped similarly to the K-80 Sporter and Pro Sporter forends, is also thinner. Note how little wood there is on either side of the barrel – looking down on the forend from the top. Next to the forend of a Model 32 Krieghoff, note how much more walnut there is on the 32 forend compared to the Parcours. This thinness also trimmed an ounce or more. Consequently, a bit of weight was removed from both ends of the gun. Does the thinner, lighter Parcours forend mean a livelier gun? Maybe.

The Parcours barrels are also lighter. All barrels with this model will be 32-inches. On my digital postal scale the barrel set on my test gun went 3 pounds 2.5 ounces. That is not only very light for a set of 32-inch barrels, it's several ounces less than the 32-inch barrels that come on the K-80 Skeet, Trap and Sporting models. The K-80 Pro Sporter had 30-inch barrels went 3 pounds 6.5 ounces. So that's a 4-ounce difference and the heavier Pro Sporter barrels were 2-inches shorter.

I have no way of measuring barrel thickness but both bores on the Parcours I'm testing for this report went .7315 internally. Yet another barrel change is that the Parcours will come with fixed chokes. Krieghoff told me these barrels will be Modified and Improved Modified. My test gun, received before the first main shipment of the new Parcours, had even tighter chokes – .704 in the bottom barrel for .0275 points of constriction; the top barrel at .695 for .0365 constriction. Again, I was told the fixed chokes in the first shipment from Germany will not be that tight. Note that on the K-80s with screw-in chokes there's a bit of a "flare" at the muzzles so there's still plenty of metal to accommodate the screw choke threads.

The Parcours barrels will not have this flare since the chokes are fixed. Total weight of the test gun was 8 pounds 0.5 ounces.

Model 32 and K-80 barrels have always come with no side panels. The Parcours has soldered ribs between the barrels. Because of the relatively tight chokes, I shot very few 25 yard birds. Most all of my shooting was at clays 35 to 45 yards off. Using 1-ounce reloads of #7½ Magnum shot in the Federal paper case at 1,140 feet per second the breaks were very impressive. The adjustable comb stock was set up so I saw a stacked mid and front bead. I may have set the gun up to shoot lower if I had the opportunity for long-term use.

I also put this test gun to work on pest pigeons one morning. The gun helped me kill 11 of the feathered marauders, and most of them were stone dead in the air. Further, there's no question in my mind that the Parcours model will make a great hunting gun. Doves in South America come to mind or doves anywhere really. Ducks?? This is a pretty fancy over/under to carry into the duck marsh.

The top rib is tapered from 8mm to 6mm, so very little tapering. Also this model is available in both true right and left-hand stock versions. The engraving on my test gun is called "Vintage Scroll," and that's a $1,400 upgrade over standard K-80 engraving. Krieghoff shows many different engraving patterns on their Website – www.krieghoff.com.

SPECIFICATIONS

Gauge: 12 gauge
Action: Over/under with sliding top lock
Weight: 8 pounds 0.5 ounces
Barrels: 32 inches
Chokes: Fixed: Modified and Improved Modified
Stock dimensions: Adjustable comb. Length of pull: 14.375. Adjustable drop: 1.675 x 2 inches
Suggested Retail: $10,995 with standard engraving
Manufacturer/Importer: Manufactured in Ulm, Germany. Imported by Krieghoff USA in Ottsville, Pa. www.krieghoff.com.

In addition to shooting the new Parcours extensively on clay targets, the author also put this new over/under to work on pest pigeons. He thinks this Parcours model will make an ideal dove gun. (Photo from Krieghoff.)

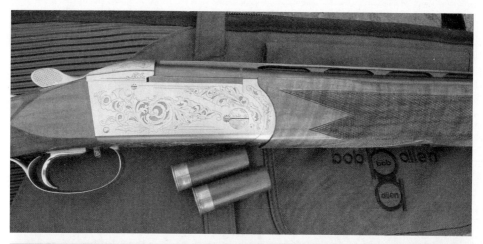

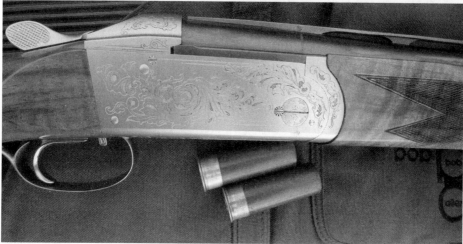

The Parcours test gun receiver with upgraded "Vintage Scroll" engraving.

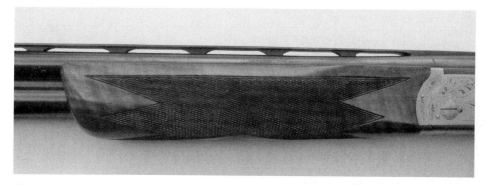

The shape of the Parcours forend is pretty much a dead ringer for the forend on the K-80 Sporter and Pro Sporter models, but the Parcours forend is thinner and lighter.

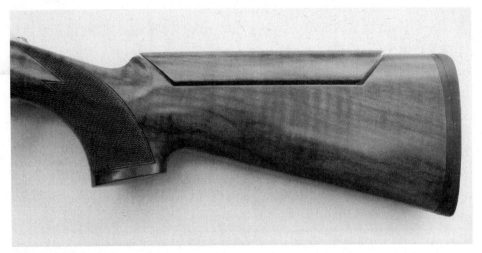

The butt stock is thinner than on the other K-80 models, but the adjustable comb feature has been retained.

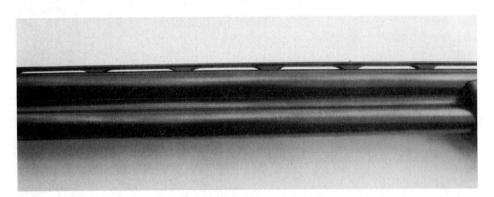

The Parcours model features soldered rib side panels, while all the other Krieghoff models have no side ribs.

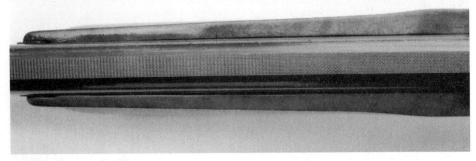

Note the minimal amount of forend walnut on the Parcours above compared to the amount of wood next to the barrels on a Model 32 Krieghoff. Thus the Parcours forend is both lighter and slimmer.

KRIEGHOFF K-20 PRO SPORTER

Whenever I had a shotgun malfunction during the 1980s my long time competitive team mate Don Lavely would remark, "Someday you'll get a Krieghoff." Naturally any of those early shotgun problems of mine were not with a Krieghoff. In the 1990s I finally bought a Krieghoff, and then another and another and another and another – yes five of them. I still have four.

I've heard some sporting clays shooters down play the K-80, saying it's too heavy, or too this or too that. But the K-80 and its predecessor the Krieghoff model 32 have broken a figurative zillion targets over the years. The K-80's popularity continues, and it's the shotgun thousands of shooters dream about acquiring some day in their future. Most all of you already know that the Krieghoff 32 was built around the Remington model 32. Those Krieghoff 32s began reaching our shores in the mid 1950s. Within 10 years they were the toast of clay target shooters all over the country, at least for those who could afford one.

In 1980 the K-80 arrived. All through the years that the 32 was produced Krieghoff made numerous internal improvements. But there was never a model change, and all the improvements were never hyped or advertised. The big difference between the 32 and the K-80 was a receiver that was heat treated to make it harder and thus even more durable. This heat treatment made a gun that previously lasted for a figurative forever hold up even longer. I could be wrong, but I don't think there's a competition receiver that's as hard as a K-80, or one that's similarly heat treated. It's a fact that these receivers are so hard that they have to be engraved before the heat treating. That's why you can't buy a used K-80 and have the receiver upgraded with aftermarket engraving. You can do this with a model 32 Krieghoff, as well as probably any other

over/under that you buy used.

The K-20 was introduced in 2000. I always thought that the year of introduction was how the K-20 got its name, but Dieter Krieghoff told me that the K-20 was named because it is a 20 gauge. Not long after 2000 the K-20 also became available with 28 and .410 barrels. The K-20 also has the same super hard receiver, via heat treating, as the K-80.

Why a 20 gauge in a competition gun where all the important events are in 12 gauge – sporting, trap, skeet, F.I.T.A.S.C? Because of the relatively short ranges involved many of today's skeet competitors shoot a tubed 20 gauge in skeet competition 12-gauge events. Of course, these skeeters shoot the same gun in 20 gauge events, and then change tubes to compete in the 28 and .410 events. A K-80 with full-length subgauge tubes is a pretty heavy gun. Heavy is good until shooters reach octogenarian status when most start thinking about shooting a lighter gun. Enter the K-20, especially a three-barrel set.

A second popular spot for the K-20, and this was not an afterthought, has become Argentina and the untold number of doves in not only the state of Cordoba, but many additional areas of the country that have opened up to tremendous high-volume shooting over the last 10 years. Most of the 20-gauge shells in Argentina are 25 grams – just a tad over ⅞ ounce, which are more comfortable to shoot than a 32-gram 12-gauge load in a high volume situation. Further, the K-20 is no light weight. Most of them are well over seven pounds. With such a K-20 firing 500 25-gram loads at the endless doves in a morning or a day is no problem, even for those of us who are super recoil sensitive.

Only a few years ago we saw the emergence of the high adjustable rib/high adjustable comb 12 gauge guns; a la the Caesar

Guerini Impact, the Krieghoff Pro Sporter, the Kolar Max Sporting, the Blaser SuperSport, the Perazzi MX2000/3 and others. So why not a K-20 Pro Sporter?

Why indeed, as that's the shotgun I've been testing for this report. Fresh out of the box one of my first impressions was the look of the receiver itself. In addition to heat treating today's Krieghoffs metal parts receive a nickel coating. This coating makes them just about impervious to corrosion but also makes for a very impressive receiver finish. Of course, K-80 and K-20 blued receivers are also available.

The receiver photo shown here has the typical engraving pattern on the "Standard" K-20 (and K-80). Nickeled parts, in addition to the receiver, include the opening lever, trigger guard and forend iron. The blued metal parts are the top lever, the pins and screws on the receiver sides – and the barrels – including the new high adjustable rib on the K-20 Pro Sporter.

The stock on my test gun is in a fairly light shade via a satin epoxy finish. The grip has a degree of re-curve, plus there is a grip swell on both sides. The forend is Schnabel in shape, but I believe other forend shapes are available. Note the step down at the top rear of the stock. All the new high adjustable rib/high adjustable comb guns have this step down – this, of course, to accommodate the face height position for the higher rib. All these guns also have adjustable comb stocks, another needed feature to accommodate the adjustable rib. I was able raise the back of the comb slightly higher than the front, creating a nearly level comb stock. The recoil pad is a Decelerator that's ½ inch wide, rounded all around to facilitate easy gun mounting, plus the rear of the pad has a bit texture to help keep the gun solidly in place once the mount is complete and/or the first shot is fired. The pad is off set from the rear of the stock with a ¼-inch black spacer.

The trigger can be moved fore and aft to make it easy to attain your perfect grip-to-trigger distance. The trigger appears to be of stainless steel. The barrel selector is a switch just in front of the trigger. The top tang safety is non-automatic and can be locked in the fire position for serious clay target-only shooting. Trigger let off was with no creep, very crisp at 4 and 4½ pounds – typical of both K-80s and K-20s.

Prior to this K-20 Pro Sporter I tested two different K-20s – both of the traditional rib style. If memory serves me right both were in the 7 pound 12 ounce range. This K-20 Pro Sporter hefts 8 pounds 4 ounces, so it's no light weight. The 30-inch barrels went 3 pounds 6.5 ounces and the forend was 11.2 ounces. Both bores were .620 which is a bit of overboring. Traditional 20-gauge bores a few decades back were .615. Five extended titanium screw-in chokes were included with my test gun; two Improved Cylinders at .611 – for .009 constriction, a Light Modified at .606 for .014 constriction, a Modified at .603 for .017 constriction and an Improved Modified at .591 for .029 constriction.

The high adjustable tapered rib has a metal mid-bead and a white front bead. To change rib height loosen the set screw at the rear of the rib and then move the tiny wheel at the front of the rib. Move this wheel up to lower the pattern, down to raise the pattern. My test gun was one of the first to enter the country and did not have this "wheel" feature.

I had a number of folks shoot this test K-20, and I banged quite a few rounds through the gun myself. As expected, there were no malfunctions. Better yet the gun brought lots of smiles to faces as clay bird after clay bird was smashed with such ease. The K-20 Pro Sporter or the traditional K-20 – these are guns most any serious shotgunner would love to own.

SPECIFICATIONS

Gauge: 20 gauge with 28 and .410 barrels also available
Action: Over/under
Weight: 8 pounds 4 ounces
Barrel: 30 inches. 32 inches available
Chokes: Five screw-in titanium supplied
Stock: Length-of-pull 14.375. Adjustable comb stock with drop down at top rear
Suggested Retail: $11,295
Manufacturer/Importer: Krieghoff in Ulm, Germany. Imported by Krieghoff International in Ottsville, Pa. www.krieghoff.com.

Close up of a Standard Grade K-20 receiver with the step up to the high rib shows this is the Pro Sporter model.

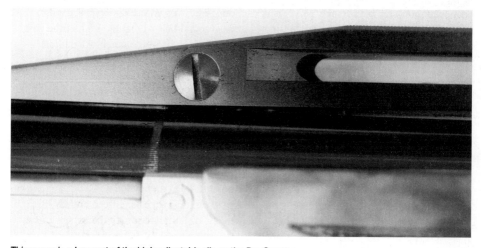

This screw is a key part of the high adjustable rib on the Pro Sporter.

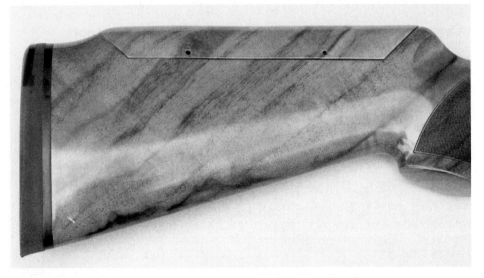

The adjustable comb is part of the Pro Sporter adjustable rib/adjustable comb package.

PERAZZI MX28B

Lithe and striking, voluptuous and attractive, startling and stunning. No I'm not describing a Hollywood Starlet, but the Perazzi MX28B. The over/under wasn't out of the box yet, and I was struck by how many descriptive adjectives I could come up with. In past years, I had groveled over the original MX28s, which were of the so-called SC2 persuasion and thus very far out of my pocket-book range. The new MX28B is still a bit out of my price range, but getting closer. Maybe the same goes for you.

Built on a tiny 28-gauge frame, this is a light little wand, but when I shot it the first time on clay targets I was pleasantly surprised by the relatively light recoil. Of course, this is not a clay target over/under. In the truest sense of the word the MX28B is one of the new game guns. Of course, the original MX28 in SC2 configuration is also a true game gun, but only recently are shotguns like this being called game guns – at least by me.

To backtrack a bit, the original game guns were the side-by-sides of the Edwardian Era – 12 gauges with 2½-inch chambers

that were actually developed for driven bird shooting in the British Isles. Those guns were so well suited to not only driven shooting, but upland gunning here in the USA as well, that writers like Michael McIntosh, Cyril Adams, Terry Wieland and others extolled their virtues in numerous magazine and book mediums.

Of course, the problem with one of those game guns of yesteryear is who can afford one? The Woodward, Purdey, Holland, Boss and others of that ilk are half the cost of today's 3-bedroom ranch. Also, there never were very many of these old game guns, and today, 100 years later and more, there are even fewer. The current Perazzi MX28B game gun retails for more than what I paid for the house I still live in, bought in 1961, so more than 50 years of inflation has taken its toll. My starting salary at U.S. Steel's College Graduate Trainee Program is poverty-level money today.

Even if anyone can afford an MX28B today, it's tough to justify the expense. But it doesn't cost a nickel to dream. And I'm dreaming. So I'm sure you are now looking for at least a little specification-type information. My test MX28B weighs in at 6 pounds 8 ounces on my digital postal scale. There are lighter small bore over/unders around – even 12 gauges – but this 6½-pounder is just about the weight of some 12 gauge Purdey side-by-side game guns of the bygone age.

Since I hate to put this lithe Perazzi down I carry it around the house a lot, probably mounting it 100 times some days. Balance is about ½-inch in front of the hinge, so a little forward weight – not bad when a woodcock tops the alders preparing for its escape. Generally, a bit of front heaviness results on quicker movement to the fast-escaping bird feathered or clay. The barrels are 29½ inches though Perazzi goes by the metric system so this one is 75 cm. The top rib is not tapered – 7mm breach to muzzle with metal bead at the front. There are full non-vented side ribs in front of the forend and separated barrels under the forend.

The barrels weigh 2 pounds 12.5 ounces. Again, many a set of light side-by-side Game gun barrels weighed similarly over 100 years ago though in 12 gauge. The bores measure .547 with my Baker Barrel Reader. Traditionally 28-gauge bores measure about .550 so there's no so-called overboring here. The forend is slim at 1.53-inches, and note the forend shape trims weight a tad, but only a tad, as weight is 9.7 ounces.

The forend wood appears a perfect match to the figure of the butt stock walnut – probably Turkish. The checkering is probably done by laser, and these machines are both precise and very expensive. Use a 2X loupe and you'll find the execution just about perfect. The checkering is also very fine line. There's no super sharpness to the checkered tops so the gun is comfortable to carry all day without gloves.

The walnut is hand-rubbed oil, beautifully done with all the pores completely filled. While the MX28B does not have

SC2 engraving, Perazzi did use a very nice looking grade wood on this new model. The pistol grip is relaxed/open, but the crowning touch to the stock is the checkered butt. Again, the checkering on the butt plate is very fine line, plus there's an opening to insert the stock removal tool that is included with all Perazzi shotguns. Care is needed in setting this type of checkered butt stock down on any hard surface. You would not want to chip the wood when doing so. It's good to make the point at this time – store all of your guns muzzle down – the muzzles on a double layer of thick shag carpet pieces. Doing so keeps oil from soaking downward from the receiver into the wood.

Speaking of the receiver, all those from Perazzi have a similar look – the elegant shape of the receiver sides and the shape of the fences just behind the barrels. The "B" in MX28B stands for "basic." The blued receiver thus has only borderline engraving on the receiver sides, plus engraving on and around the outside of the trunnions, the forend iron, the fences, the top tang, the opening lever and the trigger guard. SC2-type engraving is much more lavish and expensive, and several different styles of SC2 engraving are offered. Incidentally, SCO (a more expensive type of Perazzi engraving) translated from Italian to English means Competition Over/under with Gold Engraving. In Italian SCO is an acronym for Sovrapposto Competizione Oro.

The heart of any Perazzi is the locking system. I've never seen a Boss over/under, but, evidently, the Perazzi lock up is similar if not the same. Barrels pivot on trunnions, as almost all of today's over/unders do. Two bolts extend forward from about the midpoint on each side of the receiver to lock into lugs milled on both sides of the monobloc just under the ejector areas. Further recoil lugs on the sides of the receiver lock into matching areas on the sides of the monobloc. This has proven to be a lock up that's capable of holding up to more than most lifetimes of shooting. Perazzis have always been popular in trap, and many Perazzi trap guns have fired hundreds of thousands of rounds. The bonus for upland shooters is that the system has no underlocking lugs, thus the receiver is lower in profile – theoretically putting the shooter's hands closer to the bottom barrel – said to enhance natural pointing characteristics.

And let's not forget the triggers for Perazzi triggers are known worldwide for their excellence. Depending upon the Perazzi model, the buyer can have two trigger choices – strong and super reliable coil springs or the company's leaf-spring rendition. Both are known for their crispness and breaking glass-like let offs. The MX28B I have on consignment has such breaking glass-like triggers – on the MX28 models they are the coil spring type. My test gun's triggers go off at less than four pounds.

The gun comes with flush-mounted screw-in chokes – nickel plated and so slippery to reduce plastic wad build up. Perazzi uses a numbering system for their chokes – the smaller the number the more open the chokes. The test gun came with two chokes marked "0" that measured .547 – same as the bore – so Cylinder or Skeet. The #2 went

.540, the #4 went .531, the #6 went .527 and both the #8 and # 10 were too tight to get my Baker Barrel Reader probe into. A choke changing tool is provided. Also, fixed choke barrels are an option.

But I'm not finished covering all the features yet. Today, with any Perazzi, you can name your own personal stock dimensions, and there's only a four to six month wait for this. This means, at no extra cost, you're getting a so-called "bespoke" shotgun. Further, there are many barrel-length choices and several forend style choices.

Like me, most readers can only dream of someday owning a gun like this. But by Perazzi now offering the MX28B at a much reduced price compared to the MX28 with SC2 engraving and SCO walnut – no doubt the price is doable for more upland gunners than before.

SPECIFICATIONS

Gauge: 28 gauge
Action: Over/under
Barrels: 29½ inches. 26 – 34-inch barrel lengths available.
Stock: Standard grade walnut in hand rubbed oil. 14.75 x 1.375 x 2.125. Custom dimension stocks are available at no extra cost
Retail Price: $14,800 with screw-in chokes.

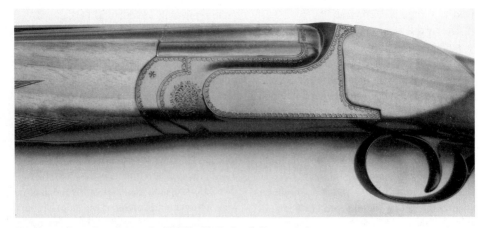

The elegant Perazzi receiver on the MX28B with the borderline engraving.

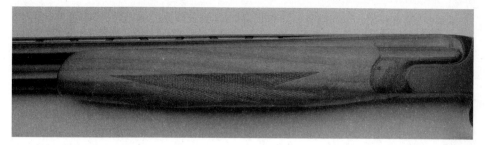

The thin and light MX28B forend.

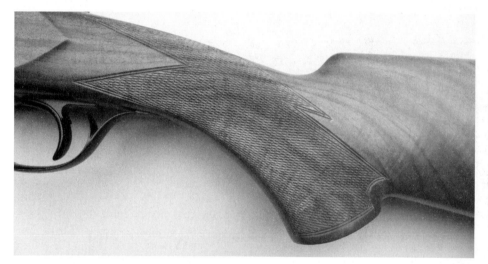

The relaxed/open grip.

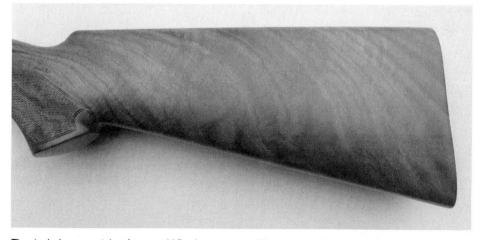

The stock shape was taken from an old Purdey game gun. This spectacular piece of walnut is finished in hand-rubbed oil and all the pores are completely filled.

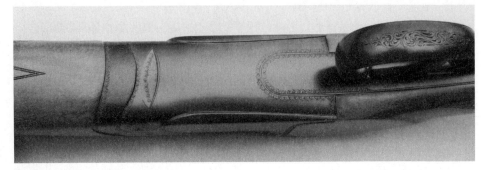

The bottom of the MX28B receiver.

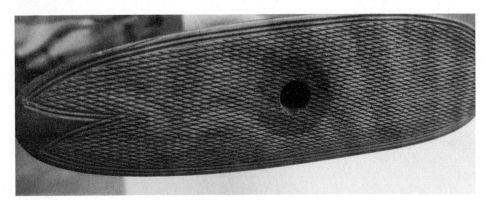

The gun's crowning touch might be this finely checkered butt plate. The hole is for insertion of the stock-removal tool.

Veteran grouse hunter Paul McConville gets ready to put the MX28B to work.

Paul McConville with the Perazzi MX28B.

Loading up two 28 gauge shells into the Perazzi MX28B

Gil and Vickie Ash are the husband and wife team who have taken the world of innovative shotgun teaching by storm. Gil has some valid opinions on this Game gun thing I've been talking about – particularly with regard to stock configurations. Here's what he told me.

Target stocks have been developed for rising targets in trap and skeet, thus higher combs. But sporting clays has many flat and dropping targets where high and thick comb stocks don't work as well. He and Vickie are sure that a gun that simply shoots where you are looking, i.e. a 50 / 50 pattern, is not only best for sporting clays but for most all hunting situations as well. Guns with slightly lower and thinner combs permit this.

The Ash's average 125 gun fits a year, and if a stock alteration is required they've had to lower the comb on well over 90 percent of those guns. Gil and Vickie both think that manufacturers of guns with lower and thinner combs are the right direction to go.

PERAZZI MX2000 S/3C

What can be said about a Perazzi that hasn't already been extolled elsewhere? The MX2000 is the shotgun of choice for Champions like George Digweed, Wendell Cherry, and who knows how many others. Perazzi over/unders of every description have been winning clay target championships over and over since that run started in 1964 with Olympic Trap Champion Ennio Mattarelli. In Olympic shooting, Perazzi has an unmatched record.

I was well into my 60s before I could afford one – an MX8 I bought from USA Perazzi guru Giacomo Arrighini, which he fit with a set of 28.5-inch Live Pigeon barrels and a stock that matched my personal dimensions. That gun has since accompanied me on numerous dove and duck shooting trips to South America, plus totaled virtually thousands of pest pigeons here at home. I guess I should have or should send that MX8 in for servicing, but I never have. No one has ever seen that gun's innards since it was put together in Italy. The MX8 has a drop-out leaf-type trigger, and I bought a spare trigger spring for it, but that spare trigger is still brand new and never used. All this I say because my experience gives credence to the already well known durability, reliability and winning ways of a Perazzi.

That said I'm of the opinion that each Perazzi I've picked up over the years has had an unmistakable feel to it. Could I blind-folded he handed several over/unders – and still pick out a Perazzi just because of this *feel*? Maybe so. So with that introduction let's take a close look at the Perazzi MX2000 S/3C.

The MX2000 is the preferred model of many great shooters. This model does not have the drop-out trigger. The triggers are fired by strong and massive coil springs. The model name/number S/3C – the "S" means Sporting, the "3" means three notches front and back of the adjustable rib (for raising/lowering), the "C" standing for screw-in chokes.

Yes, this is the high adjustable rib/high adjustable comb Perazzi. The rib has three notch adjustments at the rear and the front of the rib. Adjustments are quick and easy, using a small tool provided, to create pattern impact of 50 / 50, 60 / 40, or 70 / 30. Seven screw-in chokes are provided; the chokes numbered 0 for Cylinder/Skeet which went .737 internally – the same as both bore sizes, the choke numbered 2 went .731 for .006 constriction, the 4 went .723, the 6 went .715, the 8 went .707 and the 10 went .698 – for 39 points of constriction. These chokes are flush mounted, but unlike many flush-mounted chokes I check these have respectably long taper and parallel sections, always important to better patterns. Chokes are also nickel plated to help guard against too much plastic wad build up. Extended screw-in chokes are available.

Check the look of the adjustable comb stock with the front of the adjustable portion coming all the way to the front of the comb. Most adjustable combs don't look like this – with the front of the adjustable portion ending an inch or more before the front of the comb. The back of this adjustable comb may extend back further than most. The stock is finished sort of light in color. The grip is tight in profile, preferred by most of today's competition shooters. The forend on the test gun is slim and rounded off, but other forend styles are offered.

The checkering is well done, very fine line, and the coverage is extensive on both sides of the grip and all around on the forend as you will note in the accompanying photos. The recoil pad is open cell, very soft and absorbent, just over ½-inch thick and separated from the butt stock via a black spacer. Length of pull is 14¾ inches. There is a small palm swell on the right side of the test gun. Left side palm swells are available.

The test gun's receiver is in nickel finish, best for corrosion resistance, but a classic blued receiver is also available for the same cost. Perazzi's Al Kondak calls the hand-done engraving "classic scroll." There's a good amount of it on both receiver sides and bottom, plus the trigger guard and opening lever, both of which are in blue, as is the forend iron. The contours of the receiver are typical Perazzi – a style that has been copied by a number of over/under makers. My MX8 does not have a barrel selector, but the MX2000 does on the top tang. Move right or left for barrel selection. The safety itself non-automatic, as all competition over/unders need to be.

The lock-up was first developed by Boss in England in a bygone year. Perazzi was first to pick on that locking system, since followed by Zoli. Barrels pivot on trunnions, as do nearly all current-day over/unders. However, two bolts extend forward from a mid-point along the inner receiver sides. Upon closing, they move into lugs milled into the monobloc at the bottom position of the ejectors. The gun's recoil lugs are milled into both sides of the monobloc. They match up with opposing surfaces milled into both sides of the receiver. This lock up is extremely strong and why Perazzi over/unders are known for lasting so long. Further, with no under locking lugs Perazzis are known for their "low" profile receivers.

Barrels are almost 32 inches. Perazzi goes by the metric system – thus barrels are actually 81cm. Bluing is deep but not shiny, thus mitigating glare in competition situations. The adjustable rib is not tapered and goes 7mm. There's a metal mid-bead and classic front white bead. At the adjustable rib's mid-point; it is grounded to the top barrel, adding considerably to the rib's strength and stability. There are vented side panels between the barrels, that venting stopping about eight-inches from the muzzle, plus barrels are separated under the forend. Chambers are 3-inches. Checking visually, forcing cones do not appear to be overly long.

But perhaps one of the most interesting aspects about the MX2000 S/3C and most all other Perazzis is that the guns are totally customizable. Of course, that means the stocks can be customized to what the individual desires, although a lot (not all) of that customizability is moot with the adjustable comb stock. There is no extra cost for a customized stock. Wait times are 4 to 6 months for this. Different forends are offered. Different barrels are offered. Higher grades are also offered, with longer waiting periods. Obviously, Perazzi has MX2000 models with traditional ribs, which, I think, are the ones that Digweed, Cherry and a number of other champions shoot.

The first time I shot the test gun I ran

more than 30 targets before I missed, un-usual for me shooting a new gun for the first time. Equally unusual that on four or five different targets I thought I missed – maybe should have missed – those targets broke despite what I thought. Why? I think it has to do with a Perazzi moving more naturally, more easily to so many targets. What a bonus. If you ever feel that way about any gun – better buy it.

SPECIFICATIONS

Gauge: 12
Action: Over/under
Weight: 8 pounds 12.5 ounces
Barrels: 32 inches
Chokes: Seven flush mounted
Stock: 14.75 length of pull. Adjustable comb
Suggested Retail: $13,642
Manufacturer/Importer: Made by Perazzi in Brescia, Italy. Imported by Perazzi USA. www.perazzi.com.

The engraving on the MX2000 receiver, with classic receiver lines that have since been copied by many.

The right side of the MX2000 receiver.

The bottom of the MX2000 receiver displays additional engraving.

The shape of the MX2000 forend and the height of the adjustable rib.

The adjustable comb stock. Note the shape of the adjustable portion. Also note the light-colored hand-rubbed stock.

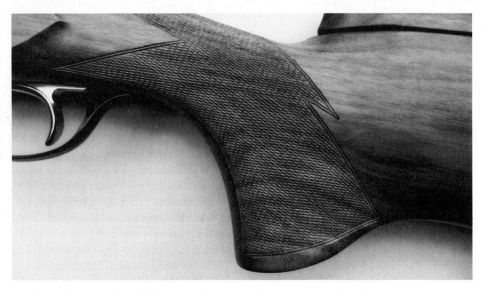

The shape of the grip on the MX2000 shows the amount of re-curve and the fine cut checkering.

PERAZZI MXS AMERICAN SPORTER

Since the Perazzi MXS is titled "American Sporter" in advertising we can assume this one is aimed at the USA market, as opposed to the European or world market. Further, this is the least expensive Perazzi sporting gun to come along in many a figurative moon, taking us back in time to before inflation increased the cost of shotguns and most other products so significantly. I remember buying an MX8 from Giacomo Sporting for $4,000, and not all that long ago – less than 15 years. I also bought a number of Krieghoff model 32s, some new-in-the box for half what a used 32 will cost today.

That said the MXS Perazzi American Sporter has hit the market at $6,900 – suggested retail – far less than an MX8 or MX2000 Sporter. How does Perazzi reduce the price on the MXS? The MX2000 Sporter and the MX8 are more or less "bespoke" over/unders. The buyer gets to specify barrel weight, barrel configuration, can get personal stock dimensions, forend type, bore

diameters, upgraded wood quality and more.

Al Kondak at Perazzi USA researched the type of Perazzi Americans had been buying over the years, so the MXS American Sporter is sort of the consensus of what USA sporting shooters want in a Perazzi. There is only one forend choice, one bore size, three barrel lengths, a blued or satin receiver, vented side ribs. The reduction in options is thus the way Perazzi has decreased the price. It's a more off-the-shelf Perazzi than the other models, but it's still a Perazzi through and through.

Two options exist beyond what's above: – four screw-in chokes at $569 additional and an adjustable comb at $368 additional. My test gun has both these options, plus the satin receiver and 32-inch barrels. The overall look – the MXS is a Perazzi. The locking system is similar to the MX5, MX6 and MX7A with a square – not rounded – monobloc – not the same as the MX2000 or the MX8. MXS barrels pivot on trunnions, two bolts move forward upon closing to engage two lugs milled into each side of the monobloc beside the lower barrel.

The forend is well shaped, has shallow finger grooves, the forend iron shape and method of opening is the same as on my MX8. That forend weighs 12.4 ounces and is about 11-inches in length; 2 inches wide at the rear tapering slightly in width toward the front. Despite the finger grooves, the forend shape/look is similar to the Browning Lightning forend – one of my favorites. Once in place there was no forend wiggle.

The receiver and barrels are of the same high carbon steel used on all the other Perazzi models. As mentioned there's a blued receiver version while my test gun wears the receiver with the satin look, which is actually a nickel coating, obviously known for corrosion resistance. Traditional buyers might want to opt for the blued receiver. Both "Perazzi" and "MXS" are boldly emblazoned on both receiver sides, the same "MXS" on the receiver bottom. The top tang is also in satin, but this is a trigger-plate action with that bottom portion in blue – as is the opening lever and the non-automatic safety. Move the safety switch back and forth for barrel choice selection.

So far the MXS is offered only in 12 gauge – barrel length selections of 28¾, 30 and 32 inches. Both bores of my test gun measured .736 – which means considerable overboring. The four screw-in chokes were marked 2, 4, 6 and 8. The #2 measured .728 via my Baker Barrel Reader (BBR) – so .008 constriction over the .736 barrel. The #4 measured .721 for .015 constriction. The #6 went .713 for .023 constriction. The #8 went .706 for .030 constriction. Additional screw ins can be purchased from Perazzi and most other aftermarket screw choke sources. The Perazzi chokes were just over 2½ inches in length. In measuring those chokes with my BBR I could feel lengthy taper and parallel sections. The chokes were extended beyond the muzzle about ¾-inch; the extended

portion was well checkered for easy finger in/out, but I tightened the chokes in place with the wrench provided and the chokes never loosened in my shooting. If you select the MXS model with fixed chokes you get Modified and Improved Modified. I'm surprised that the average American sporting clays shooter does not prefer more open chokes – fixed or screw-in.

The barrels showed no rippling, indicating best polishing. A solid rib between the barrels extended back from the muzzle 7½ inches – then it was between-the-barrel vents back to the forend – no side panels under the forend. The 32-inch barrels weighed 3 pounds 11.5 ounces on my digital postal scale. The top vent rib is tapered from .440 at the breech to .285 at the muzzle. On top there's a steel mid-bead and a white bead at the muzzle. The top of the vent rib is cross hatched from stem to stern to help reduce distracting glare.

The Turkish walnut stock wears an oil-like finish, and you have a choice in butt stock length of pull – either 14 ⅝ or 14¾ – as well as a right or left hand stock. From that I assume there's a reference to the grip swell and which side that swell is on. There may also be cast difference factors between the left and right hand stocks. There's a re-curve to the pistol grip. There's lots of fine checkering on both sides of the grip, as well as on the forend. The checkering is at 24 lines-to-the-inch. The width at the back of the stock is 1.68-inches, so plenty wide. The textured black recoil pad is ⅝-inches wide, separated from the stock via a black spacer.

The adjustable comb is a bit different and the design guarantees against slippage or movement. To make an adjustment use the included hex-head tool to remove the top adjustable portion. Also included are two each of four different heights of spacers that fit over the posts in the adjustable portion. I used a 2mm spacer under the front post, a 4mm spacer under the back post, which created a somewhat level comb. I like the level comb idea because such a configuration allows the stock to recoil more past your face – as opposed to up into the cheek. For the look of the adjustable comb check the butt stock photo.

The trigger is made with strong coil springs – not removable as with some other Perazzi models – but the same trigger type as used on all Perazzi over/unders without the trigger group removal option. Triggers are of the inertia type, let off just under 4.5 pounds on my Lyman Digital Trigger Pull Scale – nice and crisp. Balance was well forward of the hinge pins or trunnions.

Stock dimensions if the adjustable comb is not selected are $1\frac{3}{8}$ x 2 – or $1\frac{1}{2}$ x $2\frac{1}{8}$. So there really are plenty of options with the MXS; two lengths of pull, two differing comb dimensions, three barrel lengths, two receiver looks.

I shot the gun 200 times. As suspected, not one hiccup. Also as suspected the MXS handled, swung and shot just like any

Perazzi I've ever tried. As Al Kondak of Perazzi puts it, "This gun offers the same top performance and lifetime of reliability as Perazzi's top-of-the line shotguns." For those of you yearning for a Perazzi and want to save thousands of dollars it's certainly worth checking out this new American Sporter at your local dealer.

SPECIFICATIONS

Action: Over/under

Gauge: 12 gauge

Weight: 8 pounds 7.5 ounces

Barrels: 32 inches. – $28\frac{3}{4}$ and 30 also available

Chokes: Fixed: Modified and Improved Modified. Or four screw-in chokes at additional cost.

Stock: 1.375 x 2 or 1.5 x 2.175. LOP: Either 14.675 or 14.75. Adjustable comb available at additional cost

Suggested Retail: $6,900. Add $569 for the four screw choke version, add $368 for adjustable comb.

Manufacturer: Made by Perazzi in Brescia, Italy. Imported by Perazzi USA in Azusa, Calif. www.perazzi.com.

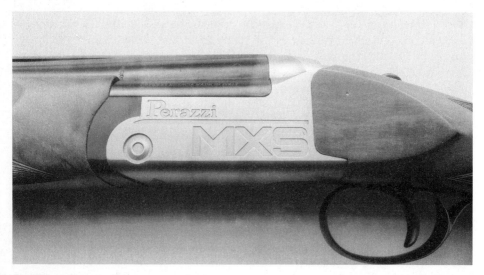

The MXS receiver.

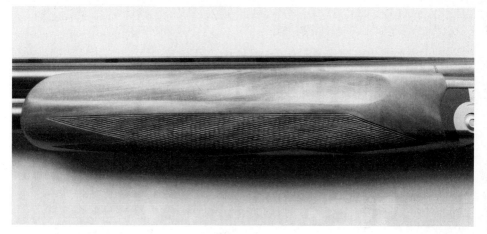

The shape of the MXS forend incorporates a slight finger groove.

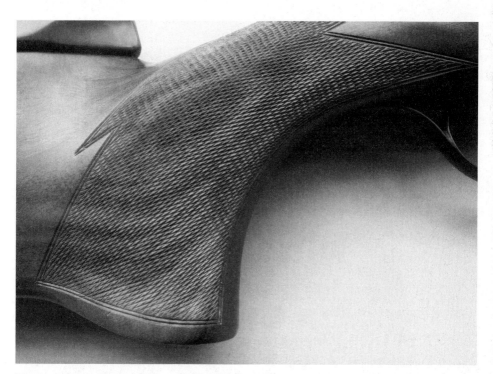

The checkering on the pistol grip is well done. Note the amount of re-curve.

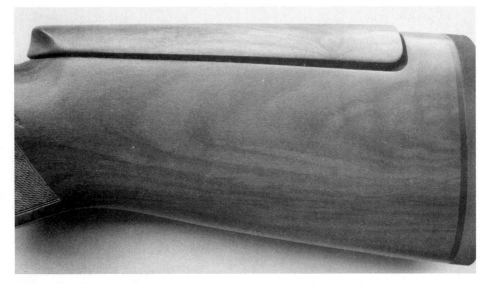

The butt stock with adjustable comb.

The screw-in chokes are long, at just over 2 ½-inches, with significant taper and parallel sections, brightly polished.

RUGER'S NEW RED LABEL OVER/UNDER

When Bill Ruger first introduced the Red Label over/under in 1977, the break from tradition was that a 20-gauge came first. Traditionally a company brings out a 12 gauge, followed by a 20 gauge some years later. Maybe later yet – if ever – the smaller gauge 28 and .410 are introduced. That initial 1977 Red Label 20-gauge was built on a blued steel frame, but many years later, about 1992, bright stainless became the receiver material. The 12 gauge was not introduced until 1982. The 28-gauge Red Label, in my view the best of the bunch and made on a scaled-down 28 gauge frame, appeared first in 1992. There was even a Sporting Clays model in 12 and 20 gauge (I think the latter is pretty rare). These, with 30-inch barrels, were offered from 1994 until 2007. Bill's son Tom Ruger was enthusiastic about Sporting Clays so he probably had something to do with pushing for this model. It came with extended Briley screw-in chokes. There were a few other Red Label iterations including the Woodside, one with a straight grip, an All-Weather Stainless with a black composite stock, and a couple of hand engraved ones.

But production of the Red Label stopped around 2010. There were maybe a couple of reasons. First off, Ruger had so many back-orders for its small frame semi-auto pistols that a major manufacturing effort was turned in that direction. Secondly, Ruger engineers wanted to tweak some of the Red Label's design features to make it better and bring the price point down. Suggested retail about the time production stopped was $2,015.

Ruger has accomplished both objectives. However, in outward appearance the new Red Label is pretty much a dead ringer for the one we've seen for decades. The classic lines of the receiver are the same. There are a number of round body receiver models these days, but Ruger had it with the Red Label way back in the 1970s.

With the originals, the recoil lug built into the bottom of the monobloc passed right through a square cut milled into the bottom of the receiver. With the new model, the recoil lug has been redesigned. It does not go through the receiver, but nestles into an area milled away from the receiver bottom. The barrels continue to pivot on trunnions and two bolts are inside the receiver to lock into two recesses milled into the outside of the rear bottom of the monobloc. These bolts that come from inside the frame's front upon closing have some similarity with the highly-regarded-for-strength Boss over/under – and similarities exist in lock up of both the modern day Perazzi and the Zoli.

Also note that this time a 12 gauge came first, but a 20 will probably appear in a few more months and hopefully not years. While only 26- and 28-inch barrels were available on the previous Red Labels (save for the Sporting Clays model already alluded to), with the new Red Labels 30-inch barrels have been added to the 26- and 28-inchers, a sign of the times with shotgunners wanting longer barrels.

There are no side panels between the barrels, but there is one post between under the forend. The vent rib barrel on my 30-inch consignment gun has a steel mid bead and a steel muzzle bead. The barrels weigh 3 pounds 8 ounces on my digital postal scale. The forend, measuring about 10-inches, weighed 9.4 ounces. The gun went 7 pounds 12 ounces.

In addition to the blued barrels, there's also a blued trigger guard and blued safety button. The opening lever, previously in blue, is now stainless. The safety is automatic, as all Ruger O/U safeties are. Different from traditional O/U safeties. Ruger's is a lever switch to move right and left. This is the same safety used for the previous Red Labels.

I remember that many of the Red Labels I tested years ago, 12s, 20s and 28s, seemed to have very good looking American walnut. As you can see from the butt stock, now it's pretty Plain Jane. The recoil pad is new – a Decelerator that's nicely rounded off. It includes the slick plastic insert at the top, plus the rest of the pad's rough texture certainly keeps it in place without slipping for ensuing shots. The pad is separated from the stock via a black spacer. My test-gun stock has a significant amount of drop. With my Robert Louis Shotgun Combo Gauge I measured nearly 2 inches drop at comb and 2¾ inches drop at heel. The Ruger Website claims higher dimensions, so maybe the extreme drop in my stock was a mistake.

The grip is well checkered, and the accompanying photo will give you a good indication of the amount of re-curve. The forend is also well checkered, both at 21 lines-to-the-inch. The forend is a tad thinner than the originals. The forend iron is also of brushed stainless.

Getting back to the barrels. They are overbored to .745, which is a lot compared to most any overbored barrel I've checked with my Baker Barrel Reader. Craig Cushman of Ruger tells me they have taken a bit off the outside diameter away as well, all to make the barrels a bit lighter, thus livelier in feel.

Because of modern CNC milling machines, tolerances are now tighter for the new Red Label, and manufacturing is easier and faster. The original receivers were made in two parts then welded together. Obviously it took a lot of time to polish away the weld marks. The new Red Label is milled from a one-piece casting. The changes, big and small, have resulted in a significant price reduction. The new gun retails for $1,399 (as opposed to $2,015 for the ones at the end of production a few years ago), and could possible sell for hundreds less – all for a fine over/under made right here in America.

Also, this is a very low profile receiver, which puts the hands in closer relationship with the barrels – very good theoretically. As you have seen in the monobloc close up, the recoil lug extends minimally below the bottom barrel.

Five flush-mounted screw-in chokes are included. Ruger has always supplied two Skeet chokes in their five-choke mix, also including the standard Improved Cylinder, Modified and Full. As already covered the barrels went .745 internally – the two Skeet chokes .740, so .005 constriction; the I.C. went .736 with .009 constriction; the Modified went .724, so .021 constriction, and the Full went .710 for .035 constriction.

There's no doubt Ruger has come up with a terrific package with the new 12-gauge Red Label. The gun looks great (just like the old one really), and it comes through your dealer at a great price, as well as the all-American-made label. Yet another new bonus over the originals, this one comes with a handsome fitted case.

SPECIFICATIONS

Gauge: 12 gauge
Action: Over/under
Weight: 7 pounds 12 ounces
Barrels: 30 inches. 26 and 28 also available
Chokes: 5 screw-in – Two Skeet, Improved Cylinder, Modified and Full
Dimensions: 14.50 x 1.50 x 2.50
Suggested Retail: $1,399
Manufacturer: Ruger in Newport, N.H. www.ruger.com.

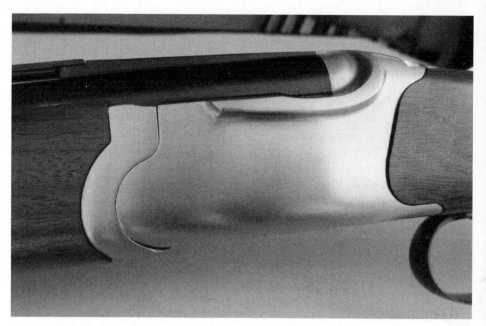

The new Red Label receiver looks pretty much a dead ringer for the original.

The original Red Label had a blued opening lever, while the new model has one of stainless steel – matching it to receiver and forend iron.

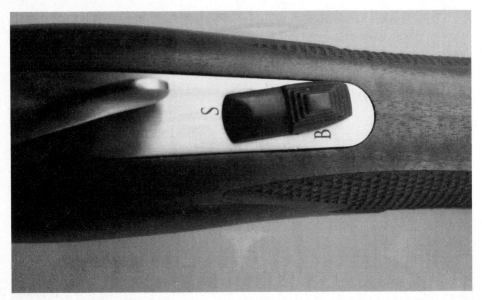

The safety is a bit different from traditional over/under safeties, but the same as the original Red Label.

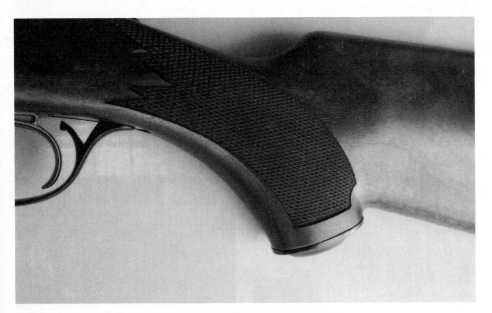

The re-curve of the pistol grip with excellent checkering at 21 lines-to-the-inch.

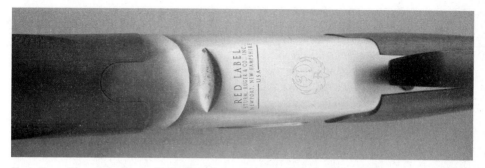

The bottom of the receiver shows the Red Label's round-receiver characteristic.

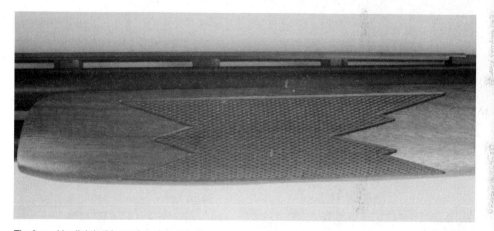

The forend is slightly thinner than the original.

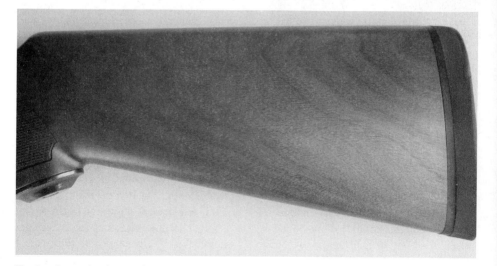

The American walnut butt stock.

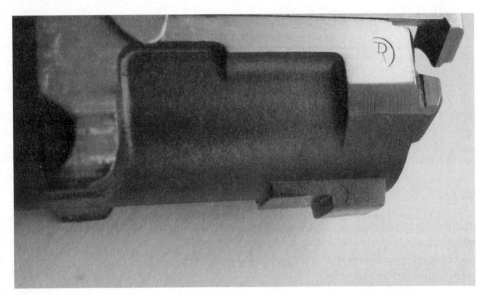

Note the small recoil lug at the base of the monobloc.

The Red label comes with five screw-in chokes: two Skeet plus an Improved Cylinder, Modified and Full.

The bottom of an original Red Label receiver, with the milled-out slot to accept the longer recoil lug that gun had.

REMINGTON VERSAMAX WOOD TECH

The original Versamax was well suited to clay-busting stuff, but the latest Versamax offshoot, the Wood Tech model, is even better suited to sporting clays, 5-Stand, F.I.T.A.S.C., as well as skeet and even trap. Why?

The 12-gauge Versamax derives its name from its "versatility" of handling all manner of shotgun shells; 2¾, 3 and 3½ inch, and the model accomplishes that versatility with a totally new, totally different type of operating system. However, there's much more versatility built into the new Wood Tech – than only being able to operate successfully with all manner of shotshells.

For starters, the Wood Tech doesn't even have a walnut stock. Made of some type of composite, the finish allows the stock to look like walnut. The stock is, however, pretty light, perhaps improving on the gun's liveliness. But let's get back to the versatility aspect. Note the black insert at the comb that black insert lies flat with the top of the Wood Tech stock. This black comb insert just pops right off, and in the impact protective case the gun is delivered in are two additional black comb inserts, allowing you to make the comb higher.

Another versatile aspect of the Wood Tech is that it comes with three plastic length-of-pull insert spacers, so you can make the length of pull longer by ½, ¾ or 1 inch. Successively longer screws are even provided for this.

There's more. Need to change the amount of cast – or if you're left-handed want to rig the stock with the correct cast for southpaws? No problem. Change out the metal insert that goes between the front of the stock and the rear of the receiver. Additional inserts are provided. The top of the receiver is drilled and tapped, thus you can add a relief-type sight, a red dot, a scope – whatever. The butt stock has a built-in swivel stud at its base, another on the forend cap screw. You won't need these or a sling on the sporting clays field, but think of that added versatility if you want to take the same gun waterfowl, predator or turkey hunting.

Of course, most all of today's shotguns come with screw-in chokes, and this Wood Tech is no exception. On the plus side, these are Pro Bore™ chokes made to fit the overbored Pro Bore™ barrel. Four extended chokes are included, and they are marked on the extended portion with the amount of constriction. For example the Skeet is marked .004 (constriction over the bore), the Improved Cylinder is marked .009, the Light Modified at .014 while the Full is unmarked on the extended portion but it's marked Turkey/Predator on the part of the choke that ends up inside the barrel. This latter choke is also extended a bit further out. I measured that latter constriction at .675. The bore is overbored to .735 – so that's .060 constriction, one heck of a lot of choke. Maybe the most I have ever measured.

The gun weighed 8 pounds .5 ounces, so it is plenty light enough for serious clay target work. The forend went an even 8 ounces. Once tightened in place there was no forend wiggle, plus the cap is screwed in against detents ensuring the grip cap will not loosen. The 28-inch barrel went 2 pounds 15 ounces with the Skeet choke in place. The barrel is TriNyte coated for added corrosion resistance. Internal parts are Teflon/nickel plated, also for corrosion resistance, as well as smoothness of operation. The aluminum alloy receiver is black anodized and lengthy at just over 9-inches – don't forget this receiver has to accommodate the lengthy 3½-inch Magnum shells.

Note the extra-wide opening in front of the trigger. The safety button you will see is also oversized. The bolt is black. The synthetic stock has over molded grips at both the pistol grip area and the forend. These have a nice rubbery feel resulting in no slippage. The barrel wears a vent rib with steel mid bead and glow-type sight out at the muzzle. The rib tapers from .375 at the breech to .275 at the muzzle.

Let's talk a bit about the operating system. Right in front of the chamber there are seven holes. When a 2¾-inch shell is fired the crimp opens up, but all seven holes come into play bleeding off gases to operate the action. However, when a 3-inch shell is fired, the crimp opens up to block the three port holes closest to the front of the chamber. Thus less powder gases are used (or needed) to operate the action with this more power-ful shell. When a 3½-inch 12-gauge shell is fired the crimp opens up to cover four of the port holes closest to the front of the chamber, leaving the front three holes to operate the action – all that's needed with this even more powerful shotshell. No other shotgun offers this unique type of gas-operating system.

I was shooting 1-ounce reloads at only 1,115 feet per second, so they were very light. Still the Wood Tech operated without malfunction every time. Further, the recoil was very light. I had others shoot the Wood Tech with factory 12-gauge target loads. Unsolicited from me, both shooters said the gun was very light in recoil. In fact I'd say those shooters were more impressed with the low recoil than I was.

Of course, the unique gas-operating system is major in low recoil with the Versa-max, but the recoil pad is very instrumental

as well. Before talking about the recoil pad it's important to convey that I never cleaned the gun, yet the mag tube still looked clean due to the self-cleaning action. Remington says it has fired the Versamax thousands of times without cleaning.

The recoil pad is the same one used on the other Versamax models, as well as on some 870 pump gun models. Called the Super Cell Pad, it is super cushiony and very recoil absorbent. The pad is also fairly thick at nearly 1.4-inches.

The NRA's *American Rifleman* magazine calls the Versamax Wood Tech their "Shot-gun of the Year" I can see why. In shooting this test gun 200 times there was never a malfunction. Further, the gun has a lively feel. Despite the light reloads I was shoot-ing, the empties were tossed with authority many feet – so no touchy ejection problems were encountered. I really like the idea of the black comb inserts that easily popped on and off to change drop at comb heights. From my perspective I'd suggest the lowest comb insert for hunting, the medium height insert for sporting and the highest comb in-sert for trap. With the latter you will still be able to see the rising trap target as you pull the trigger. The comb inserts go a very long way into making this one of the most ver-satile 12 gauge shotguns on the market. No wonder Remington calls it the Versamax.

SPECIFICATIONS

Gauge: 12 gauge
Action: Semi-auto, gas operated
Weight: 8 pounds .5 ounce
Barrel: 28 inch Pro Bore
Chokes: Four Pro Bore supplied
Stock: Adjustable LOP via inserts between the recoil pad and the back of the stock. Adjustable comb heights with three comb inserts supplied.
Suggested Retail: $1,630
Manufacturer: Remington Arms, Madison, N.C. www.remington.com.

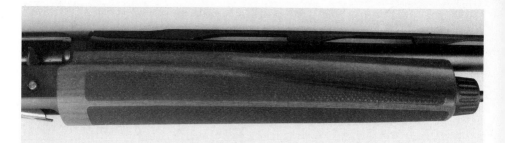

The Wood Tech forend.

The Wood Tech butt stock features the overmolded grips with the rubbery feel and the black comb insert.

Two additional, higher black comb inserts are included in the Versamax package. These comb inserts just pop in and out.

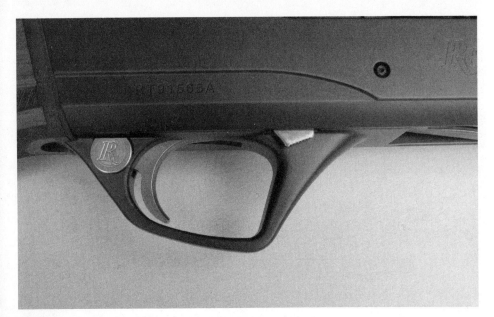

Note the oversized safety and the wide opening in the trigger guard.

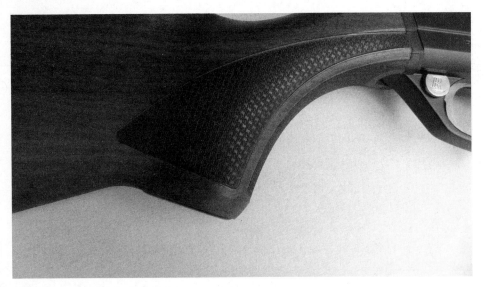

The overmolded grip on the butt stock.

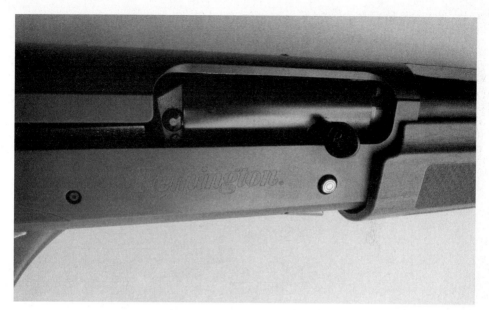

The bolt is black.

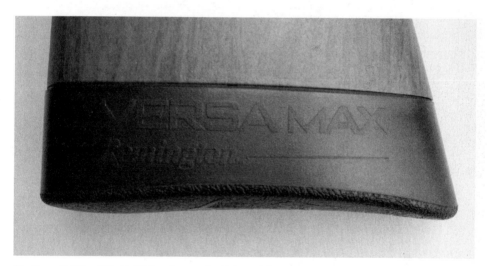

The Super Cell Recoil Pad is thick and very soft with lots of give upon recoil.

Four ProBore chokes come with this Wood Tech Versamax.

CHAPTER ELEVEN

USED SHOTGUNS FOR CLAY SHOOTING

L et's look at a few of the used shotguns which many believe will be ideal for sporting clays. Perhaps one or more of these suggestions will pique your interest, either for yourself, one of your offspring, or your significant other. One or more of these suggestions might surprise you.

BROWNING CITORI

When someone approaches me about what used shotgun to purchase, especially for an entry level over/under, a used Citori seems to always come first to my mind. Relatively speaking these shotguns are reliable no matter how much they have been shot previously. While Browning has added many various sporting, trap and skeet models to their line, all Citoris are made on the same rugged action which features a full-width crossbolt, as opposed to the barrels pivoting on trunnions, as well as a full-width bolt that moves forward upon closing to engage the huge lug milled into the bottom of the monobloc. No doubt most importantly, dual recoil lugs that are milled into the bottom of the monobloc extend all the way through two square-cut openings in the bottom of the receiver. Incidentally, for many years Citoris were made without a monobloc. The chamber section in years past was an integral part of the barrels, always known

as chopper lump barrels.

The best entry-level choice here would probably be a basic used Lightning model. That one has a slightly open grip and the rounded Lightning-style forend. From a strictly looks standpoint, I've always thought this was also the best looking Citori. A solid used 12-gauge Citori will not break any serious sporting shooter's bank account.

REMINGTON 1100

As well more than four million have been made, a good Remington 1100 is easily found on the used-gun market. While an 1100 may not stand up to the pounding a Citori will take, parts for the gun are easy to find and relatively inexpensive. What makes the 1100 great is that this one has excellent *feel,* and don't discount this gas-operated gun's minimal recoil.

Other gas semi-autos have come along over the years, and quite a few of them. The vast array of these newer semi-autos has put the 1100 on the figurative back burner among sporting clays shooters. But new or relatively new shooters are not in sporting clays Master Class, or skeet or trap AA Class. For shooters who are rather new to the game or who want to get a new person started with sporting or the other clay target games the 1100 is both ideal and a bargain.

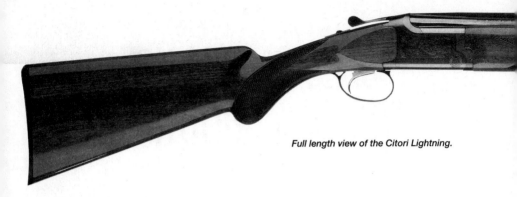

Full length view of the Citori Lightning.

No telling how much game the millions of 1100s have brought down, or how many clay targets these semis have pulverized. From time to time it's possible to pick up a used 1100 at an eye-popping price. Just because the used 1100 price might be low compared to today's new and high-tech autoloaders, doesn't mean you'll be buying that figurative pig in the poke. These guns handle well. They need to be kept clean, but no semi-auto is easier and quicker to clean than an 1100.

KRIEGOFF MODEL 32

Evidently the competition shotgun world has seen the value of Krieghoff's original model 32. Fifteen years ago these over/unders could be bought for about half what these guns demand on the used market these days. Still, I think the 32 can be a bargain because almost all new competition shotguns have escalated in price quite a bit over the last five to 10 years.

Internally the 32 is much the same gun as the modern-day Krieghoff K-80. Further, obtaining model 32 parts is never an issue because in almost every case a K-80 part will fit a 32. The guns are engineered with that feature. The one main difference with a K-80 is that it has a case hardened steel surface. The 32s do not. Consequently, the

K-80 is undoubtedly more durable, but there are many, many Krieghoff 32s that have not only withstood the test of time, but have fired hundreds of thousands of rounds or more.

And the 32s are still a Krieghoff, through and through. There's great feel and there's great factory support from Ottsville, Pa.

BERETTA 682

The 682 was one of the first Beretta over/unders that ended up being highly favored among shotgun competitors. Introduced in 1982, the concept of two relatively small round bolts that extended forward upon closing, nestling into two milled out circular areas on the sides of the top chamber area caused some to question the strength of this locking system. In effect it's the shoulders of this Beretta series that act has recoil lugs.

The 682 model has certainly withstood the test of time. Not only is the lock up strong, this is another shotgun with outstanding feel. Further yet, with no underlocking lugs (Krieghoffs, and a few others, do not have underlocking lugs either) receiver depth is minimal. Theoretically this puts the forend hand slightly closer to the barrels, enhancing the gun's point ability. At least that's the theory.

Generally a 682 will weigh less than a Krieghoff 32 or K-80. Many sporting clays shooters tend toward slightly lighter over/unders since considerable muzzle movement is required on many sporting courses, especially when it comes to doubles.

BERETTA 303 SEMI

While the many different models of the 391 and the newer A400 Xplor are very hard to beat, don't consider the old Model 303 a no-account. This is one excellent gas-operated semi-auto. Though they are getting tougher and tougher to find on the used market some diligent searching can put you on to one of these early Berettas. It's no wonder the 303s are difficult to find as so many serious shooters have discovered them. I know one lady who scoops up every one she can. Who knows how many she has stashed under the bed and in various closets.

Despite the 303 being well recognized in competition clay target circles, the price tag they usually wear won't shrink your wallet or melt your plastic. As with many of these used suggestions stocks can also be purchased after market in case you want a higher or lower drop at comb and/or heel. A different recoil pad can often be the answer to a longer or shorter length of pull as well.

WINCHESTER SUPER X-1

This selection should be of no surprise to many of you. Quite a few serious sporting clays buffs shoot the Winchester Super X

A Custom Stock?

With any of these shotgun suggestions, once you make the purchase, shoot the gun for a reasonable length of time and affirm that you like it, maybe your gun-buying nest egg will have been built up a bit by then. If all of the above is true, you might next consider a custom-made stock for the used sporting gun you've come to love.

But there's another consideration here. If you've made an average deal on the used gun itself, you are probably going to get your money back out of it should you decide to sell it. If you invest in a custom stock, it probably is going to be impossible to get that money back out , especially if your personal stock dimensions are too much different than what the average guys feels is right for him. Despite this potential problem, it is probably a good idea to invest in a custom-made stock to your dimensions if you really like the gun you are shooting and if you hit well with it. Will you hit better with a new gun? Or will you hit better with a gun you certainly like that has some custom tweaks made here and there so that stock fit is even better than before? You have to decide this.

Before you invest high three figures or even four figures into a stock for your used gun don't forget that a longer or shorter recoil pad can create the ideal length of pull you want. If it's a higher comb that you want to try, don't forget adding moleskin to the gun's comb. Moleskin is even soft and not abrasive to your face.

Model 1. With its all milled parts (relatively), this was a gas semi-auto that was ahead of its time. These guns have long been recognized for their durability. Nu-Line Guns (www.nulineguns.com) now has lots of parts in inventory for this model. Maybe they can even make some parts when needed.

The Super X-1 is another of the shotguns that I favor for its good *feel*. This one tends to be soft on recoil and it wears good looks. Enough said on this one since it's fairly well known to so many of you.

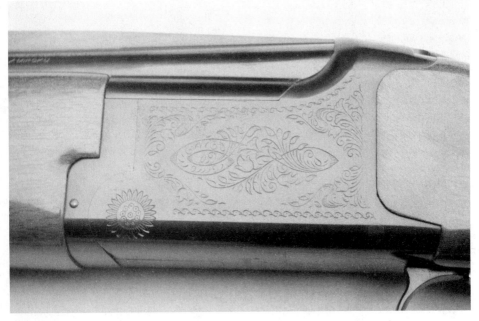

Close-up look at the Citori receiver.

The look of the Krieghoff Model 32 receiver.

A new stock on a used gun helps customize fit for the new owner.

Don Lavely prepares to shoot his Remington 1100.

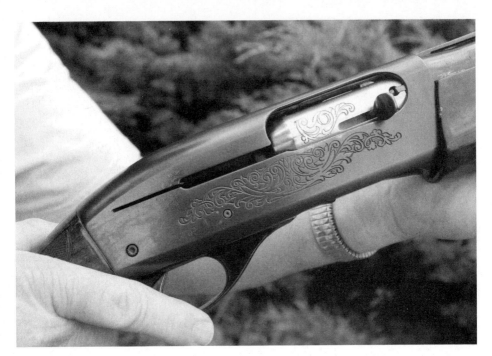

Close up view of the Remington 1100.

It is the blued "shoulders" on this 682 Beretta Silver Pigeon S receiver that also act as recoil lugs.

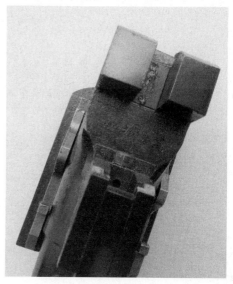

The two recoil lugs on the base of the Citori monobloc dovetail into the two square areas milled out of the bottom of the Citori receiver. The result is a tall receiver from top to bottom, but nonetheless a very strong one.

The two squares milled out of the bottom of the Citori receiver accept the dual recoil lugs milled into the bottom of the monobloc.

CHAPTER TWELVE

THERE'S MORE TO RELOADING THAN JUST SAVING MONEY

It may be an incorrect approach to break reloaders down into two categories, but let me propose that one category of reloaders shoots factory ammo in tournaments, while their reloads are shot in practice. But there's another category of reloaders who shoot reloads for both practice and registered competition. In this latter category I'm guessing there can be a lot of differences. There are expert reloaders and the not-so-expert reloaders. It's the really expert reloaders that I'm addressing.

Cliff Moller at Briley Manufacturing suggested this approach to me. Cliff considers himself in the first category above. He shoots factory ammo in tournaments and reloads for practice. He went on to tell me he feels poorly any time he shoots factory ammo in practice, it's like he's guilty of not being the proper custodian of his company's money. When it comes to reloading, he uses a Spolar, noted for the high number of shells it can produce in record time, but he has not experimented at all and uses the same primer, powder, wad, hull and shot recipe that Spolar set up for him at their factory.

Advance to a day Cliff was practicing with some other folks and Cliff runs out of his own 20-gauge reloads. He was shooting with skeet All-American Lindsay Plesko. They were shooting doubles, and Cliff was lamenting the fact that he couldn't hit any-thing – which, believe me, is a total stretch. Anyway, Lindsay offered Cliff a box of her 20-gauge reloads, which she apologized, "This box – they are all my rejects – they look bad – but you will find they shoot well." Obviously, from a cosmetic standpoint these were not the perfect crimp shells she used in gaining All-American status.

So Cliff slips two of them into his tubed Perazzi and voila, he cleans up – never missed a bird the entire round. Further, he told me those Plesko reloads were just obliterating targets, but he wasn't being bounced off the gun which is so important in any doubles shooting. Up until this point Moller had not considered that Lindsay had put any extra thought into those 20-gauge reloads, but he soon discovered that she had spent an unbelievable amount of time, money, energy and patterning work into developing this 20-gauge reload and no she's not about to share her recipe. Why should she? You need to spend the time, money, energy and pattern paper work that she did to find out.

One point here is that Plesko has more total confidence in this reload than she ever could have in a factory load, and we all know what confidence means in any clay target game. Another point is that she's a woman, and how many of you males considered that such a person could concoct better reloads than you? Or how many of you females think that reloading is just for the guys? Don't forget, she's an All American. There's something very positive going on here.

In patterning Lindsay is striving for pattern evenness, a lack of any pattern holes, and a lack of pellet concentration. I think with most of her early reloads she didn't get that result. One or two patterns with one reload showed this was not the powder, wad, primer, shot combination she was looking for. So it's back to the reloading machine to come up with a new recipe to try (always sticking with published recipes). Also, in addition to changing the load, she also tries changing the choke. She uses pattern paper, not a pattern plate, and she says the Houston Gun Club has an excellent pattern facility. Does your club have that feature? Lindsay has been experimenting and developing reloads for years, but it has only been recently that she has achieved a reload that she is especially happy with. She started off with a single-stage reloader but now uses a MEC 9000G.

Another example is John Castillo. He and Cliff are very close, and Moller told me that John is constantly working on perfecting his reloads – checking velocities, being true to himself about any recoil reduction sensations, but, most important, spending an inordinate amount of time at the patterning board to determine how his reloads are producing. You are probably already aware, but if you're not – Castillo is another All American.

Moller suggested, and I'm sure he's right, than there are many, many skeet shooters who are just as professional in concocting truly great ammo after plenty of experimentation – the proof of this pudding in the hundreds of pattern papers or pattern plates that have been perforated over the years. Reloaders in this category know when they have come up with something better. Because they know their confidence can't help but soar when they get down to serious practice or start shooting a tournament.

Another Moller suggestion was that he thinks most of these reloaders in this latter category reload slow, maybe even on a single-stage reloader, though not necessarily. Sometimes I hear talk from a guy who claims he reloads X number of shells in 30 minutes – the X-factor always being a high one. In my view we should not reload for speed. We can only do our best at this pursuit if we really slow down, carefully take our time. I'll bet Lindsay Plesko and John Castillo reload very carefully.

How many squib loads do you turn out per 1,000 rounds? The number should be zero. One or two at most. Anyone encountering five or more squib loads per 1,000 rounds is hardly an expert reloader. I'm not talking about primer dents and the primer not going off.

There are many of us who genuinely enjoy reloading. I often fib at folks. "The only reason I shoot clay targets is so I have something to reload." While not entirely true, perhaps you get my point. Reloading is enjoyable. After all, we're essentially creating something from individual components that don't look, feel or react like the finished product. Personally, I spend an inordinate amount of time using my brain pounding this keyboard, then going over and over what I've written. Plus there's the computer scut work that is part of every modern business. Consequently, I usually can't wait to get away from this computer, pull the black cover off one of my reloaders and sort of put my mind in neutral while I start working the operating handle and inserting wads – slowly of course.

I'm guessing that many of you feel the same way. You work so hard at what you do that it's relaxing to get away from the turmoil and stress to just sit down and crank out 100 or so shells. Some with stressful jobs will disagree, if they do not reload. Many non-reloaders look at this pursuit as dreadful, mundane, boring and/or other negatives. But reloading is what you make of it, and I guarantee that thousands and thousands of shotgun shooters love to create their own shotshells.

Further, if you take up the past time, work your way slowly toward the expertise of Lindsay Plesko and John Castillo. You won't make the progress they have made in a week or month or even a year, but life is a journey and becoming an expert like the above two can be your journey.

IN CASE YOU ARE NOT A RELOADER

Most skeet shooters are reloaders, at least the ones I know. This is not true with trap shooters and with sporting clays buffs. Why? While trap shooters were once very big on reloading, the price of competition factory 12-gauge shells has gone up. The price of many imported 12-gauge shells, as well as some USA-made 12 bore shells that are not designed for competition shooting, have not gone up nearly as much. Consequently, many of the trap shooters I know just buy 12-gauge imported or lower-priced USA-made stuff. In many cases this is true of sporting clays shooters where most of the events are for 12 gauge. Plus most sporting clays tournaments do not permit reloads. This was once true of the World Skeet Shoot – only factory fodder – but that rule was relaxed decades back.

The high cost of today's factory .410 and 28 gauge shells makes reloading these two gauges in particular more than sensible. As reloaders we can make great 28 and .410 loads for a fraction of the cost we have to pay for factory ammo in those two gauges. If you do not reload you should consider it.

Don't start with the 12 or 20 as reloads in those gauges do not offer as much savings as reloading the 28 and .410. So start reloading 28-gauge shells, in case you are not already doing that.

Further, the 28 is an excellent gauge for a lot of clay target practice. The 28 hulls are not as easy to come by as the 12s and 20s, but they are available. The ¾ ounce of shot in the 28 means less shot is used, although 20-gauge wads and reloading data are now offered for ¾ ounce 20-gauge loads. Still, comparing the savings of 20-gauge factory ammo over 28-gauge factory fodder – the 28 reloads save you more money.

SOME RELOADING TIPS

Sewers aide

Dan Ahern wrote me about having shot bridge (get stuck) in the shot drop tube, especially when reloading the .410. However, shot can bridge in the shot drop tube in other gauges when larger shot sizes are used. With the 28 gauge, I can get away with size 7½ maybe 99.9 percent of the time without any shot bridging. If I go to #7 magnum shot, I have seen bridging more than once. So I stick with #7½ magnum as the biggest shot I load in the 28 gauge. With my 20-gauge reloads for pest pigeons I stick with #7 Magnum for my largest shot size – no bridging. With 12 gauge pest pigeon loads I have no trouble with #6 Magnum bridging. Of course, most all of you know that when shot catches (bridges) in the shot drop tube it's going to come out with the next shell we load. What a mess results.

Dan Ahern's girlfriend came up with a shot-bridging solution. She suggested a product called Sewers Aide which prevents thread from breaking against the needle because of its slick properties. Dan puts Sewers Aide on a cleaning patch and pushes this through the shot drop tube with a cleaning rod about every 200 rounds. He says the shot bridging problem has thus been solved, evidently the Sewers Aid providing a more slippery surface inside to the shot drop tube.

Pattern control powder baffle

There can be a problem of powder leakage around the charging bar of MEC reloaders. Ron Reiber at Hodgdon Powders told me to check with Kevin Lewis at Downrange (Duster Wad makers). Downrange bought Pattern Control, another shotshell wad maker, in 2003. With that purchase the Pattern Control Powder Baffle was included. Many of you may already know about this product. The technology of the spring-loaded insert at the base of the Powder Baffle is what helps prevent powders from leaking out around the charge bar. Powder leakage here is especially a problem with ball-type powders like Winchester 296 and Hodgdon's 110, although powder leakage around the charge bar can occur with other powders as well. No doubt many of you use this Powder Baffle. An interior baffle in this product keeps the same weight of powder just above the powder bushing no matter how much or how little powder is in the powder bottle. The Pattern Control Powder Baffle largely solves the problem if powder leakage around the charge bar.

Downrange

Since we're talking Downrange and Duster Wads let's take a close look at wads this company offers. Certainly many of you rely on Duster wads for your reloading, but just as certainly many of you do not. Thus why not make you shooters in the latter category more aware of what Downrange offers?

For example, did you know that this company offers biodegradable wads? No, these are not fiber-type filler wads. They look just like a normal plastic wad, with wad fingers and a bottom section that seals perfectly and is at least partially collapsible to ensure perfect crimps. Called OXO-BIO, there are five different style wads in this category, some for internally-tapered hulls. OXO-BIO wads are offered in 12, 20 and 28 gauge, including a wad for $\frac{7}{8}$-ounce 12-gauge loads. There are also Duster replacement wads for most Winchester, Federal, and Remington hulls.

Another wad category is their Spolar Gold. These wads are of premium quality and custom made to plastic specifications suggested by Spolar – the reloading machine manufacturer. They are super slick for better feeding, leave little or no plastic residue in barrels and screw-in chokes, and the wad is designed to protect the shot all the way to the end of the barrel, at which point the wad fingers flare. This flare, combined with the very light weight of the wad, creates a parachute effect – with the wad dropping harmlessly away from the pellets, allowing a denser and shorter shot string.

Another Downrange (Duster) wad category is their Value Wads. In this line are knock-offs of the Remington Figure 8 and the Federal S3. Made from a "baseline" plastic these will help reloaders keep costs down.

So far I'm only touching the surface of all the different wads offered by this company. Also in the line are wads formerly made by Windjammer, Versalite, Pattern Control and the new XL series. The XL wads, there are five of them, allow 12 gauge reloads from $\frac{7}{8}$ ounce to $1\frac{1}{8}$ ounce. These XL series wads are made to fit virtually all the different hull styles. There's more on the Website – which I suggest you peruse – www.downrangemfg.com.

Mec Simple Addition charge bar

You've maybe seen their ads for decades the "Simple Addition" Charge Bar for MEC reloaders. There are 43 MEC Powder Bushings and 23 MEC Shot Charge bars. With the Simple Addition you just buy one. Via adjustments on either end of this adjustable bar you can dial in both the powder and shot charge you've taken from your published reliable source of reloading data. Each bar comes with a chart for both powder and shot allowing 487 settings. This one bar can be used for all gauges, plus you can load not only lead but steel and bismuth as well. The unit is lead shot adjustable from $\frac{1}{2}$ to $2\frac{1}{4}$ ounces. Check the accompanying sketch for a better idea of how this "Simple Addition" works. Their website is www.multi-scalecharge.com.

A good shotshell crimp is only the beginning to producing a top performing reload. Next comes the pattern board, and then followed by experimentation to produce a better patterning load; seeking patterns without "holes," patterns with no pellet concentration, patterns with evenness throughout, and, hopefully, with less recoil.

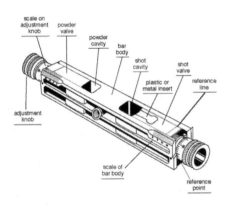

Schematic of the Simple Addition Multi Stage MEC charge bar.

The Pattern Control Powder Baffle is attached to a MEC powder bottle. The spring-loaded insert (top of the photo) helps prevent powder leakage around the powder bushing/charge bar. A baffle inside this product also helps with consistent powder charge weight drops.

CHAPTER THIRTEEN

COMPANIES IN THE CLAY TARGET BUSINESS

There are an untold number of businesses that cater to the shotgunner. Perhaps you know a number of them – or not. This section is devoted to making you aware of a few of the businesses that are especially well known for their knowledge of clay target products and how they are able to help clay target shooters – whether that help might be in shotgun selection or any of the related products that can help you break more targets. Let's get started.

BRILEY MANUFACTURING

Briley Manufacturing had its beginnings in the early 1970s. These were the days of a booming oil economy all around Texas, but especially around Houston. Jess Briley worked at many jobs making products for the oil industry at that time. He was a gifted machinist, but more importantly Jess was called upon time and time again to figure something out, usually how to make a product, and usually it involved some type of problem his engineering-degree bosses could not answer.

Cliff Moller of Briley Manufacturing told me that Jess never stayed long at these jobs. Always opinionated, Jess often battled company engineers when they did not agree with his vision on how to tackle projects. This tended to make him unpopular. With the oil industry booming, he simply left, quickly finding another job with a company that was

doing something interesting. A man with his talents was always needed.

Jess was invited to a local gun club where they were shooting skeet. One trip was all it took and he was hooked on clay target shooting. In those days, the four-gauge game of skeet required four guns, usually four Remington 1100 semi-autos were used, or a four barrel set – usually a Krieghoff Model 32 with barrels in all four of the skeet gauges. Neither of these was an option as four semi-autos or a Krieghoff four-barrel set were not in Jess Briley's price range.

Jess more or less did little else but work and read, a combination that no doubt helped his ever-thinking brain to solve problems, in this case a skeet gun price problem. He ended up buying a well-used Winchester 101 over/under. Using a milling machine in his garage he drilled out iron pipe to 20, 28 and .410 gauge bores, then milled the exterior of those pipes (tubes) to fit the barrels of the used 101. That's how Briley got started in the shotgun business.

During the early 1970s a guy in California, Claude Purbaugh, came out with full length aluminum skeet tubes in 20, 28 and .410 that were made to precision fit inside 12-gauge over/under barrels. Purbaugh tubes came with separate extractors that were not permanently attached to the sub-gauge tubes. Those types of extractors might not have been that much of a big deal at the time for shooters, but Jess Briley started thinking there had to be a better way. Thus he invented sub-gauge tubes with integral extractors. All the sub-gauge tubes made for decades now come with the extractors attached to the sub-gauge tubes. If you have ever inspected the extractor attachment to one of these tubes you know this had to be quite an engineering feat – to come up with the idea in the first place – as well as figure out a way to mill out the extractor slots – and do that cost effectively.

Jess was still working an oil industry job at the time, now about 1972, but he started turning out aluminum sub-gauge tubes right from his garage. By 1974 this was a hobby, but that hobby started to pick up momentum about the time. Cliff Moller met Briley's daughter Linda. They married when Cliff was a senior at the University of Texas. Not many months after Cliff's graduation Jess offered, "Why don't you come to work for me in my garage?"

Thus, with a handshake, a partnership was born. They are still partners, and Jess still comes to work every day. It was a number of years after 1972 before sub-gauge tubes became overwhelming popular. "There were plenty of months when neither of us could draw a paycheck," said Moller.

One very big problem with their production was that skeet was seasonal. At that time the World Skeet Shooting Championships took place the third week in July. After that skeet shooting went dead. It was not until many years later that the World Skeet Shooting Championships were moved to October, a move that was spearheaded by Hal du Pont who was the mover/shaker at the National Skeet Shooting Association (NSSA) at that time.

Briley's sub-gauge tube business fell off dramatically after the World Skeet Shoot in July. For four to five months there's was too little work, so employees had to be laid off. Most of them were quite skilled machinists so by the time Briley was ready to hire them back at the start of the next clay target shooting season those previous employees had found other work. So new folks had to be hired and trained anew. Further, making sub-gauge tubes was never a booming business. There simply aren't that many skeet shooters in the world, and once these shooters own a tubed over/under they're set for life. Neither the tubes nor the guns wear out. Even today only a few Briley employees are involved in the skilled job of making sub-gauge tubes.

To make a real business out of Briley Manufacturing more had to be added. That's where screw-in chokes saved the Briley day. Many of the popular shotguns of the day (sporting clays had still not reached our shores) came with relatively thin barrels. Consequently, threading a shotgun for screw-in chokes didn't offer enough metal to safely do it. But Jess Briley put his figurative thinking cap on and eventually came up with his idea of thin-wall screw-in chokes. Not only was the metal thin on these chokes (thousands of these special chokes are still made today by the way), Jess designed them with square threads, which made them plenty strong despite the chokes themselves being thin.

Right along with the thin-wall movement or very shortly thereafter shotgun manufacturers were beginning to offer their new shotguns with screw-in chokes. A number of those manufacturers came to Briley for advice and at least some of those contracted with Briley to actually make their screw-in chokes for them. This was a big shot in the Briley financial arm.

In the later 1980s, sporting clays had arrived and that's when the screw choke business shot through the figurative roof. Even today, screw choke making means about 50 percent of the Briley Manufacturing business. But it was the arrival of sporting clays that allowed this screw choke business to mushroom. The fact that thousands of sporting clays shooters bought sub-gauge tubes for their over/under sporting guns so they could compete effectively in small gauge sporting events didn't hurt the Briley bottom line a bit either.

But sub-gauge tubes and screw-in chokes were only the Briley start. "If we have been successful it is because we keep turning over every stone," said Moller. "Believe me Jess and I have made some business mistakes. But we are on the creative side of the firearms business. Everyone who is creative makes mistakes. That's part of the 'creation' business. Consequently, a creative person must never fear failure because failures are going to occur from time to time. Sure, we have our production side, too, also very important, but we wouldn't have anything to produce if it wasn't for our creativity, especially Jess's creativity."

I have personally been close to the Briley business for over 30 years, and while I'm familiar with Jess Briley's genius I know that Cliff Moller has genius of his own. His mind is sharp – always thinking, always calculating. Next a guy named Claudio Salassa came along with an idea for Briley, and Cliff jumped on it. From South Africa, Claudio wanted to us the Briley facilities to accurize pistols for competitive shooters. More or less this is done by machining parts to extremely tight tolerances, for which Briley was already well known. Claudio thus heads up the Briley handgun division today.

The next figurative rock to be successfully turned over was Briley going into the gunsmithing business. Over the next few decades, the Briley name has become well known for not only working on handguns, but especially their work on shotguns – which can involve repair, re-sleeving barrels,

tightening actions, especially any type of gun work that you don't want to entrust to your local guy.

In 1997, a storied gun club was about to go under financially – the Greater Houston Gun Club. The renowned Grant Ilseng taught there all through the 1970s and 1980s. Most of the traps had been sold as the gun club cannibalized itself. Cliff and a small group of very intelligent shooting companions (both men and women) collaborated to convert this shooting tomb into a thriving vibrant club its membership can be proud of, as well as serving as an American model of how to resurrect a gun club in trouble. This involved a group of 10 to 12 members on the new Board of Directors that put their money, hearts and souls into the project. This group had many board meetings trying to resolve the gun club's financial crisis. There were emotional meetings, as well as many differing ideas about how to pull the gun club out of the financial doldrums. What Cliff learned in all these meetings is that some of his ideas weren't always the best, some of the other Board members ideas weren't always the best, but with 10 to 12 very smart folks all on the same page, the Board always made the best decisions. This is an excellent life lesson for any Board members of a gun club. Learning that your ideas aren't always the best ideas can be discomforting at the least, but other ideas could be the best for your gun club.

One of the Briley partners in Spain was trying to persuade Briley to take on distributorship of Mattarelli traps in the USA and Mexico. But Cliff wasn't much interested, mainly because the rest of the business was doing very well, and he didn't want to take the time to start yet another new project. But when Cliff was too busy to check out the samples Mattarelli sent Jess told him, "I'll look at these Mattarelli traps." A few minutes later Jess came back and said, "You better take a look at these. They're pretty special."

And thus became the start of the Briley/Mattarelli relationship. When the Greater Houston Gun Club was able to build their first sporting clays course that layout was set up with one of the first sporting models that Mattarelli ever made. That sporting course was a great testing ground for Briley/Mattarelli, and many trap design changes and innovations came from experiences at that club. The sale of Mattarelli traps thus became yet another part of the burgeoning Briley business.

Next came electronic coin boxes to help gun clubs better control payment for the number of targets shot. This technology was started in Europe, but Briley improved on the design of coin boxes, made them more reliable when exposed to the elements. In more recent times Briley has perfected the use of wireless "wands" that release targets in response to the shooter's voice command of "Pull." Perfect target releases do not tend to be as important on sporting clays as often targets are hidden behind vegetation or whatever, plus some targets start from very long distances. Obviously, in skeet and trap shooting the release of the target with no time delay is extremely important. "We are working on new voice releases for trap shooting that are going to be much less expensive than those currently in use and being sold."

"Our release wands work great on sporting clays courses as they can count targets, all to the benefit of the gun clubs," said Moller. This is the Briley I-Pull System which was brought to Moller via email by Barak Dar, an Israeli immigrant electronic engineer from Minnesota. This system counts targets by listening to the recoil of the shot.

In Briley advertisements you have probably seen photos of the Briley Showroom store. Yes, this is yet another part of the figurative rock turning that has turned into another significant element of the overall Briley business. The guns most often seen in the showroom are highly desirable, but older guns – though other shotguns are in abundance as well. John Herlitz is the "Chief" of this retail store business, a recent transplant from Beretta USA. "Everyone here is proud to have John on our team," says Moller. "His attitude and personality are a perfect fit with Briley."

Briley Manufacturing is thus an integral part of what is Americana – a business that was started with a unique and original idea, as well as on a figurative shoestring brought to fruition with hard work, long work hours, creativity, ingenuity and the business sense of continually turning over figurative rocks, not always successful, but new ideas intended to keep the business growing and growing.

Where will Briley be five years from now? "I have no idea," Cliff came back. "We'll just keep trying to turn over those rocks for ideas. Some will work out. Some will not. Either way I have no idea how any of our new innovations will turn out, but we have no fear of failing here."

Jess Briley, founder of Briley Manufacturing, has always been an outstanding mechanical problem solver. That's Jess Briley in the foreground working at the drafting board, with Cliff Moller in the background looking on.

Hannah Manion is one of the sales stars at Briley. In addition to working out of the Houston office, Hannah is on the sporting road a lot marketing Briley products.

The Briley retail store is located in the front portion of Briley Manufacturing.

This target release was invented through Briley. The system is capable of throwing every target perfectly timed, but perhaps more importantly the system counts the number of shells fired. This counting of the shells fired, and thus targets thrown, is very important to a gun club's bottom line.

Steve Power, Sales Manager Non-Regulated Products Division, has been with Briley for decades and is highly regarded in this company.

MORGAN OPTICAL

Harold Morgan sold his first pair of shooting glasses in 1979, and he's still going strong. This is a family business, and Harold has his two sons, Wayne and Tom, working with him. It is an interview with Wayne that forms the backbone of this report. Harold Morgan, an optician, and his sons devote full time to the shooting glass business.

Based in the western part of New York – in Olean, the company enjoys walk-in shooting glass trade, but their main sales are done via the phone and through the Internet. Morgan Optical ads appear in most all the shooting magazines, but Wayne Morgan did tell me after I asked where the bulk of their business came. "No question – it's satisfied customers and their shooter friends that they refer to us."

Harold Morgan met Bud Decot at the Grand American and was impressed with what he was doing to help shooters see targets better, rather than shooting with their dress glasses. By the 1990s Morgan Optical started using Randolph Engineering products. Now for many years Morgan Optical has worked with Randolph's Rich-

Briley Manufacturing.

ard Waszkiewicz helping to develop their Ranger and Sporter frames. Today Morgan is the largest dealer of Randolph shooting products.

"These glasses are all American-made – which our company thinks is very important," said Wayne.

"We've found that a satisfied customer is apt to tell his shooting friends," said Wayne. "On the contrary, an unsatisfied customer will probably speak his displeasure about the glasses he bought to everyone in the gun club. Customer satisfaction is Number One with us."

At Morgan Optical, lens materials include CR-39, polycarbonate and Trivex. While all three of these lens materials can be used, it's also important to note that Randolph offers four different frame styles, each of which can be ideal for specific shooting circumstances. Any of these

frames can be purchased with a myriad of different non-prescription lens colors, and this is a significant part of the Morgan Optical business, but what the company specializes in is prescription lens shooting glasses. Depending upon the prescription needed, making the ideal shooting glasses for a customer can be wrought with pitfalls. This is where Morgan Optical excels, not in the pitfalls but in customer satisfaction. Another specialty of Morgan Optical is dealing with very high Rx prescriptions. Many other shooting glass makers cannot make lenses with a high Rx. When such shooting glass makers can't make such a prescription they often refer their customers to Morgan Optical.

"There are a number of ways to make a prescription shooting lens. None of them is necessarily wrong. But our decades of experience results in our being able to select the right way to make lenses for varying circumstances – as well as knowing what lens material is best for a specific shooter," said Wayne.

The Ranger Sporter frame is great for a number of circumstances, but this frame was developed especially for prescription shooting lenses. Offered in black and brushed pewter frame colors, the Sporter is also an ideal every-day frame. Temples are wrap-around so the glasses stay firmer in place. I don't like glasses that keep slipping down on my nose, thus constantly require pushing the frames back upward. As a shooter you have no doubt experienced these types of frames.

Where the optical center of a lens is placed is critical, and Morgan Optical can vary the optical center of your lenses. "Depending upon what game you shoot – trap, sporting clays, skeet, cowboy action, hunting, rifle, handgun and more," said Wayne.

There are 11 different lens colors available from the company including Pale Yellow, Medium Yellow, Orange, Vermilion, Light Purple, Dark Purple, Brown, and CMT. The newest colors to hit the line are the HD 58 and the HD 59 Light. Further, the company offers a virtually unlimited line of custom colors. Obviously, clear non-tinted lenses are also available.

One of the new lens colors Wayne is particularly excited about would be their Autumn Gold Transition. "Seeing better is all about contrast," said Wayne. "These Autumn Gold Transition lenses are great because they give exceptional contrast. Also since these are 'transition' lenses they turn darker as light intensity increases. They are ideal for many hunting situations, some clay target shooting situations, but what we are finding is that this lens color, because of the increased contrast, is excellent for driving early and late in the day, even at night, as well as when it's foggy, rainy or cloudy.

One customer called me to say that he was driving home from a trap shoot during a South Dakota snow storm. Visual conditions were pretty bad so he figured what the heck, he'd try his new Autumn Gold Transition lenses. He told me there is no question that he could see farther through the snow with those lenses."

Another new lens shade Wayne and Morgan Optical are very high on would be their CMT shade. CMT is the acronym for Color Mag Technology. "The bottom line with CMT lenses is that up to 250 percent of orange light can pass through. Since most clay targets are orange that means very enhanced target recognition," Wayne explained. There's a good explanation of how this CMT stuff works to a shooter's advantage on the Website at www.morganoptical.net. And there's a great deal of additional information about the various Randolph frames, lens colors and more.

Morgan Optical also specializes in polarizing lenses in High Contrast Brown, which are offered in varying frames, as well as clip on type glasses. This High Contrast Brown lens is not overly dark, but with a polarizing lens you don't need as dark a lens.

Yet another item from Morgan Optical that is certainly taking off would be their clip-on frames/lenses. There have not been many shooters who have given positive marks to clip-on type glasses, but that situation is changing. That's because these Morgan clip-ons are made specifically for shooters wearing the Randolph Sporter frames. The idea is to buy one pair of clear lenses to fit your Sporter Rx, and then add clip-on glasses in various colors as needed. What makes these new clip-ons ideal is that the lens surface is just as big as your Sporter lenses. Consequently, when you view virtually any target – a high bird, low bird, a bird off to the side – all you see is the color of the lens clip-on you are wearing. In other words you never see the clear lens at all since the clip-ons totally cover the clear lenses. There can be big cost savings here, as most of the lens colors are available with these clip-ons. The Autumn Gold Transition, Polarized and CMT clip-ons are more expensive.

Morgan Optical does not farm anything out. Everything is done in-house. The company grinds their own prescription lenses, puts the notches in interchangeable lenses, and even does their own lens tinting. Tom tends to do a lot of the lab work and shipping. Father Harold does lens notching and final frame/lens tuning, while Wayne concentrates on sales.

The company does work with youth giving discounts where appropriate, especially to kids belonging to 4-H, but also with youth involved in the STCP and AIM programs. "Youth are the future of our sport. All shooters and companies involved in the shooting business need to help introduce more youngsters to our sport," said Wayne.

Wayne considers himself very lucky as a shooter because his dad took him and his brothers trap shooting right from when they were very young. As he and Tom gained shooting experience, Harold would take them to the Grand American, which was then held in Vandalia, Ohio, and their dad would pay for them to shoot the entire program. Harold also paid for all their shooting at the huge Pennsylvania Trap Shooting Championships shot near Williamsport, PA. In 1981, Wayne Morgan won the Junior Pennsylvania Handicap Championship. A number of state, regional and national trophies are still on display at Morgan's physical location – 920 West State Street in Olean, N.Y. "These days it's almost cost prohibitive for a father to do that with two sons," Wayne told me. "What with not only entry fees but travel costs, accommodations, food and more the expenses have sky rocketed compared to 30 years ago."

Morgan Optical has their own building at 403 Mallard Lane in Sparta, Ill. where the Grand American is now held and Harold, Tom and Wayne spend the better part of a month of August there. One or more of the Morgans have been making this pilgrimage for 33 years. In addition to working with trap shooters, Morgan Optical has customers in all the clay target disciplines, plus the company works a lot with pistol shooters, muzzle loaders and archers. "If the shooting discipline requires iron sights, a typical trap shooting prescription won't work," said Wayne. "But we have the know-how to create an Rx lens that's ideal for such shooters.

"Every bird counts in today's high competition stakes," said Wayne. "Scores have gotten better for a number of reasons, and one of those reasons has been shooters being better able to see the targets. That's where Morgan Optical comes in."

The Edge frame from Randolph Engineering. The Edge frame allows the lenses to be placed slightly closer together.

The clip-ons that Morgan Optical offers are specially designed for the Sporter frame. The clip-on lenses cover the entire clear lens on the Sporter. The idea is to buy one Sporter frame with your "clear" Rx prescription and then add the tinted lens clip-ons that you need. Consequently, there is considerable savings compared to buying several pair of Rx lenses.

The Sporter with the Polaroid Bronze clip-ons attached.

The Ranger Sporter frame is perhaps Ranger's mos popular model. These clear lenses are prescription lenses.

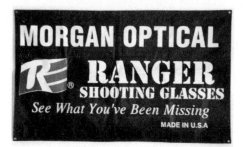

The Morgan Optical banner flies at Sparta.

PILLA AND ZEISS

In 2009, after Pilla sport glasses had reached new peaks in lens and frame technology, the firm was sold. Not much was heard from this company once the new owners took the reins. But Phillip Pilla and his family repurchased the company, and Phillip told me, "While there were no improvements in lens or frame technology after the company was sold in 2009, I feel we've made five years of technological improvement just in just a few months."

Earlier in this century, Pilla had been approached by Germany's Zeiss Optical to make a joint effort with new lens and frame technologies, but apparently the planets were not properly aligned for that marriage at that time. But Pilla and Zeiss has become the perfect match, and what the two companies are doing is going to markedly benefit shooters.

"Seeing is the great equalizer in shotgun competition," is the way Phillip put it to me. "We've taken eyewear to a new level. The result is now 'equipment' (as opposed to just eyewear) that allows shooters to actually see better."

The key to this new lens technology is a new lens material called VIVX. This lens material utilizes a proprietary formulation that manages light while further enhancing color. The claim is that optical clarity is increased by 15 percent, plus this VIVX lens material is 15 percent lighter in weight than even polycarbonate. The result is the VIVX

platform delivers a richer even more defined high definition color filtration system that's specifically designed to enhance clay targets. Other lenses have done this in the past, but Pilla claims that these new VIVX lenses, all because of the new technology behind them, take these lenses to new clarity and enhancement levels without color distortion. Pilla says color can be over pronounced. When that happens definition is lost. These lenses are perfectly balanced to provide exact levels of rich color while maintaining clarity around the edges.

Interestingly, the VIVX lenses were designed in conjunction with the new Outlaw X frames that are different from any you have seen in the past. The VIVX lenses are total wraparound in style. The significant lens curvature makes designing such a lens quite difficult. Consequently, these new VIVX lenses had to be pioneered with the wraparound style in mind. Pilla says these VIVX lenses, despite the lens curvature, are perfect edge to edge and it took new technology to perfect this. There's no light bending – vertical lines remain vertical – horizontal lines remain horizontal – all the way to the edges.

There is almost no frame to the Outlaw X/VIVX combination. To the wrap around lens is a built-in rubber nose piece as well as a built-in rubber sweat band on top that keeps the lens away from the face to help against fogging. With no frame in the sight picture that means vision is completely unobstructed – right, left, up and down. Further, integrated vents in this unique sweat band go the extra mile in preventing fogging.

So what about the temples? Again, you've never seen temples like these before. Called Snap-tech technology, two buttons on the forward part of the temple snap into receptacles on each side of the VIVX lenses. Note the width of the temples at the forward end. This width makes snapping the temples on and off the VIVX lenses easy, plus this is the way the VIVX lenses are changed. The lenses don't pop out, the temples are removed from one lens and then attached to another VIVX lens.

There's more. The temple material is carbon fiber and weighs almost nothing. Little if any distracting stray light can sneak in from the side due to the temple design and the full wrap around built into the lenses. The temples can be pulled out a notch at a time for a perfect fit. Note also that these temples have two drop-down portions at the rear for an even better snug fit. Further yet, the temple tips are made of rubber with a titanium inner core, which is bendable, again to attain a perfect individual fit that's comfortable.

Three Outlaw X kits are available. In all VIVX lenses that color filtrations are used the lenses are not simply made with color baked on. This is new filtration science. The Outlaw kit comes with three differing lens colors. The "Enhanced Definition Kit" offers a red lens with 22 percent light transmission for full sun conditions; a somewhat lighter red lens shade with 42 percent light transmission for cloudy days and a yellow colored lens with 78 percent light transmission for low light days.

A second kit is the "Max Orange Kit." All three lenses in this kit are of a red/orange shade, each with varying degrees of light transmission; 22 percent for full light conditions, 38 percent for medium light conditions and 62 percent for lower light conditions. The third "Specialty Lens Kit" comes with three differing colored lenses – a blue/purple with 46 percent light transmission to be used in medium light, a yellow high contrast lens with 58 percent light transmission for overcast flat light, and a red lens with 52 percent light transmission for medium lighting under a clear sky.

The Panther X frame comes with a slightly different shape to the VIVX lens, plus this model has wrap-around-the-ear temples, but still with interchangeable lenses via the Snap-tech temple technology. Both frame styles can be used with the company's new integrated prescription system featuring an Rx insert with no metal parts and thus is much lighter in weight. The frame for the insert is made out of the same lens material as the VIVX so there's a seamless integration of that prescription lens. In the accompanying photo you can see the insert Rx lens, but I'm told the Rx portion disappears when actually wearing this set up. The Rx insert lens will be clear. The prescription insert slides into the rubber sweat band portion and thus by design the Rx is positioned very close to the shooter's eyes – which Pilla says is the ideal solution to Rx needs.

Only Pilla will market every single VIVX lenses by Zeiss. Further, Zeiss authenticates ever single lens. They do this via an engineer and microscope looking for even the slightest of imperfections; spotting, inclusions, color nuances or differences, marks, scratches and more. Only once a Zeiss engineer has approved these VIVX lenses are they authenticated with a Zeiss "Z." Without the Zeiss "Z" on the lens, it's not a Zeiss lens.

Drop tests? The VIVX lenses will also protect your eyes. To pass this test a 500-gram steel projectile with a hardened bullet-shaped tip is dropped onto the lens from over four feet. For abrasive resistance, Zeiss developed yet more new technology. No lens is scratch or abrasion proof, so always handle your glasses with extreme care. But with the new abrasive-resistant coating Zeiss puts on the VIVX lenses, they simulate abrasive damage with a 1Kg eraser, stroking the lens for 20mm of the surface. They do this eraser stroking of the lens 25 times to prove the excellent abrasion resistance. In the event your lens does get scratched there is a warranty.

Another ruggedness test is subjecting the lenses to simulated long-term use. Rain and dew are simulated repeatedly at 50 degrees Centigrade and damage from sunlight is simulated by Fluorescent UV lamps at 60 degrees Centigrade (140 degrees Fahrenheit). Not only are the VIVX lenses not altered by these tests, lens coatings are not affected either. In addition to scratch-resistant coatings, anti-reflective and Hydro-Pel coatings are on these lenses. The Hydro-Pel coatings mean that water runs right off – important when shooting in the rain. Hydro-Pel also results in reducing smudging from finger prints and this coating is hard further enhancing scratch resistance and the added hardness makes the lenses easier to clean. Check out the Website at www.pillasport.com.

This is the look of the Outlaw X with wraparound unobstructed lenses and the unique temple design.

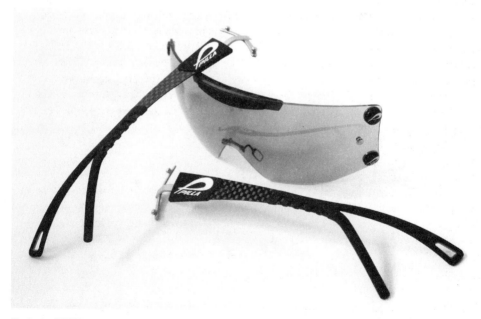

To change VIVX lenses you snap off the temples, rather than removing the lenses from the frame. In the Outlaw X technically there is no frame. Thus the VIVX is all lens offer an unobstructed view.

Note the sweat band in this top view of the Outlaw X.

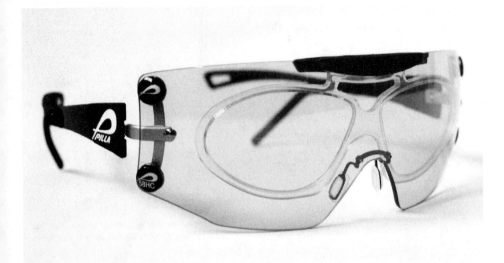

Although you can see the slide-in Rx insert in the photo, Pilla says the Rx portion mostly disappears when worn.

The Panther style comes with wrap around temples, but still features VIVX lens technology.

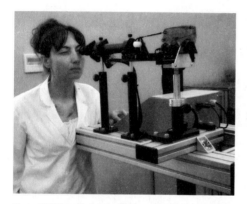

Every VIVX lens is inspected by a Zeiss engineer for any imperfection.

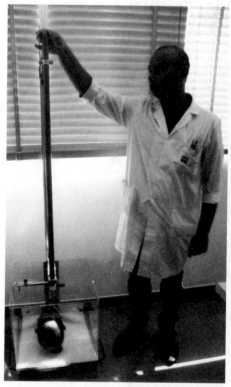

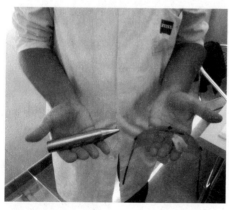

This 500-gram steel projectile with hardened point is dropped on the VIVX lens to test for strength and shatter resistance.

The steel projectile is dropped from over four feet to test the VIVX lens for impact and shatter resistance.

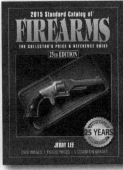
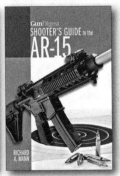

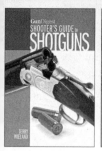

**GUN DIGEST SHOOT-
ERS GUIDE
TO SHOTGUNS**
U2146 • $19.99

**GD SHOOTER'S
GUIDE TO RIFLES**
V6631 • $19.99

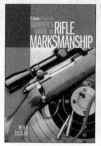

**GUN DIGEST SHOOTER'S
GUIDE TO RIFLE
MARKSMANSHIP**
U2928 • $19.99

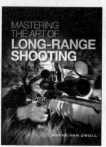

**MASTERING THE ART
OF LONG-RANGE
SHOOTING**
U2148 • $29.99

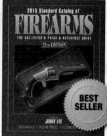

**2015
STANDARD CATALOG
OF FIREARMS**
T1347 • $42.99

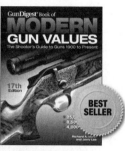

**GUN DIGEST BOOK
OF MODERN GUN VALUES**
U5559 • $34.99

**GD BOOK OF THE
REMINGTON 870**
V8197 • $32.99

**GUN DIGEST PRESENTS CLAS-
SIC SPORTING RIFLES**
W7930 • $24.99

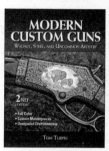

**MODERN
CUSTOM GUNS**
U3979 • $59.99

**ABCS OF
RIFLE SHOOTING**
U8579 • $27.99

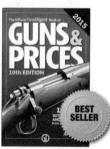

**THE OFFICIAL GUN DIGEST
BOOK OF GUNS & PRICES 2015**
T6947 • $26 .99

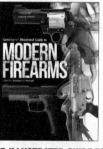

**GD ILLUSTRATED GUIDE TO
MODERN FIREARMS**
V9118 • $32.99

**GUN SAFETY
IN THE HOME**
T0031 • $15.99

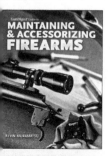

**GUN DIGEST GUIDE TO
MAINTAINING &
CCESSORIZING FIREARMS**
T0033 • $32.99

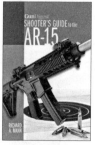

**GUN DIGEST
SHOOTER'S GUIDE TO
THE AR-15**
U7713 • $19.99

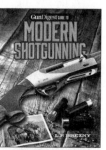

**GUN DIGEST GUIDE TO
MODERN SHOTGUN-
NING**
U9369 • $32.99

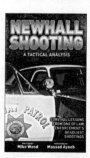

**NEWHALL SHOOTING:
A TACTICAL ANALYSIS**
T1794 • $24.99

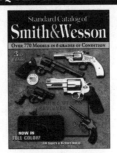
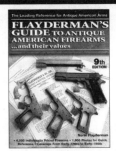

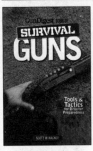

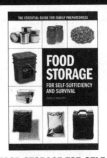
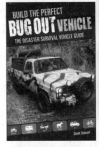
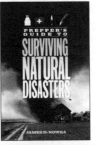

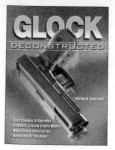

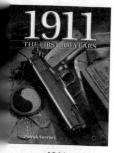
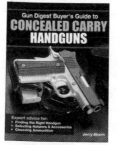
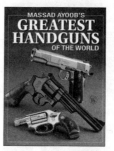
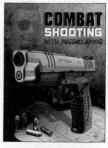
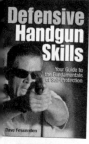

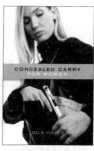

799.202834 SISLEY

Sisley, Nick.
Shooter's guide to
shotgun games

R4001889724

SEAST

SOUTHEAST
Atlanta-Fulton Public Library